Community Development in Ireland

Theory, Policy and Practice

Edited by
ASHLING JACKSON & COLM O'DOHERTY

GILL & MACMILLAN

Gill & Macmillan
Hume Avenue
Park West
Dublin 12
with associated companies throughout the world
www.gillmacmillan.ie

978 07171 4974 2

Index compiled by Cover to Cover
Print origination by Carrigboy Typesetting Services
Printed by GraphyCems, Spain

The paper used in this book is made from the wood pulp of managed forests.
For every tree felled, at least one is planted, thereby renewing natural resources.

A CIP catalogue record is available for this book from the British Library.

Contents

Foreword

The secret of a successful book can sometimes be timing. Good research and clear, accessible writing are key ingredients, of course, but sometimes a book just seems exactly right for its time. On that basis – in fact, on the three bases mentioned above – *Community Development* deserves to be a success.

We are at a moment of transition in Ireland. There are communities coping with disadvantage – sometimes extreme disadvantage – all over the country that lived on the promise of regeneration. They're not giving up, but all of those communities have been betrayed by the collapse of the public–private model of investment that was so dependent on rising property prices.

At the same time, the state players – government at central level, local authorities, the health and caring services, even the Gardaí – are increasingly crippled by a lack of funding. The voluntary and community sector is also struggling to cope with the depth of the recession.

Resources, in short, are being squeezed. But demand is growing.

During the years of the Celtic Tiger, we introduced a phenomenon I sometimes call 'drive-by poverty'. Go to any of the communities where poverty is most embedded in Ireland and you'll find that one of the things they have in common with each other is a fine ring-road or, in some cases, a dual carriageway that bisects them. You can drive past poverty in Ireland at 40 miles an hour without incurring the risk of a penalty point.

Of course, a lot of these communities have other things in common. We built many of them facing inwards, cut off from the communities around them. We institutionalised poverty in those communities and, as a result, we all know addresses that carry a stigma with them – it's four times as hard to get a job if you come from those places.

When we were rich, of course, we didn't need community. We needed retail and holiday homes abroad and lots of cheap mortgages.

Now, all of a sudden, we have never needed each other more. For our own sake we have to rebuild an understanding of what makes communities work, and how we can make them better.

And we can, of course. Yes we can.

I drive a lot around Ireland in the course of my work, and everywhere I go I've noticed the same thing. I remember one weekend in the summer of 2010, as the recession was biting deep. There was an international summer school in Carrick-on-Shannon, in honour of the great John McGahern, that brought several hundred of us on a voyage of discovery through the places he loved and where he produced some of the finest writing of the last 50 years.

The summer school alone attracted several hundred visitors to the town – but there was much more. The streets were colourful and lively, the pubs thronged and welcoming, and the harbour was chock-a-block with boats from the Shannon. Children everywhere were being entertained by face-painters and clowns on stilts, and food stalls on the roadside were doing a lively trade.

Athlone, the following day, was the same. Again there was a festival, with flags and stalls from all the countries of Europe. But above all there were people, young and old, walking the streets, enjoying the sights of a lively Irish town. The whole place had a real buzz – you couldn't drive through it without wanting to stop and savour the atmosphere.

Yes, there's a recession, but driving around Ireland gives you the strong impression that people aren't lying down under it. They're getting on with life, investing in their own communities, rediscovering the importance of their own place, and generally giving the impression of a people who have by no means given up hope.

Hope is to be found in community. Rebuilding hope means rebuilding community and what it means, for everyone. And we're going to have to do a lot of that ourselves. Because we have come to associate quality of life almost exclusively with money, we are going to have to relearn a lot of the values on which we built a strong sense of community in the past. It's a cliché, of course, to talk about the *meitheal* – that spirit that obliged neighbours to support each other when the harvest had to be brought in. But the *meitheal* was lost in Ireland and was replaced by the contractor with the enormous combine harvester.

Now we have to relearn that quality of life is about more than money. And we have to do it for ourselves. Community development won't be funded in the future the way it was in the past. There will be no time for process, for empowerment for its own sake. We need community development to produce results.

And if that's the challenge we face, isn't it good to know there are tools at hand? Ashling Jackson and Colm O'Doherty have done us all a huge favour by pulling together this collection of essays on one of the most pressing needs we face. It's finely balanced between academic research and at-the-coalface practice, and each essay is focused on learning.

But just as important, the entire collection is readable, clear and sound. It will be immensely valuable to everyone who works in the community and voluntary sector, for instance, and will also, if there's any sense in the world, inform public policy.

We're great in Ireland at picking up the pieces after damage has been done, and we're always willing to spend buckets of money on the task. On the other hand, strong communities are a fail-safe preventative mechanism and we've never invested enough. One of the lessons of *Community Development* is that resources aren't everything; when you have resourcefulness instead, and the commitment to community is matched by a level of scientific skill, a better future is truly possible.

Fergus Finlay
CEO, Barnardos

1

Setting the Scene

Ashling Jackson and Colm O'Doherty

> As free citizens in a political democracy, we have a responsibility to be interested and involved in the affairs of the human community, be it at the local or the global level. (Wellstone 2002)

We are two academics who at various points in our careers have been directly involved in community development work. Our long-standing interest in community development has been inspired by our social experiences in different communities in England, Wales and Ireland. Both of us are delighted to bring together in this book the ideas, interests and frameworks which are currently shaping community development programmes and projects in Ireland.

While it is tempting to look back in a nostalgic fashion and declare our experiences to have been uniformly positive, some elements of these communities were not affirmative, and as a result some of our experiences were neither comfortable nor fruitful. So right from the outset, it is important to acknowledge that the power of the idea of community is such that it can make us look backwards in a nostalgic way, or forward in an idealised manner. The notion of community is itself contentious: it can be understood as soap opera theme, as a political aspiration or, as in recent times, as a social policy instrument for the implementation of an active citizenship agenda. Definitions of community are legion and often contested. It is sufficient to state here that what people feel about a community determines, to a large degree, whether or not it is a community. Communities can be defined by location and physical proximity, but also and importantly, they are units of belonging where intangibles such as feelings, attitudes and perceptions connect members in a network of relationships. Community should not, however, be regarded as providing us with some kind of blueprint for utopia. To regard it in this way is to fail to recognise that all utopias, from Plato's *Republic* to More's *Utopia* and beyond, have one thing in common: they are predictable social settings from which change is absent. Contemporary Irish society is not a utopia, and the changing and diverse nature of community in Ireland is readily visible.

'Community development can be defined as a process in which people join together to improve conditions and create change at the community level' (Checkoway 2011:5). This definition succinctly captures the essence of community development work. Different definitions of community development will be used by the various contributors to this book, each of whom will draw attention to the key elements of community development work.

Community development may be evident in local initiatives or in the work of formal agencies with diverse racial, ethnic, religious, or other groups, and in rural and urban communities in industrial and developing areas.

> Community development has some core concepts on which there is relative agreement, such as 'starting with people', the idea that the process should originate in the experience of people; 'strengthening community', that community is a unit of solution; 'joining together', that individuals acting collectively can accomplish more than one person acting alone; and 'creating change', that change is both desirable and possible (Checkoway 1997; DeFilippis and Saegert 2008)' (cited in Checkoway 2011:ii6)

Communities and people within communities can mobilise and be mobilised in a variety of ways. For example, they can provide community-based services, advocate on issues that affect them, raise awareness and critical consciousness, and lobby the government for social change. There is no single strategy to create change; there are many (Checkoway 1995; Zukin *et al.* 2006).

For community development workers, community development is a *way of working with* communities, so that the community can become empowered, be competently proactive and, if necessary, reactive to the issues that affect it. Sound community development practice will see community development workers facilitate, manage, advocate and mediate for change in communities, most especially marginalised communities. They will do this by assisting the community to identify (if it is not already evident) a common need, something that is important to the community; to facilitate the community to identify ways to address this need; to empower and build capacity so that the community as a whole or, at the very least, individuals within the community can act to address the identified needs, all the time ensuring that the community takes ownership of the solution or process to effectively address its needs.

Given that social change has been so rapid in Ireland since the 1960s, and that the social context of communities has changed so dramatically over the last few decades, the theory of community development work, and policies affecting the operation of community development organisations and community development practice, have also changed rapidly. Therefore, when choosing an orientation for this book, we decided to adopt a theory, policy and practice approach. Community development practice is more and more shaped by social and economic policy, as well as by our own ideology as community development workers. In compiling the chapters that make up this textbook, we also employed a key principle of community development work, that of collaboration, by working closely with experts in the field. Contributions from key practitioners and academics in the community development area provide examples of best practice in various aspects of community development, while taking cognisance of the altered landscape of working in community development settings in Ireland. Current restrictions on funding, compared to what was available a decade ago, is an example of this altered community development landscape. The chapters in this book reflect current theoretical conceptualisations in the area of community development, the latest policy implications for the community development sector and, importantly, models of best practice for working in various community development settings.

Community development practice is framed by the social context in which it occurs. Ireland is in itself an interesting case study, in that until recently 'two social processes have partly overlapped in Ireland in the last two decades: one is a general modernisation, with its greater individualism and secularism; and the other is a tremendous surge in economic growth, with its spiralling materialism, consumerism and increased choice' (O'Connell 2001:7). Combined, this meant that Ireland experienced very rapid economic, social and cultural change in recent decades (O'Connor 2006; Fahey and Layte 2007).

This book looks at community development in Ireland *now*, in the aftermath of the Celtic Tiger and at a time when Ireland is in the throes of a well-established recession. Chapters 2 to 6 explore the evolution of community development and the current social context in which practitioners work. In Chapter 2, we see how a culture of competitive individualism, very much a characteristic of Celtic Tiger Ireland, undermines collective and individual well-being. Community development can be an effective response to this. However, community development has been evolving in a particular way in Ireland. Chapter 3 explores the nature and type of community development in Ireland, drawing particular attention to how community development has moved away from the politicised action that informed its birth in Ireland in the 1980s. Theories and understandings of well-being are introduced in Chapter 4 to enable the reader to understand the impact of social context and circumstances on well-being. The link between well-being and government policies is established here. Importantly, this chapter shows how community development processes can strengthen the capacity of people to be involved in social transformation activities that redistribute power and enhance well-being. While community development practice is framed by the social context in which it occurs, it is also framed by the environmental context in which community development workers carry out their work. Chapter 5 examines cultural diversity in Ireland and draws attention to the increasingly important value of culturally competent practice when working in community development settings. While the majority of chapters in this book deal with community development in the South of Ireland, Chapter 6 focuses on the impact of community development in a conflict setting, exploring specifically the evolution of community development in Northern Ireland, as well as the nature of community development practice there.

Chapters 7 to 10 review examples of various aspects of community development work in new and emerging settings. Chapter 7 describes how an intensive family support project was set up and implemented in two areas suffering from sustained poverty and disadvantage using core community development principles. Collaboration between professionals, and between professionals and the community, is promoted here. Collaborative working is further explored in Chapter 8, which identifies best practice in collaborative working in Ireland and examines the impact the international collaborative model of co-location is having on community development practice in Ireland. Chapter 9 focuses on one of the major additions to the community development sector in Ireland over the past two decades – family resource centres. This chapter analyses the contribution local community members make to the successful running of these centres on behalf of their local community, as well as to community development practice in Ireland. Chapter 10 discusses family resource centres, community development and restorative justice as possibly congruent activities. The chapter draws some conclusions as to the compatibility of community development and restorative justice in principle and practice, and makes recommendations as to how practice might be developed in this area.

Community development and community education are inextricably linked. In Chapters 11 and 12 various dimensions of community education are explored. Chapter 11 introduces the reader to a number of critical theories relevant to adult and community education. The importance of being a knowledgeable and critical practitioner, equipped with the necessary knowledge that informs practice, but also possessing a developed sense of criticality, is highlighted. Community education, particularly if a peer education model is employed, can be a very powerful force for social change. In Chapter 12, five Traveller women share their experiences of becoming Traveller community health workers and peer educators, and what this means for them and their local Traveller community. Here we can see how peer education can be an effective way of promoting self-help and mutual aid in community settings.

Community development practice should be rigorously conducted and ideally be evidence-based rather than evidence-informed. Chapter 13 explores how community-based youth and family interventions can introduce and utilise an evidence-based approach to community development workers' work, by engaging in a system of tracking the perceived social support levels among adolescents attending their project. In this practical way, community development work can move from being evidence-informed to being evidence-based. In Chapter 14, evaluation, an essential element of sound community development practice in assessing the effectiveness of the community development endeavour, is promoted as a way to empower communities. Empowerment evaluations specifically can be an effective way to ensure ownership by the community at all stages of a project. In the recessionary times in which we live, empowerment evaluations may well become a cost-effective approach to evaluation in community development practice.

Community development can be a powerful social force in any society. It may well be a panacea for that sense of normlessness, the feeling of having no control and of events being very unpredictable, that is experienced when one is living in a rapidly changing society and which is exacerbated by living in a marginalised community in a rapidly changing society. Our concluding chapter, Chapter 15, reflects on community development as a key characteristic of civil society, and the importance of it as a mechanism to improve the social situation of those living in marginalised communities in Ireland.

This book aims to provide thought-provoking insights into the complexity and richness of community development practice in Ireland, a practice that is framed by theory and by current social and economic policy. It is not an exhaustive account of the myriad of community development work that occurs, or the variety of community settings in which that work occurs. We do hope, though, that this book will give a flavour of the current state of play of community development practice in Ireland. Importantly, we hope the best practice guidelines provided in various chapters will assist the reader to achieve best practice standards in their current or, indeed, future community development work.

2

The Value of Community Development

Colm O'Doherty

It is always worth itemising happiness, there is so much of the other thing in a life, you had better put down the markers for happiness while you can. (Barry 2008:148)

CHAPTER SUMMARY

Community development and well-being are natural bedfellows. Community development enhances individual and collective well-being by strengthening communities in ways consistent with the core principles of: collective action, empowerment, social justice, participation, equality and anti-discrimination. (CWC 2008:22/26)

COMMUNITY DEVELOPMENT AND WELL-BEING

The purpose of community development is to improve people's social and emotional well-being – their happiness – by promoting positive change through a process of social emancipation. We are regularly made aware by politicians, church leaders and other influential figures who comment on the decline of community that we need to do something to counteract this movement away from the 'warm circle' (Bauman 2001:11) of respect and belonging associated with collective life and the cultural resources which sustain it. Putting down markers for happiness and manifesting our shared humanity are two of the key organising principles for community development.

However, the key organising principle of our dominant economic system is that society works best when each person individually seeks to maximise their own utility or satisfaction in the marketplace. Under this economic order, vulnerability or insecurity, which is part of the modern psychological condition, is directly related to our personal failings. Coping with the insecurity of contemporary life requires us to constantly re-assess our individual circumstances and forces us:

. . . to seek biographical solutions to systemic contradictions; we are looking for individual salvation from shared troubles. That strategy is unlikely to bring the results we are after, since it leaves the roots of insecurity intact; moreover, it is precisely this falling back on our individual wits and resources that injects the world with the insecurity we wish to escape. (Bauman 2001:144)

This individualistic approach to well-being sits well with a dominant economic model which equates happiness with economic growth and consumerism. Our sense of self-worth is bound up with self-management and the acquisition of commodities. In this model, gross national product is seen as a true indicator of the level of human happiness. For many people their social standing and sense of identity is no longer reflected in the quality of interactions with others and the real knowledge of each other that they can experience in a community to which they belong. A person's social standing becomes an ongoing project, the project of the self; and the project of the self hinges on the successful forging of an identity which affords a person social recognition. Consumerism, and the traits and activities (for example shopping for brands/logos) associated with it, provides a ready-made identity platform for obtaining and retaining a social standing which in turn occupies a central position in the pursuit of a happy life.

Too often consumerism is regarded as though it reflects a fundamental human material self-interest and possessiveness. That, however, could hardly be further from the truth. Our almost neurotic need to shop and consume is instead a reflection of how deeply social we are. Living in unequal and individualistic societies, we use possessions to show ourselves in a good light, to make a positive impression, and to avoid appearing incompetent or inadequate in the eyes of others. Consumerism shows how powerfully we are affected by each other. Once we have enough of the basic necessities for comfort, possessions matter less and less in themselves, and are used more and more for what they say about their owners. Ideally, our impressions of each other would depend on face-to-face interactions in the course of community life, rather than on outward appearances in the absence of real knowledge of each other. The weakening of community life and the growth of consumerism are related (Wilkinson and Pickett 2009:225–6).

Counterbalancing the utilitarian or materialist perspective is a significant and growing literature on happiness, or subjective well-being (Layard 2005; Searle 2008; Bauman 2008; Jordan 2008; Layard and Dunn 2009; Wilkinson and Pickett 2009; Delaney 2009), which rejects the excessive individualism of the economic growth model.

By excessive individualism we mean the belief that the prime duty of the individual is to make the most of his or her own life, rather than to contribute to the good of others. Of course some degree of individualism is necessary for survival, and individual choice and self-determination are vital ingredients of a good life. But individuals will never lead satisfying lives except in a society where people care for each other and promote each other's good as well as their own. The pursuit of personal success relative to others cannot create a happy society, since one person's success necessarily involves another's failure. Individual freedom and self-determination bring many blessings, but they can only exist if balanced by a proper sense of care and responsibility for others (Layard and Dunn 2009:6).

Layard and Dunn's *Good Childhood* report (2009), a landmark inquiry into children's experiences of childhood in the UK, identified excessive individualism as the source of a whole range of problems for children: problems relating to family breakdown, teenage antagonism, dishonest advertising, excessive competition in education and inequality all stemmed from excessive individualism. This culture of individualism, 'in which each person is supposed to realize themselves through the development of their special potentials' (Jordan 2008:8), is derived from the 'invisible hand' economic model of Adam Smith (1723–1790). Smith's *The Wealth of Nations*, published in 1776, set out to explain the singular increase in economic growth occurring in Western Europe. *The Wealth of Nations* analysed the inter-relationship between three key elements – the *factors of production*, the *market* and the *state* – of mercantile society. Smith's influential examination of the emerging market capitalist system has become a manifesto for contemporary capitalism and shapes the cultural flows in which social value is defined. Bauman points out that:

> The 'invisible hand' of the market operated by selfish individuals in search of their own wealth and pleasure seemed to be rather reluctant or impotent to save humans from the horrors of reciprocal cruelties. Most certainly, it managed neither to liberate most humans from the bondage of passions, nor to make completely happy those few whom it succeeded in freeing. (Bauman 2008:49)

The shortcomings of this economic model in promoting well-being were documented in 1974 by Richard Easterlin. He identified a counter-intuitive relationship between economic growth as measured by gross domestic product (GDP) and measurements of happiness in affluent countries. As income and economic growth rise, well-being remains stalled. The Easterlin paradox – as this insight was termed – suggests that societies in developed countries like Ireland are operating within an economic model that is not capable of improving the quality of life of their members. The growing literature on well-being has challenged the economic account of how value is created and distributed. According to the economist Richard Layard (2005), the critical dimensions affecting our well-being or happiness are health, income and the quality of our relationships. Material success and social failure in many rich countries flags up the need 'to shift attention from material standards and economic growth to ways of improving the psychological and social well-being of whole societies' (Wilkinson and Pickett 2009:4). Wilkinson and Pickett (2009) argue that economic growth and increases in average income make only a limited contribution to well-being in rich countries.

This is because as these countries have grown richer their societies have become more unequal: Wilkinson and Pickett (2009) show how the quality of social relations deteriorate in less equal societies.

Trust is a valuable collective good because it lubricates our day-to-day social and economic exchanges, facilitates co-operative relations and generates social capital. Social capital, as defined by Putnam (2000), refers to social rules, networks of reciprocity (I will do something for you on the basis that in return you do something for me) and trustworthiness. Putnam sees social capital as being akin to neighbourliness. He identifies personal as well as collective benefits, for example through networking, and that the concept of social capital has links with the notion of community (Packham 2008:32).

There is a ample evidence that social capital constitutes a major resource for communities and that it promotes health and well-being, reduces levels of crime, sustains social cohesion and advances solidarity (O'Doherty 2007). Trust is diminished by the divisiveness of inequality. Here in Ireland, Delaney (2009) examined the health and well-being of the Irish population during the boom years of the Celtic Tiger. Using statistical data from administrative and survey sources he considered whether this period of growth had improved well-being and welfare in Ireland. He found that:

> If one looks at psychological distress measures, Ireland fits neatly with the pattern of relationship between economic growth and well-being described by Richard Easterlin in his seminal papers on the topic. The substantial period of economic growth throughout the late 20th century may have had a strong welfare component to the extent that it funded advancements of elder life expectancy. However, there is no evidence for large increases in psychological well-being from the data available. (Delaney 2009:12)

Stalled happiness or well-being is associated with an individualistic version of social value based on the traditional assumption that economic growth is the way forward for the creation of a better society. If we understand culture in its broadest sense as a whole way of life, we can see how the individualistic culture associated with the economic model places little or no value on the interpersonal sources of social value that are associated with local and increasingly globalised networks of formal and informal support. Money and what it can buy is, in conventional economics, the fixed measure of value that makes it possible to establish the relative price of all commodities. Like all social systems, money capitalism is cultural in the sense that its economic activities are made meaningful to participants through cultural processes – in this case, processes that overstate the value of commodities and devalue the interpersonal goods produced through positive social interactions. These interpersonal goods are experienced through relationships, groups, associations and communities. They constitute an interpersonal economy which creates social value by developing cultures of mutuality, respect and belonging. Community development sets about improving well-being by generating and implementing changes which impact on people's collective life and cultural resources. Before setting out the features of community development that improve well-being it is important to acknowledge what we know and understand about the idea of 'community'.

COMMUNITY

'Community' has become a somewhat elastic term, but its ubiquitous usage is testimony to its enduring importance in our lives. It is an evocative idea conjuring up positive images and feelings of identity, belonging and understanding shared by all its members. Belonging offers members security and exclusivity. The feelings of belonging associated with community membership can kindle divisiveness and become a triggering factor in racial, ethnic, class, gender, religious and ideological tribalism and xenophobia. These negative social outcomes can be influenced by a type of social capital that supports and produces inward-looking social networks.

Referred to as 'bonding' social capital, it reinforces solidarity and ties between homogenous groups. As such it can be utilised at one end of the spectrum by nefarious organisations such as the Mafia or the Ku Klux Klan and at the other end by golf clubs that foster exclusivity. In between these two extremes it can underpin golden circles of exploitative individuals or sustain the strong ties between families and within ethnic groups and immigrant communities. 'Bridging' social capital, on the other hand, enables participation and involvement in outward-looking networks such as the civil rights movement in the USA (O'Doherty 2007:25).

In addition to these two sources of identity formation and social cohesion, Field (2003:66) draws attention to a third type of social capital, 'linking social capital', which is derived from relationships with agencies and organisations up and down the social and economic scale. 'Linking' social capital connects people to contacts, from outside their own social milieu, that supply resources capable of enhancing the well-being of their communities. It is manifested through alliances between communities and individuals or groups with formal power, especially power over resources that can be used to encourage social and economic development. Hence the social value of communities or networks is bound up with the characteristic type of capital mobilised by their members. An exclusive sense of identity which rejects other groups or the whole culture may be upheld by bonding social capital which is based on inward-looking ties. Bonding social capital serves to reinforce homogeneity, while bridging social capital encourages and facilitates contact across diverse social networks and communities. Community development produces or harnesses social capital for collective benefit.

To sum up, then, community can be understood as a body of people with an ongoing relationship stemming from shared interests or something in common. The relationship may be based around a locality, a shared identity or experience of discrimination.

HOW COMMUNITY DEVELOPMENT IMPROVES WELL-BEING

The three features of community development that enable people to be active and to take action that increases well-being are:

- Self-determination: it assigns a positive value to people acting for themselves as opposed to having things done for or to them.
- Collaborative action: it has a collective rather than an individual focus.
- Getting a better deal for people, especially those who are collectively missing out in some way. Engagement and commitments are guided by moral and political principles rather than technical or ideological concerns.

Self-determination

Community development workers operate as facilitators with people in relation to what *those people* decide to become involved with, helping them to realise *their* collective goals (Twelvetrees 2008:3).

Community development works best when it is the people themselves, rather than a professional worker, who choose the means and ends to improve their own communities. So whatever occurs is on their terms and, more often than not, on their home territory rather than in a clinical or office setting. People are enabled to develop community responses and projects improving collective well-being in the natural setting of their social and physical environment. Community ownership of family support and outreach youth work services is encouraged when such community development programmes are situated in the neighbourhood rather than being located in an official building miles away.

Collaborative Action

Formal and informal relationships, comprising the currency of community development, make it easier for people to communicate and co-operate with each other and thereby generate purposeful collective action. The collective focus of community development is instrumental in empowering citizens to shape and determine positive social change in their communities. As Bauman puts it: 'We all need to gain control over the conditions under which we struggle with the challenges of life – but for most of us such control can be gained only *collectively*' (2001:149).

Moral and Political Principles

The third feature of community development follows from the other two. Community development is concerned with people's lives in a community and the distribution of resources and power within the community itself and between the community and the wider society. Community development, through participative processes and structures, seeks to challenge inequitable power relationships and empower marginalised and excluded groups within the community and mainstream society.

To put it more simply, community development ensures that people as members of a geographical or other form of community (interest, faith, ethnicity, gender, class, virtual) get a better deal through their own collective efforts.

ESTABLISHING THE VALUE OF COMMUNITY DEVELOPMENT

Community development processes produce social value which supports healthy societies by building community capacity for children, youth and adults. Community capacity is the interaction between human capital (community members' levels of skill, knowledge and health status), social and institutional capital (leadership, motivation and networks) and economic capital (local services, infrastructure, resources) available to be used in collective ways to improve the well-being of any particular community.

As I discussed earlier, the logic of the economic model does not allow for a sympathetic evaluation of the arguments in favour of collective life and the cultural resources that sustain it. Because the economic model fails to explain behaviour that occurs outside the formal or monetary economy, it can measure the growth of national product but it cannot measure the growth of happiness or well-being.

When the social value of community development programmes is viewed solely through the lens of objective criteria, we are unlikely to see how and to what degree the programme has increased the happiness or subjective well-being of participants. Case studies that provide us with a rich description of the context in which the programme was located and in which the participants lived are a respectable method of social research. To increase our understanding of the value of community development, for the communities themselves and wider society, ongoing medium-term fine-grained qualitative research into social networks and community activities and their contribution to social capital is required.

CONCLUSION

In this chapter I have examined the transformational manner in which community development increases happiness and well-being. It does this by producing, through its programmes, the collective goods of intimacy (the close feelings generated by partners, family members and friends), respect, the culture of civility and belonging (the sense of loyalty, commitment and trust between members of the same group, community or society). The social value of community development can be contrasted with the individualistic version of value derived from the economic model.

Individualism – a very uniform, reductionist and ultimately banal version of the value of life – has failed to subvert a multitude of other collective ways of experiencing social value and sustaining it through relationships, groups, associations and communities (Jordan 2008:230).

Under the aegis of the economic model the dominant ideas and policies of speculators, builders, bankers – who believe they know best – have infiltrated our thoughts as *common sense* when they make no sense at all. The proposition that banks, developers and financial services could be trusted to advance our general well-being is now exposed as a fantasy. The value of community development is that it creates alternative sources of social value and develops collective cultures which offer genuine opportunities for citizens to *put down markers for happiness.*

3

Investigating the De-Politicisation of Community Development: What Happened? Where Do We Go Now?

Déirdre O'Byrne

CHAPTER SUMMARY

This chapter examines the nature and type of community development which has been happening in Ireland in the past thirty years with the specific aim of establishing whether the process has been eroded or whether it is still rooted in its defining principles. In order to establish an answer to this question, the chapter explores the results of primary research conducted with a community project on the Northside of Cork City, along with research insights derived from participant observation arising from the author's experience as a community worker for the past twenty years, the last six of which have been spent as a support community development worker in the Munster region. The research findings suggest that community development has moved away from its defining principles as set out in the UK in the 1960s and 1970s by authors such as Curno (1978), Craig and Mayo (1995) and others; and that it has moved away from the politicised action that informed its birth in Ireland in the 1980s. The chapter will offer insights as to how and why this has occurred.

INTRODUCTION

Many academics and community organisations (Harvey 2010; CWC 2010) have concluded that the Community Development Programme (CDP) in Ireland is in crisis. Related questions include: How have cutbacks in funding arrangements affected CDP groups? What has been the effect on projects in relation to community development principles and the practice of social analysis and use of social policy training? What are the effects of the growing demands on CDPs to engage in services provision and to cope with increasing managerial demands from the state? What effect will new organisational structures and the ceding of local management groups' power to local development companies have on empowerment and community development?

The hypothesis explored in this chapter is that community development has been de-politicised and de-radicalised and has lost its social change ethos. Specifically, community development, since its evolution in the UK in the 1960s, has at its core a commitment to challenge social structures that disempower people (Popple 1995). Community development has come to have social justice as a central component; it is committed to giving ordinary people a say in decisions that affect them and strives to include and empower citizenry individually and collectively. This has meant that community development challenges the status quo and works to provide fairer alternatives. Campaigning, lobbying, advocacy and mobilising the media for support have heretofore been part of community development. These methodologies have been eclipsed in recent years in Ireland in the era of 'partnership' between the community sector and the state.

HISTORICAL AND POLICY CONTEXT

The roots of community development in Ireland are often associated with Muintir na Tíre, which was founded in 1937. It operates through principles of 'neighbour-liness, self-help and self-reliance' (Muintir na Tíre website). The organisation is rooted in rural development and originally borrowed from the agricultural co-operative movement in Ireland that dates back to the turn of the nineteenth century (Plunkett 1914). This approach to community work was later epitomised in the work of Fr James McDyer (1982) in Glen Columcille in Donegal in the 1960s. The first 'community workers' were employed by the Health Boards in the early 1970s, and community work also became a concern of the state in other ways, through the Vocational Educational Committees (VECs), the first EU Anti-Poverty Programme, and in adult education courses run throughout the country (Whelan 1989).

A more 'organic' and rooted community work emerged from the ashes of economic and social decline in Ireland in the 1980s, starting in large areas of deprivation in Dublin and other major cities. Inner-city Dublin communities in particular had been ravaged by a heroin epidemic and high levels of unemployment and deprivation. Community members took to the streets protesting against the failure to tackle these issues (Duggan and Ronayne 1991; Kelleher and Whelan 1992; Tallon 1993). These conditions acted as a spur to the organic growth of community development. Similarly, community work grew in Northern Ireland as a response to the establishment's failure to address poverty, inequality and discrimination (Lewis 2006:4).

The Department of Social Welfare responded by setting up the CDP in 1990 (DSCFA 1999:3). At the outset, social justice and empowerment were enshrined in the programme's working definitions of community development (DSCFA 1999). Community development projects were set up in marginalised areas in Dublin, Cork and other large cities (DSCFA 1999), and the number of projects grew to reach 180 in 2010 (Pobal website).

Also from the early 1990s, 'local development' became a key element of state policy. Area-Based Partnerships[1] were established and charged with promoting community development. These became known as the 'partnership companies'[2] and their stated modus operandi was community development (Walsh *et al.* 1998).

In the context of Irish social partnership at this time, beginning with the Programme for National Recovery (1987), the state proclaimed its commitment to tackling social exclusion and poverty. Community development increasingly became a major component at the core of a number of national programmes addressing development in disadvantaged communities. This commitment became embedded in all subsequent Programmes for Government throughout the 1990s and 2000s. The state fostered the development of a number of different mechanisms to support community development throughout this time.

Arising from the Programme for Economic and Social Progress (PESP) 1991–94 and the Programme for Competitiveness and Work (PCW) 1994–96, Area-Based Partnership companies and 'mini-partnership' companies were set up to deal with local development; the Leader local development programme was established in rural Ireland; and family resource centres were set up nationwide. The community sector was given a voice through the establishment of the City/County Development Boards (2000) at local level and the accompanying Strategic Policy Committees (SPCs). At the national level, the 'Community Platform' was in 1996 given statutory recognition as the voice of the voluntary/community sector in partnership negotiations and this pillar was formally recognised as a discrete 'social partner' at the turn of the millennium.

Three main national programmes (Pobal 2010) were instigated which claim commitment to principles of community development: the CDP;[3] the Local Development Social Inclusion Programme (LDSIP)[4] and the Family Resource Centre Programme.[5] The CDP was the most prominent programme of its kind – in which, at least theoretically and from a social policy perspective, community development was given a central role – and it will therefore form the main focus of this chapter; but comparisons will be drawn with the other two programmes.

UNDERLYING THEORETICAL INFLUENCES INFORMING BEST PRACTICE

Community development in Ireland was strongly influenced by the UK experience in the 1960s. From the work of groundbreaking left-wing theorists of the welfare state in the UK at the time, such as Crosland (1956), Titmuss (1968) and later Marshall and Bottomore (1991), there emerged strong arguments for the mainstreaming of 'community development' as a legitimate practice response to empowerment and anti-poverty issues. The Calouste Gulbenkian Report (Younghusband 1968) had a profound effect in legitimising the emerging practice of community work in Britain, which crystallised into a long-term commitment to supporting vulnerable communities to help themselves.

Community development was the main focus in community work. Most of the theorists and academics writing on community development at the time possessed a strong belief in its potential for radical social change. This can be gleaned from the work of writers such as Marjorie Mayo (1975), Paul Curno (1978), and Gary Craig *et al.* (1982), with the latter presenting us with dilemmas of community work, ideology and local politics which are as poignant in contemporary Ireland as they were in the early 1980s. The work of these theorists defined community development from that time onwards and laid bare the work that it encompassed, doing so in a way which worked strongly from a neo-Marxist perspective and rooting the practice in the structural problems of the welfare state (Butcher 2007). These authors were writing in the UK at a time when Marxist ideology was popular and the power of the unions was also strong. During this time, community development was far less professionalised; it was driven by a strong left-wing theoretical ethos as espoused by these writers; the area of community development, unlike social work, resisted professionalisation and the methodologies utilised regularly crossed over into community action. At a time when neo-liberalism had not yet been born, these were the halcyon days for community development.

The educational work of Paulo Freire in Brazil was firmly anchored in community development. Freire, like most other community development academics in the UK, was Marxist in his orientation. However, he has often been termed a 'cultural Marxist', much like neo-Marxist thinkers such as Gramsci and Althusser (O'Brien and Penna 1998). These academics have also been described as 'critical reformists' (Hurley 1992). However, unlike classical Marxists, Freire and the others were not of the view that a social revolution and the overthrow of capitalism were necessary to achieve an egalitarian society. Like Gramsci, Freire's central belief was that the apparatus of the state – its educational institutions, media and communities – could be exposed to popular radical education that could 'conscientise'[6] wide sections of society to challenge the hegemony of ideas which bolstered the economic interests of the ruling classes. These liberatory ideas strongly influenced community development principles as there are close associations between liberatory ideas and strategies for empowering communities.

Critical Consciousness

Like Freire, Saul Alinsky was not an advocate of Stalin's revolutionary violence, but he was a neo-Marxist and was more committed to Gramsci's ideas. He relied on what he termed 'gradualism', 'infiltration' and 'the dialectic process'. He believed in using and working a dysfunctional system from within, gradually eroding problems until they disappeared. He advocated dressing arguments with 'moral clothing to reach his goals' and was disdainful of the kind of liberal thinking that leads to inaction on inequality and injustice (Alinsky 1969). He was equally disdainful of what he called 'suicidal' or 'rhetorical' radicals. In his book *Rules for Radicals* (1972), he refers to the folly of radicals thus:

> The Revolutionary force today . . . is reminiscent of the idealistic Christians, yet they also urge violence and cry, 'Burn the system down!' They have no illusions about the system, but plenty of illusions about the way to change our world. (Alinsky 1972:xiii)

Whatever the merits of the approach, some writers have argued that there are inherent dangers in mainstream community development practice, such as co-option and de-radicalisation (Meade and O'Donovan 2002; Meade 2005; Kirby 2007; Kirby and Murphy 2008). This view has been expressed in the Irish context of the corporatist model of government with the involvement of the community/voluntary pillar at social partnership level. In this context, it is argued that community development has survived largely because of programmes that have been funded by the state and mediated through government structures where the community sector has been represented in social partnership talks. However, the fact that the voluntary/community sector is the weakest of all social partners – it has neither the economic clout of the Irish Business and Employers Confederation (IBEC) nor the worker power of the Irish Congress of Trade Unions (ICTU), and is totally dependent on the state for funding – has put it in a subordinate position to the other partners. As such, the state has forced the representatives of the sector to accept its will, which essentially 'co-opts' the whole sector into the demands of the state. These demands involve: greater financial accountability and value for money measures; less focus on social education; more service provision; and detraction from a political focus.

Community development theorists such as Ledwith (2005) and Butcher (2007) in the UK and, in the Irish context, Forde et al. (2009) and the Community Workers' Co-operative (CWC) (2008) all draw heavily on the critical approach within sociology. This approach deals with the root causes of inequalities and poverty. It has a strong structural focus on social class, the economy, redistribution and the political values which inform social policies.

Influenced by these theories, ideas and principles in the Irish context, Mary Whelan's description of community development is very often quoted and seems to stand the test of time. It is clear and unambiguous, and it differentiates and distances itself from many interventions (which in themselves are valuable) at community level.

> The objective of community development is to contribute to social change leading to social justice. The process of doing this involves participation and collective action by people in exerting control over economic, social and political issues that affect their lives. (Whelan 1989:145)

Implicit in this statement are concepts of positive social change and decision-making powers which involve participation and empowerment as an outcome of the process. Twelvetrees (1985), Tucker (1989), Duggan and Ronayne (1991), Faughnan and Kelleher (1992), Popple (1995) and Craig and Mayo (1995) have put forward similar contributions which encapsulate the above concepts.

Across a broad array of contributors it is possible to identify key elements common to all definitions.

Box 3.1. Social Change Characteristics of Community Development

- Empowerment of communities[7] through input into decisions that affect them.
- Participation is crucial to empowerment.
- Empowerment extends to capacity building (including training and education) of community members, with a strong emphasis on moving people out of poverty.
- Access of input into policy making to challenge structural inequalities, thus challenging the root causes of poverty.
- Promotion of democratic and accountable management structures comprised predominantly of voluntary 'non-professional' management committees/boards to which an ultimate decision-making power is entrusted.
- The 'process' being as important as the 'outcome' in defining the practice.
- The strong belief that these arrangements are consistent with social change leading to social justice.

THE STATE'S DEFINITIONAL TERRAIN OF COMMUNITY DEVELOPMENT

The Irish state did build at least some of these principles into its stated definition of community development. This informed the funding and delivery of such projects on the ground. How far it has strayed from this definition is the focus of this chapter. The definitions to which the state has subscribed, at least on paper, are clear from the following:

> Community development is about promoting positive change in society in favour of those who usually benefit least. However, it is not just about making concrete changes in the quality of people's lives. It is also about how this is done, i.e. both task and processes are important. Community Development seeks to challenge the causes of disadvantage/poverty and to offer new opportunities for those lacking choice, power and resources. (DSCFA[8] 1999:3)

This definition contains the phrase 'positive change', mentions the importance of 'process' and the 'challenge' to the root cause of poverty, and alludes to the provision of opportunities to those lacking resources. These are elements that are consistently repeated by many theorists and practitioners, as we shall see below. Similar to the CDP definition, LDSIP describes community development as:

> . . . a developmental activity composed of both task and a process. The task is the achievement of social change linked to equality and social justice, and the process is the application of the principles of participation, empowerment and collective decision making in a structured and co-ordinated way. (Pobal 1999:16)

TENSIONS AND CHALLENGES TO COMMUNITY DEVELOPMENT OVER TIME

The definitions above display a statutory commitment to community development best practice, which is broadly consistent with the defining theories outlined earlier in the chapter. There has been a growing concern in recent years, however, that this commitment has become less apparent in reality. This has been influenced by the direction of Irish social policy, which has become increasingly more neo-liberal, and this has not left community development untouched (Kirby and Murphy 2008).

Within the confines of social partnership (CWC 2000) and the inclusion of the voluntary/community pillar in the social partnership process[9] towards the end of the 1990s, a consensual politics emerged (Kirby 2005; Kirby and Murphy 2008). These authors have highlighted how a move to consensual dialogue has to a large extent eroded radicalism and the political hard edge of social change efforts. Meade and O'Donovan (2002) have highlighted their belief that the community sector has been co-opted by this process. These views suggest that from the late 1990s community development essentially became so consensual that much of the social change ethos was lost.

This erosion of community development as a radical agent of social change has happened alongside an erosion of social justice values (Collins *et al.* 2010) and the triumph of the neo-liberal agenda (Allen 2009). In this context, a consensual community development response was rendered even more powerless by the failure of welfare state policies to redistribute (O'Connor 2009). There was never a greater need for real community development, but it seemed to be becoming increasingly less effective (Jacobson *et al.* 2006). This was bolstered by the celebration of individualism during the Celtic Tiger years (O'Reilly 2004) but also by 'stroke' politics (O'Carroll 1987). The latter is a form of political patronage whereby a TD or councillor in a local area 'pulls a stroke' on behalf of an individual to obtain a tangible reward – such as planning permission, the awarding of a medical card or a local authority house – from the state. Higgins (1982) and Hazelkorn (1986) have detailed over many years how this process relegates entitlements and rights to the level of a competition between individual citizens who are essentially set against each other by the public representative acting as a 'broker' between the 'client' (the citizen) and the 'patron' (the state) in order to achieve a reward. The process erodes emerging social solidarity between citizens (Hazelkorn 1986) and negatively impacts on the collective approach of community development.

The challenge of social development during and after the Celtic Tiger period has been at the heart of community development. Harvey (2004) used EU poverty reports to demonstrate that Ireland had the highest rate of relative poverty during this time; and according to Allen (2009) and Kirby (2002, 2004), there was strong evidence to show growing social inequalities in terms of income and wealth. Kirby (2004) further supported a view of growing inequality when he cited Seers and Joy (1971:7) in claiming that the traditional yardstick for social development is 'growth with equity' and in that context he contends that equality has deteriorated during these years. These claims are further supported by an OECD (2008) report on income inequality in which Ireland is ranked twenty-second in a list of thirty countries, putting it in the highest one-third, and indicating perfect inequality. In addition, O'Sullivan's report (2007) clearly shows inequality of income and wealth in Ireland. These contentions would seem to support the view that radical challenge during this time was not effective.

Galbraith's 'culture of contentment' (1992) and growing levels of inequality developed in Ireland during this period. Emily O'Reilly (2004) contends that the rapid growth of 'consumerism' nurtured a strong commitment by government to economic growth without adequate compensatory mechanisms for those who were worse off. This view is echoed by Kirby (2004), who claims that community projects (funding and numbers having grown) became increasingly mute on challenging a state project that moved Ireland closer to a free market model which was increasingly based on low tax and low spending. He claims that the Celtic Tiger years' failure in terms of social development rendered the 'economic miracle' a 'mirage'.

The collapse of socialism in the early 1990s and the triumph of neo-liberalism from the 1980s onwards also contributed to the consensual nature of community development. In the words of Fukuyama (1993) it was the 'end of history', by which he meant the end of social class divisions and conflicts over distributional shares.

Alongside the triumph of neo-liberalism, there developed a growth in the pervasiveness of 'managerial' ideology (Clarke and Newman 1997). This ideology holds that the old welfare state was hopelessly inefficient and that services provided by the state should be provided also by the private and voluntary/community sectors. Within the public and voluntary/community sector, management needed to be tightened up and subjected to more precise measurements (Clarke and Newman 1997). Performance management, reporting and increased emphasis on competitiveness were all grist to the mill of managerialism.

Given that managerialism demands outputs which are subject to measurement (report writing, financial returns, human resource management, etc.), managerial mechanisms have been designed to measure the outputs of voluntary and community organisations. This is epitomised in the SPEAK[10] program implemented by the CDP and the Family Resource Centre Programme. Consequentially, Freirean community education became increasingly marginalised within community development (Kirby 2007). The work of community development support agencies testifies that the demand for human resource and management training had grown in recent years (Family Support Agency 2010). Kirby (2007) views this as an increased move towards service provision as the modus operandi of community development, coupled with the marginalisation of social analysis and community education. Gaynor (2005) concurs with the latter view, referring to it as the 'de-politicisation of community development'. Radical social change campaigning strategies, Kirby (2007) says, are becoming increasingly 'episodic' in Irish society. Similarly, the CWC (2003) recognises the growing emphasis of service provision within community development. Meade and O'Donovan (2002) have also added to this debate by claiming that increased professionalisation has led to the marginalisation of the radical social change imperative.

Since the McCarthy Report (2009), the CDP has been effectively neutered in Ireland: nineteen CDPs have been closed down completely. Most vulnerable to closure have been those CDPs involving the highest level of politicisation and focusing on social analysis and social action in regard to women's rights, Traveller rights, poverty and inequality. Others have been reined in by being compelled to surrender their assets to the government and to be managed by the LDSIP in their region. Their management boards have been relegated to the status of advisory committees. There have also been significant cutbacks in funding (O'Connor 2010; Millar 2008). These developments are summed up well by Noreen Byrne, Co-ordinator of North Clondalkin CDP, whose funding was withdrawn. Launching a campaign to protect the assets of CDPs from being taken over by the state and to prevent the closure of CDPs, she stated that many of them felt: '[t]he heavy boot of the state on their neck through the use of economic violence and we don't actually cost much money' (Byrne 2009).

EMERGING CHALLENGES

As a result of all these tensions, a number of key problems/challenges can be identified for community development which threaten both its existence and its future development in Ireland. These may be summarised as follows.

Box 3.2. Challenges Facing Community Development in Ireland

- Dominance of service provision (Ledwith 2005; Butcher 2007; Forde et al. 2009).
- The legacy of the Celtic Tiger: a cult of individualism/consumerism (Allen 2000; O'Reilly 2004; Kirby and Murphy 2008) and the culture of contentment (Galbraith 1992).
- Clientelism in Irish politics (Higgins 1982; Hazelkorn 1986; O'Carroll 1987).
- The growth of managerialism (Clarke and Newman 1997; Kitchener et al. 2002).
- The eclipse of socialism and the global dominance of neo-liberalism (Allen 2000; Geoghegan 2008; Kirby and Murphy 2008).
- The professionalisation of community development (Meade and O'Donovan 2002; Meade 2005).
- The marginalisation of social analysis (Lynch 1999; Gaynor 2005; Kirby 2007; Allen 2009).

IMPLICATIONS AND RATIONALE FOR RESEARCH

The overwhelming conclusion arising from the above evidence is that community development in Ireland is in crisis. The closure of many CDPs, and the rationalisation of others by the Irish government as part of the McCarthy Report cutbacks announced in December 2009, further bolstered the 'crisis' in community development. As is obvious, this was/is indeed a structural problem foisted on communities by the Irish government.

However, the rationale for the research used in this chapter was not informed by this concern alone. Having spent many years working at the coal face of community development in Ireland, six of them spent supporting the Community Development and Family Support Programmes in Munster, the author had begun to gather evidence which suggests that the 'structural' problems in community development run far deeper than state funding. Some of these have been alluded to in previous sections. However, the extent of the macro socio-economic discussion contained in these commentaries often masks how these structural problems play out in the actual practice of community development on the ground. How practice evidences these problems is rarely discussed in the literature. The 'warts and all' of practice needs to be examined; and this need is the raison d'être for carrying out this research. To do this, a cross section of the major community development stakeholders' views were obtained and analysed. The methodology informing this work, and its results, are discussed next.

METHODOLOGY AND THE BROAD THEORETICAL FRAMEWORK

The broad theoretical framework adopted in this research encapsulates a number of approaches. These include critical, interpretative and participatory approaches and have been informed by the Marxist approach to social structure and the Weberian interpretative approach to social inquiry (Harvey and MacDonald 1993; Sarantakos 1998; and May 2001).

The interpretative approach derives significantly from the work of Max Weber, who coined the term 'verstehen' to describe the meaning which a person attributes to any social phenomenon. In research terms, this involves ascertaining what the research subject understands, for example, to be the meaning of community development; or his/her understanding as to why or how community development may be in crisis. The Marxist structural approach examines the role of the state, the economy and the class system in understanding any social phenomenon. In the current context, this results in an examination of the state's role in the community development process.

Participatory Research

The participatory approach strongly influenced the research's methodology. This approach involves the research subjects as active partners in the methodological design of the research process. The researcher worked closely with Farranree CDP.[11]

Farranree CDP is one of five Community Development Projects situated on Cork City's Northside. All of these projects are situated in Revitalising Areas by Planning, Investment and Development (RAPID)[12] programme areas. This project's co-operation and input to the research has been central to the work.

RESEARCH METHODS

The tools of research selected for the research were:

- A focus group interview with the staff and management group of Farranree CDP.
- Six in-depth interviews with community activists, academics and representatives of state bodies.

Table 3.1. Research methods

Focus group interview (semi-structured) (1) Purposive selection	Interviews (semi-structured) (6) Purposive selection
Management and staff, Farranree CDP	<ul><li>Voluntary management member of a Cork City CDP</li><li>Co-ordinator, Farranree CDP</li><li>Principal community worker, HSE</li><li>Director of Services, Community and Enterprise, Cork City Council</li><li>University lecturer who has researched and written extensively on community development</li><li>Social researcher and author of many subject-related publications</li></ul>

RESULTS

Given the scope and brevity of this paper, only the results of the interviews are discussed. The discussion below is based on a thematic analysis of the findings of the primary research. There are seven thematic areas.

1. Service Provision or Community Development

Interviewees were asked to comment on whether the following government statement confirms that CDPs are now conduits for a service delivery model as distinct from a community development model:

> Despite the tone of some of the coverage of the redesign of community–local development programmes and the integration strategy, those involved in community development have nothing to fear from the new model. It is all about ensuring that front line services are maintained and that the important services currently being provided continue to play a vital role in strengthening our most disadvantaged and marginalised communities. (White 2010)

The university lecturer commented that that the state now views the CDP as a conduit for service provision and that the community development model has now been replaced by a community services model. She argues that this is happening even though, at the time of its design, government posited services as only one strand of the programme, which incorporated a far greater range of possibilities aimed at reducing poverty. She stated that the new approach '. . . de-sensitises against any notion of community participation or community ownership'. She added, 'The statement stinks as it rejects any notion of the broader or more political understanding of what community development is about.'

The social researcher who was interviewed disbelieves the assurances given by Mary White on the future of community development, saying that these assurances were also given to other agencies when they were absorbed within a government department, a case in point being the Combat Poverty Agency:

> No, I wouldn't believe a word of it . . . We have not heard a squeak out of the Combat Poverty Agency since the day it was absorbed, so that's why I attach no credibility to the statement by Minister of State, Mary White. Government commitments, assurances and understanding in this area have no credibility whatsoever.

The Farranree CDP co-ordinator said that the minister's statement confirms a move towards 'pure' service provision. He added that in the new LDSIP model, community development 'is gone out the door . . . all the new model talks about is quantities and numbers . . . it doesn't in any way deal with community development work . . . our job is to be a conduit or advertising agents of services'.

The senior HSE community worker argued that the state is only interested in service provision and believes that the ultimate aim is to make all local development and local services provision the preserve of the city and county councils.

The director of community services in Cork City stated that services are now the number one aim for the state in funding community projects and that the eight CDPs in the city, although not overly expensive, will certainly be impacted upon 'by the new arrangements'. He added, 'the stated aim now is to improve efficiency and improve corporate governance and reduce duplication'.

The process of reconstituting community development to become a de-radicalised model of service provision is not unique to Ireland. This process follows the experience in the UK and has been documented by many writers, including Butcher (2007) and Margaret Ledwith (2005). In the British context, both these writers argue that there was more emphasis placed on holding on to local services such as post offices and pubs, on facilitating enterprise and on developing social provision such as housing than there was on fostering democracy. Ledwith, commenting on UK policy, states:

> [T]he term 'community empowerment' is being used as synonymous with improved service delivery – which is just a small part of the community development agenda . . . My point is that without vigilance, community development will be diverted into a different role, one which focuses primarily on service delivery and fails to analyse and act on the structures of power which continue unabated to create and recreate oppression and marginalisation. (Ledwith 2005:2)

2. Identifying Community Development Consistent with Definitional Principles

The view that community development (as defined by the literature) was practised by CDPs, at least at some levels, was the overriding message from the interviews and Farranree CDP management group. However, several of the interviewees pointed out that most projects delivered, but some did not. The Farranree CDP co-ordinator believed that participation in social partnership had weakened the process to a great extent. The HSE community worker also believed that some projects achieved a rebalancing of power inequalities, which is a critical feature in the definition of community development in Motherway (2006).

Within this broad consensus there are nuanced positions. The university lecturer, for example, points out that community development had very high expectations placed on it which it could never have hoped to achieve. New social movements exist to provide an impetus for this development, she said.

The social researcher's belief that real emancipatory community development has been practised in many projects seems influenced by the fact that most community co-ordinators have community development qualifications. This belief of professionally trained community development workers promoting a radical agenda is, however, at variance with the view that professionalisation tends to have the opposite effect – of creating elite positions and de-radicalising the community development process (Meade and O'Donovan 2002).

A crucial issue in promoting community development has been the appointment of members of the CDPs' target groups to local management committees. On this measure there was mixed evidence: some CDPs were strong while others were not. Both the Department of Community, Rural and Gaeltacht Affairs and Pobal sought the representation of target groups (e.g. lone parents, unemployed, early school leavers) on local management groups. Research carried out in its region by the South and Mid West Community Development Support Agency[13] (Bon 2007:23) with management groups of CDPs and family resource centres clearly shows that representation on these groups was not heavily drawn from the target groups. Members of management groups were in most cases drawn from more socially advantaged groupings.

Overall, the evidence suggests that attempts to operationalise critical social education (Hurley 1992) and to develop a critical consciousness within communities in order to challenge the hegemony (Gramscian) of state oppression have been only partly successful in the CDP programme. Gramscian insights are used in this context, whereby the state has created a dominant view of the world through its monopolisation of the ideological apparatus, including its dominant control of the media and education. In order to counter this dominant narrative, an alternative interpretation needs to be fostered and disseminated into the public domain through the use of adult/community education. The hope is that this can empower ordinary people into understanding the policies and structures that oppress them. It is at that stage that a 'critical consciousness' develops to challenge the 'false consciousness' that the state, in concert with the most powerful in society, has created. Low performance of empowerment as an aspect of community development has been recorded in the UK by Craig *et al.* (2011), Ledwith (2005) and Butcher (2007). These publications may be linked to others that call for a more 'critical' community development practice (Forde *et al.* 2009).

3. The Effects of Neo-Liberal Values and Principles

The university lecturer stated that neo-liberal values that promote individualism fit well with the non-collective focus of the Irish state since independence and its desire 'to farm out' welfare services to the Catholic Church and others. However, where the welfare state has expanded, she believed it is becoming increasingly privatised. This has meant more regulation of community activities that are expected to respond to the deficit in public services provision, while at the same time community organisations are becoming more closely monitored. In this context, she stated: 'Community development projects can exist in opposition to neo-liberalism but [can] also be products of that neo-liberal culture.'

Similarly, the social researcher expressed serious concerns about the impact of neo-liberalism on community development, saying that 'by definition, neo-liberalism wants the state to be diminished'. He viewed neo-liberal values as 'a form of social Darwinianism in which those communities who have the least education and assets will, by definition, sink'. These views were echoed by the Farranree CDP co-ordinator, who held the view that the neo-liberal project has strongly affected government policies in relation to CDP projects. 'They have served the elite within our society rather than the more marginalised.' The HSE community worker cited the privatisation of health services as the 'new apartheid' in the Irish health system and the privatisation of services by Cork City Council as a case in point.

The only opposing voice was the director of services, who said that the state no longer had the resources to allow CDPs not to bear their share of efficiencies and implicitly acknowledged the neo-liberal emphasis in Irish economic and social policies. However, he was largely accepting of this approach and didn't see that there was any alternative. He believed that up to a couple of years ago, when the state had plenty of resources, it allowed community projects to grow in an unplanned way, but now the state had decided to re-assert its control. 'This is largely due to the Department of Finance as part of an "efficiency drive" and community development is low enough on the list at the moment.'

He defended current examples, stating that 'the conventional thought is that we have to cut public spending and social welfare programmes . . . including community development'.

Recent years have witnessed a growing body of opinion from social scientists in Ireland that Ireland since the 1990s has increasingly developed into a neo-liberal state, accompanied by a rapid deterioration in the social outcomes of welfare state policies (Millar 2008; Kirby and Murphy 2008; O'Toole 2003; Allen 2009; Begg 2009). The draconian fiscal rectitude that has surfaced as a result of the crisis in Irish public finances since 2008 has unleashed on Irish society stronger and more negative forces within this neo-liberal paradigm, such as cuts in the numbers of schools' special needs assistants and speech and language therapists, and cuts to disability services (Inclusion Ireland website).

Community development has not escaped this maelstrom and the government cut €25 million from the programme in 2010 (Harvey 2010). This has injected fear into communities and has also been felt by those interviewed for this research. The social research points here to Darwinian ideas of only the strongest surviving.

4. Brokerage and Clientelism

There was unanimous agreement that brokerage and clientelism are a negative and divisive influence on community development.

The university lecturer believed that both brokerage and clientelism 'has created the situation where your neighbour up the road becomes your competitor rather than your ally . . . the logic is that I can only get this at somebody else's expense'. In agreement, the social researcher stated that the neo-liberal model does not allow for social solidarity but strengthens the process of individualism. In addition, brokerage is inevitable given that the state 'has not empowered independent, objective regulatory bodies'. He cited the Office of the Ombudsman as an example, claiming that it is 'quite weak'.

This process, in the view of the CDP co-ordinator, has the further effect of 'taking away the fundamental rights of people when you allow cronyism or clientelism to exist which prevents people coming together on issues which affect everyone, such as housing'.

Clientelism became widely accepted as a model of Irish politics after Chubb (1970:273) described politicians as local men who looked after their constituents' interests by 'going about persecuting civil servants'. Clientelism has the potential to translate into votes. Negative positions on the question firmly confirm the views expressed by Hazelkorn (1986) and Higgins (1982), among others. Most of the responses clearly validate Higgins's claim that clientelism and brokerage 'disorganises the poor and is an impediment to aggregating their demands' (Higgins 1982:133). According to O'Carroll (1987:77–82), brokerage TDs pull 'strokes' and are viewed as 'cute hoors' by 'sneaking regarders' in the community. This reinforces the view within communities, as is evidenced here, that collective action to secure rewards for communities from the state is not favoured, given the necessity for individual citizens to secure the services of the 'cute hoor' TD to pull a 'stroke' to deliver what is usually an entitlement of the individual.

5. Managerialism and Dispersal of the Welfare State

The strong evidence for the imposition of managerial principles on community projects was echoed by the majority of interviewees. The university lecturer said:

> [F]low charts and management reports and . . . professional community work has occurred in tandem with this creeping managerialism . . . even though you could argue that professional community work could be about other things like social analysis, without managerialism at all.

The social researcher observed that 'there is an emphasis on monitoring and reporting which is generally inappropriate', which he attributed mainly to the 'pernicious role of European social programmes and technocrats who don't understand the purpose of community development . . . which use quantitative measures which are inappropriate'.

The 'contracting out' practice, emanating from managerialism (Billis 1993; Clarke and Newman 1997), was highlighted by the CDP co-ordinator, who contended that communities are being contracted to provide services on the cheap. His views were echoed by the HSE community worker. She argued that part of managerialism is about contracting out functions previously carried out by the welfare state to community and voluntary groups. She feels that what the state expects to get back, in terms of auditing and work, is 'quite a heavy burden'. She stated that this is accompanied by a lack of commitment to power sharing and that the state is averse to social change as part of community development. Her view is that the state is not really concerned with equality, and that 'we are now in a backlash phase'. In this phase the state wants the communities to do their bidding: 'A number of projects have obeyed in Cork City and have become co-opted as a result.' This has led to 'an audit culture'.

By contrast, the director of services did not believe that the increased emphasis on report writing and accounting has harmed community development. He said that this work is essential and that the co-ordinators of projects have a strong capacity to carry out this work. He did, however, point to the danger of this process giving too much power to community co-ordinators:

> There is a danger, however, that the co-ordinator becomes the key figure as distinct from the board . . . it is much like journalism where the journalist can often become the story as opposed to the story itself . . . this happened in some projects in Cork, you know.

We may observe that managerialism has been a conjoined ideology of neo-liberalism since the early 1990s. Some of the main effects have been the state's focus on value for money, monitoring and the demand for deliverable outputs (Clarke and Newman 1997). Also, the state has 'dispersed' welfare state functions previously monopolised by powerful 'bureau professional elites' (Clarke and Newman 1997) across voluntary/community services through the contracting of a services model between the sector and the state. Clarke and Newman (1997) view this dispersal as a flexible and cheaper way for the state to deliver services.

This model, often described as 'new public management' (Kitchener *et al.* 2002), is now driving the dramatic move towards the LDSIP control of CDP projects. The CDP co-ordinator was critical of the surveillance, outputs, reports and statistics now demanded by the state and said they are 'deeply offensive'. This view was echoed by all participants in the research, except for the director of services, who claimed that communities must become more efficient with resources. The HSE community worker lamented this as a retrograde move and 'an audit culture'. Her view is that long-term successes in community development cannot be measured in this way.

6. Social Partnership and the Question of Co-option

The university lecturer asserted that social partnership has had a malign influence on CDPs. In terms of having an input into national policy, she said 'some do have a say but are not really listened to'. She doesn't believe that the so-called 'filter for popular participation' has come about. She stated:

> I don't think it works. I don't think social partnership is democratic. I think it's anti-democratic. It creates illusionary spaces where certain people participate and others are actively excluded.

The CDP voluntary management member echoed this view, saying that local partnerships in Cork City:

> . . . were very bad for community development. Community representation was always outweighed by more commercial and business interests. The model is very top down; no participatory democracy and community people have, more often than not, been tokenistic members and informed rather than consulted.

The social researcher is of the view that the machinery of partnership at a local level became difficult for CDPs, which are small organisations. This process contributed to the lack of policy input by the CDP into social partnership. The problem was exacerbated by CDPs being dealt with as individual projects, meaning that the programme itself did not gain a voice. The fact that the Department at times 'did not know what it was doing' meant that the whole programme was constructed 'on shaky foundations'.

The Farranree CDP co-ordinator stated firmly that empowerment has been drastically curtailed by the CDPs entering into partnership with the state through various local and national structures. Partnership has sidelined issues, he said, because 'many people have bought into the view that it's best to sit at the table rather than to be outside it'.

The director of services, in contrast to these views, believed that social partnership increased participation opportunities for CDPs and overall partnership was very beneficial for CDPs.

There were also serious problems at the micro level: the HSE community worker and the Farranree CDP co-ordinator were in agreement that some projects either went 'chasing the money' or developed into a 'cosy cartel' with the state.

These observations resonate with the views of Meade and O'Donovan (2002) that social partnership has had a decisively negative affect on the process of real community development. The university lecturer stressed that social partnership was never about altering income or wealth shares or redistribution. Rather it was an exercise in 'managing issues such as poverty' and the 'collective spirit' was sucked out by social partnership. In addition, social partnership was focused on economy and not society and the community members had little 'economic muscle'.

This view is also echoed by Mary Murphy (2000), who points out that the ideology of neo-liberalism, with its anti-collective and individualist foci, was insidiously inculcated into social partnership agreements throughout the 1990s. The pervasive culture of individualism and the contaminating effects of social partnership were instrumental in eroding the focus on collectivism. Allen (2000) dismisses the Irish partnership paradigm as a co-option to a neo-liberal project that attempted to replicate the USA, with all its inequalities and injustices.

Kirby and Murphy (2008) point to a position entirely consistent with the research findings, that consensual dialogue and corporatist planning have significantly eroded the social change impetus in community development. Short-term contractual funding, despite the promises by the government in the Supporting Voluntary Activity White Paper (DSCFA 2000), subordinated community members to do the state's bidding.

Meade (2005) believes that CDPs have been easily co-opted by this process. Butcher (2007) has written about de-radicalisation of community development and his publication is a cry to arms to reclaim critical community practice in the UK. In this context, Alinsky's (1972) belief in the process of change from within through dressing arguments 'in moral clothing to reach goals' did not hold true. It would seem that many CDP projects that may have started the process with Alinsky's focus finished up having themselves been indoctrinated by the arguments they originally sought to use. In this context, they have become forced followers of state policy and not drivers of it, as outlined by the social researcher. Again, the parallels with the UK are striking:

Community work is too often drawn into the latest fashions of government policy agendas because that is where the funding is, rather than developing and maintaining a clear analysis to inform action. Increasingly, the emphasis on training seems to be on skills to the exclusion of thinking about the theory and politics of community work: Government now provides a community development employment base which is fragmented, short-term and insecure with the result that practice is dominated by the policy and political context rather than creating it. (Craig *et al.* 2011).

7. The New LDSIP Structures

The university lecturer stated that the LDSIP will not promote 'process' as well as 'outcome' and added, 'I don't think it's meant to'. She described the Centre for Effective Services report underlying the new structure as 'horrendous': it makes claims that are not even referenced and 'evades any kind of responsibility to address the complexities of community development'. With regard to the disbandment of local management groups, the lecturer claimed that members of community management groups are:

> . . . quite disgusted at this because it takes a huge element of power away from the management groups . . . hours and money that was involved in training management committees will be lost . . . it's offensive and patronising . . . this is the volunteer alms-giving model.

The social researcher's view was somewhat similar. He stated that the Centre for Effective Services designed the new LDSIP model and claimed that it is difficult to interpret from their report how the values of community development could possibly be maintained in the new process: community development is more concerned with 'qualitative outcomes and policy-focused analysis'. He found it difficult to understand how the new LDSIP structures will support this. He added that 'service provision may become the dominant paradigm' within local development companies.

The HSE community worker believed that within the new LDSIP model the 'process' will not be cherished at all. She feared that projects will be governed by a business model, 'where the main concern for the state is to get the best value for its buck . . . the projects are only the servants, the state is saying that it wants business outcomes'.

She also pointed out that community development is a slow model and that it takes time to show outcomes. She also believed that LDSIP is almost more about labour activation measures with a big focus on FÁS and Community Employment (CE) schemes. She added, 'I don't think it will be collective action, equality . . . they'll say, we've been there and done that . . . now we want you to do what we want to do.'

The director of services believed that as a direct result of the new structures, there will be an increased emphasis on outcomes. He added that there will be a loss in process, which had been important in getting marginalised people to participate.

The Farranree CDP co-ordinator said he was taken aback at the LDSIP structures. As a result of the abolition of the management groups, he believed that 'participation has been thrown on the scrap heap'. He added:

> The new LDSIP programme is bad for community development as it is 'an integrated service approach' and no more. Traditionally, the CDP programme was about balancing inequalities and action learning. It was about equipping people to bring about the change themselves . . . it was about challenging through collective action the inequalities that exist in our society . . . it was about those things but those things became very short-lived.

The voluntary management CDP member commented that LDSIP will keep government 'up there' and communities 'down there' and that's how government prefers it.

The new LDSIP will affect change in CDPs and has become a deliberate strategy of the Irish state in the past two to three years, according to all those interviewed. For the HSE community worker, we are now witnessing a 'state backlash', given that in recent years the state has begun to fear the social change strategies of many CDPs across the country. This view was echoed by Kathleen O'Neill, a CDP activist, in a paper delivered to a conference on community development in Ireland (O'Neill 2010). In her paper, the author, who is a CDP co-ordinator in Kilbarrack, Dublin, stated that it was the more radical projects, which continue to do political and community development work, that have had their contracts with the state terminated.

The imposition of the LDSIP model and the 'backlash' (as expressed by the HSE community worker) against community development values and processes are very obviously part of the twin effects of neo-liberal ideology and new public management (Kitchener et al. 2002) within the managerial state (Clarke and Newman 1997), as discussed previously. However, the timing of the 'backlash' and the introduction of LDSIP is interesting. The Irish public finances have deteriorated dramatically in the past two years. In an effort to convince the Irish population that they should absorb cutbacks to services, government has warned of disastrous consequences if fiscal rectitude is not implemented. This has now become the 'shock doctrine' (Klein 2007) of Irish public policy. In this context, it could be observed that 'shock doctrine' has been used as the vehicle to implement high cuts to the voluntary and community sector. This view is supported by the HSE community worker's statement that 'the government would never have got away with this five years ago'.

CONCLUSION

The previous discussion suggests that the Irish state has been by far the most culpable in endangering the survival of community development. It has removed local management groups of CDPs and taken their assets; it has terminated the contracts of a number of CDPs; it has removed their support agencies; it has introduced managerial practices; and it has failed to understand the nature of community development. What seems certain, however, is that government has detected the growing power of CDPs, and that the demise of community development in Ireland may be due to, more than anything, a perverse response by the state to a growing political influence in the process. The Irish financial crisis has been used as justification to bestow a 'shock doctrine' (Klein 2007) which many suspect is more akin to ideological influences than to the demands of fiscal rectitude.

Further research needs to delimit solutions which might focus on:

- The creation of community media sources, which is already happening to some degree, to challenge the hegemonic ideological consensus of the neo-liberal agenda
- The re-politicisation of community development arising from possible alliances between community development projects and political parties/representatives on the left in Ireland, which has increased significantly since the 2011 election.
- The increased use of direct action and a return to the original roots of community development in community action (Popple 1995).
- The forging of more working groups and partnerships with the trade union movement, a feature of community development in Great Britain in the 1960s (Curno 1978).

Community development cannot be allowed to perish.

Notes

1   Area-Based Partnerships were initially set up from agreements under the Programme for Economic and Social Progress (PESP) 1991–94 and subsequently under the Programme for Competitiveness and Work (1994–96).
2   Since January 2010, Area-Based Partnerships have been renamed as Local Development Companies, of which there are now 53 nationwide.
3   This programme was set up under the auspices of the Department of Community, Rural and Gaeltacht Affairs. (This department was renamed in 2010 as the Department of Community, Equality and Gaeltacht Affairs and again in May 2011 as the Department of Environment, Community and Local Government.)
4   Also set up by the Department of Community, Rural and Gaeltacht Affairs.
5   The Family Support Agency has responsibility for this programme.
6   This anglicised term derives from Freire's concept of *conscientização* (Portuguese), which refers to learning to perceive social, political and economic contradictions and leading to take action against the oppressive elements of reality.
7   These may be geographically based communities or communities of interest.

8 This government department subsequently became known as the Department of Community, Rural and Gaeltacht Affairs.

9 Other groups included farmers, business groups and trade unions.

10 SPEAK – Strategic Planning, Evaluation and Knowledge – is a software package that CDPs use to evaluate their performance in communities.

11 Subsequent to this research, Farranree CDP's funding was withdrawn as the management group decided not to agree to new arrangements for CDPs under the new LDSIP programme.

12 The RAPID programme includes urban areas that have been designated disadvantaged. The rural equivalent of RAPID is Ceantair Laga Árd-Riachtanais (CLÁR).

13 The research area included counties Cork, Kerry, Clare and Limerick.

4

Changing the Rules of the Game: Supporting Community Development – Empowerment in Practice

Colm O'Doherty

A sense of equality is necessary to freedom because when a society breaks down into hopelessly unequal blocs the elite in its own defence will seek to contain – that is repress – the disaffected. . . . An unequal society is an angry and fearful society, and a fearful society is not a free society. (Updike 1992)

CHAPTER SUMMARY

A brief review of the literature reveals that an understanding of and a commitment to the concept of empowerment and its grassroots strategy of participation are at the core of community development. This chapter discusses and clarifies the importance of empowerment in relation to the well-being of individuals, communities and wider society. Theories and understandings of well-being are introduced to enable the reader to understand the importance of social context and circumstances for well-being. The link between well-being and government policies is established. Finally the chapter spells out how community development processes can strengthen the capacity of people to be involved in social transformation activities which redistribute power and enhance well-being.

INTRODUCTION

Community development is best understood as a process for building relationships of trust and integrity, between citizens, communities and wider society. In community development, people's social involvement and social interaction are regarded as sources of well-being. Enabling strategies employed to build these relationships expand the capabilities of people to take control of their lives and extend their levels of participation in social and economic life. The Community Workers' Co-operative has identified key elements of community development work:

It is centred on a series of principles that seek to go beyond consultation to participation and beyond capacity building to consciousness raising and empowerment. (CWC 2008:10)

This quotation tells us that community development is not governed by profit or power but by enthusiasm for expanding the capabilities of people to lead the kind of lives they value – and have reason to value. Practice is not based on an acceptance of the natural order of things. Instead the focus is on challenging and questioning how resources, power and social rules are manufactured and distributed within communities and between communities and wider society. Empowerment changes the rules of the game and enables people to play a different game.

THE RULES OF THE GAME: UNDERSTANDING HOW SOCIETY WORKS

To understand why empowerment is important we need to start thinking about what we mean by society and the relationship between society and the well-being of individuals, families and communities. Well-being is brought about when the basic physical and social needs, which all people across the world more or less share, are met. Some social theorists, such as Dean (2010), distinguish between two aspects of human need. This distinction is expressed through the notion of 'thin' needs, which require satisfaction in order to survive; and 'thick' needs, which when met enable a person to have a sense of purpose, feel able to achieve important goals, participate in society and make a contribution to the community (see Box 4.1).

Box 4.1. Different Kinds of Needs

Thin needs:

- Shelter
- Food/water
- Healthcare
- Non-hazardous living environment
- Non-hazardous work environment
- Financial security

Thick needs:

- Having a sense of purpose
- Feeling able to achieve important goals
- Participating in society
- Having supportive personal relationships
- Living in a strong and inclusive community
- Having meaningful and rewarding work

To return to my earlier point – it is the relationship between individuals and society which determines how these needs are met. This relationship is strongly influenced by government policy.

Activity: Establishing the Link Between Policy and Well-being

Which of these statements matches your thoughts about society and well-being? What do they tell us about government policy?
Statement 1 A certain level of income is required to meet people's basic needs. Poverty, financial stress and financial insecurity have negative effects on well-being.
Do current government policies meet these economic needs?
Statement 2 Participation in education and employment are important for well-being. ·
What are the well-being issues related to education and employment?

Statement 3 Relationships lie at the heart of a person's well-being.
How do government policies affect people's relationships?
Statement 4 Housing/shelter and the wider environment make a big contribution to people's well-being.
Which government policies are likely to play an important part in meeting these needs?
Statement 5 Health is a major element of well-being.
Do government policies enable people to be healthy?
Statement 6 The well-being of individuals and wider society is affected by the calibre of government we have and whether or not ordinary people have a real say in decisions which affect their lives.
In your view, do we have a quality government? Give reasons for your view.

This activity should have started you thinking about the link between well-being and policy. A government policy forum report on well-being tells us that:

> There are essentially two aspects to the role of public policy in promoting well-being: the first is that citizens who have high levels of well-being are likely to make a positive contribution to society; and the second is that the state has a shared responsibility in supporting the well-being of its citizens. (NESC 2009:38)

However, it is quite likely that the activity above highlighted for you the reality that government policies may not always meet essential human needs as fully as they might do, or that the needs of all people in a society are not met equally: the government's policies may favour one group of citizens over another. When some essential needs, such as a reasonable income to live on, remain unmet, there are significant harmful implications for individuals and the wider society. Imbalanced or inadequate policy making disadvantages individuals, groups and communities and relegates them to the margins of society. The disadvantaged individuals, groups and communities at the receiving end of the policy are then at risk of poverty and social exclusion (Box 4.2).

Box 4.2. Poverty and Social Exclusion

> Poverty and social exclusion are two very distinct, though interrelated phenomena. Poverty generally refers to a lack of income and resources. The EU uses a relative definition of poverty and people are said to be living in poverty if their income and resources are so inadequate as to preclude them from having a standard of living considered acceptable in the society in which they live. Social exclusion is a much broader and multidimensional concept that encompasses income poverty, unemployment, access to education, information, childcare and health facilities, living conditions as well as social participation. It is multi-layered insofar as the causes of exclusion can be at the national, community, household or individual level. (Eurostat 2010)

Broadly speaking, the notion of poverty is primarily focused on individuals' and households' participation in the material economy, while the notion of social exclusion is primarily focused on their participation in the interpersonal economy (Box 4.3).

Box 4.3. The Interpersonal Economy

[E]ach person adds something to the collective value that makes up a society. How each person does so is through their interactions with others, in various social units, from families to social movements and political parties. These interactions create extra value (though they can also diminish the value experienced by some participants, for example through stigma, disrespect, unfairness or oppression). Each interaction (between two people or a group) is therefore like a small enterprise (a cooperative factory, a shop or service) in which value is produced – but (like these) it may also exploit or cheat some 'workers' or 'customers', or cause 'pollution' to some third parties.

The difference between the material economy producing goods, and the interpersonal economy producing feelings (including morale, team spirit and solidarity) and culture (ideas, images, science, art, music and drama) is that the latter produces something intangible and difficult to measure. But what the interpersonal economy produces is *real*. It determines our emotional state, it shapes our wider engagements with the material economy and the formal systems of government, and it provides us with both the *resources* and *restraints* for our thoughts and actions. In other words, our social world is shaped and patterned by the interpersonal economy. (Jordan 2007:xi)

THE RULES OF THE GAME: WHO MAKES THEM?

The main concern of Antonio Gramsci (1891–1937), an Italian Marxist who was imprisoned and died under Mussolini, was to help us understand the nature of power in society and how the dominant ideas of society permeate our thinking and convince us that the interests of the powerful are the natural order of things. This view of the world becomes part of our everyday thinking and we can no longer distinguish between ideas and thoughts which have infiltrated our minds through a process of cultural domination or hegemony (a term coined by Gramsci) and ideas and thoughts which are truly generated by our own experiences. Ruling by consent, the state prefers to use negotiating skills to produce compromise, although it has the ability to use force if necessary (Box 4.4).

Box 4.4. Hegemony

We appear to be making the rules, but our thinking is heavily influenced by the ideas of the powerful in society. Their agenda becomes our agenda, their ideas become our ideas. Control of society is not achieved through coercion and force but rather through persuading people that the views and ideas of the powerful are reasonable and sensible.

> Whereas coercion is exercised overtly through the armed forces, the police, the courts and prisons, consent is subtly woven through the institutions of civil society – the family, schools, the media, political parties, unions, religious organisations, cultural, charitable and community groups – in a way that permeates our social being and asserts hegemonic control by influencing our ideas. (Ledwith 2005:122–3)
>
> Through this process social divisions in society appear natural and given. Marginalised and excluded sections of society are convinced that these arrangements are normal and it becomes common sense that there should be differences in how people are treated in society. Inequality and social exclusion is maintained by the consent of the powerless, rather than the coercion of the powerful.

In most societies there are differences between people, which have resulted in some people being treated less favourably than others, and in some people benefiting from these differences. Different treatment paves the way for the construction of social divisions which can be formalised and policed through the legal system or be upheld through informal social sanctions. These divisions are then maintained by laws, social rules, attitudes, beliefs, values and principles. Some differences between people are naturally occurring, but socially structured differences result in discrimination, inequality and lack of equal opportunity. These differences extend across economic, political, social and cultural spheres of life and are reproduced by successive generations through sets of 'god-given' or 'natural' beliefs and values.

CHANGING THE RULES OF THE GAME

Community development workers build relationships with citizens, work together with them to identify how to solve a problem and enable them to be active and take action within their communities. Community development is, therefore, primarily concerned with enhancing the skills, knowledge, confidence and organisational capacity within communities so that they can:

- recognise how differential access to power (social, political and economic) accounts for the disadvantage, exclusion and oppression of some groups over others;
- understand how power can be mobilised to achieve the resource redistribution and service improvements that will help reduce such poverty and exclusion;
- implement successful strategies that will effectively challenge the rules of the game which create the unfair power relations.

EMPOWERMENT STRATEGIES

In the real world, while community empowerment will rarely unfold in a smooth step-by-step manner, building the resilience of communities and the confidence of residents levels the playing field and prepares the ground for healthy co-operation to replace unhealthy competition. Community development practitioners provide game-changing support for improving citizens' and communities' 'outlook'. Healthy co-operation (Box 4.5) is a positive way of accessing power sources at different levels. Good conversations and active communication channels foster constructive dialogue between professionals and communities.

Box 4.5. Healthy Co-operation Framework

1 **Between citizens themselves.** Social capital[1] (particularly bridging and linking social capital) and social trust would appear to be fundamental building blocks of a healthy community. Where these do not exist, communities can become inward-looking and unresponsive to consultation, engagement or other interventions, treating strangers – including public agencies and other external offers of support – with hostility.

2 **Between citizens and wider agencies.** Some of the best examples of neighbourhood renewal involve excellent partnerships – working between a range of different agencies – public, private and voluntary – but crucially involving members of the local community. Neighbourhood management has gained a strong reputation precisely because of this approach.

3 **Between different 'tiers' of state action.** Very often strategic planning fails to take significant account of variations between neighbourhoods. Good co-operation requires a much better joining-up between neighbourhood prioritisation and district, city and region-wide policy-making.

4 **Between the 'centre' and the 'locality'.** There has been much government rhetoric over several years about the need for decentralisation. But in fact there has been very little 'letting go'. (Oppenheim *et al.* 2010:3–4)

Individuals who intend to take responsibility for changing the rules of the game in order to gain more control over their circumstances and lives will benefit from a process of training and capacity building[2] leading towards change and learning. The starting point for this process is a guided inquiry into the different dimensions of our lives which we want to transform (Box 4.6).

Box 4.6. Individual Empowerment Strategy

Intellectual Dimension
I want to understand:

- how society works
- my responsibilities and rights as a citizen
- the meaning of personal relationships
- other people's behaviour and reactions to me

and to:

- identify my own strengths and areas where I am not so strong (weaknesses)
- learn to solve different problems individually and in a group.

Social Dimension

I want to:

- get along and co-operate with my social network
- interact with adults in an appropriate manner
- interact with others in an appropriate manner
- understand how my personal behaviour has an impact on others and develop my behaviour according to feedback.

Emotional Dimension

I want to:

- recognise my feelings (negative and positive) and how they affect others' behaviours and reactions
- learn self-control
- improve my self-esteem; have faith in my own abilities and possibilities
- have more confidence in meeting other people
- learn to trust other people more
- lift my sense of spirits.

Physical Dimension

I want to:

- improve my health and safety.

Source: Saarnio *et al.* 2006.

Collective Empowerment Strategy: Active Citizenship

The conditions necessary for fully functioning, capable communities include: high levels of social trust, equality, concern for others; ability to solve problems; participation; access to resources; well-informed residents; and a positive community outlook. In order to create these conditions residents require skills and opportunities to become active citizens[3] making connections between their individual learning and the potential for solving collective problems and achieving social goals. The interaction of different forms of capital – human, social, institutional and economic – can be harnessed to improve or maintain a given community.

Human capital is the capacity of individuals, through their skills, knowledge and health status, to contribute to the well-being of their community. *Social capital* refers to social networks based on trust and reciprocity that enable individuals and groups to collectively resolve common problems, achieve common goals and contribute to the well-being of the community. *Institutional capital* is created through organisational development and strengthening which enhances the ability of organisations to plan, undertake and sustain or build on activities that can contribute to the well-being of the community. *Economic capital* is the economic resources of the community at all levels that can be accessed to contribute to the well-being of the community.

It is important that community development practitioners take a holistic approach here and recognise that a combination of human, social, institutional and economic capital builds empowered and empowering communities (Figure 4.1).

Figure 4.1. Interaction of different forms of capital

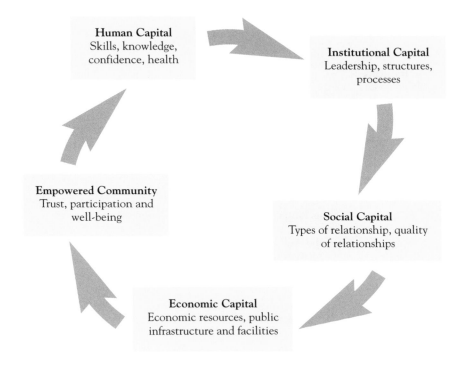

THE PROCESS OF EMPOWERMENT

Community empowerment is about both processes and outcomes – how we work and what happens as a result. It is about empowering *processes* – taking an approach that is empowering for others, not dictatorial, bossy or directive. And it is about empowering *outcomes* – changes that are enduring and that contribute positively to people's lives and environment. Community empowerment is the result of putting community development values and commitments into action. The five dimensions of community empowerment working are set out in Figure 4.2.

Figure 4.2. Dimensions of community empowerment

Confidence is about working in a way that increases people's knowledge and confidence

Influence is about working in a way that encourages and equips communities to take part and influence decisions

Community Empowerment

Inclusion is about working in a way that recognises that discrimination exists, and promotes equality of opportunity and good relations

Co-operation is about working in a way that builds positive relationships across groups

Organisation is about working in a way that brings people together around common issues and concerns

Source: CDX/National Empowerment Partnership 2008.

AN EMPOWERING AGENCY

The South and Mid West Community Development Support Agency was established in 1996, following a broad consultation process, to empower community development organisations working at the coal face. Since 1996 the agency has been engaged in community capacity building by providing support and training to over fifty community development and family support organisations in the region. Its mission statement, underpinning values, and strategic aims committed the agency to an empowering approach towards its work.

On the ground the agency provided community development projects with a team of policy and support workers. The support workers increased the capacity of projects to manage and deliver their work effectively. The policy workers enhanced the capacity of the community development support programmes to develop and influence policy at local, regional and national level. Working across two critical areas – capacity building and policy work – the South and Mid West workers built

Box 4.7. Mission, Values and Strategic Aims of the South and Mid West Community Development Support Agency

Mission
To work towards a just, equal and inclusive society through the process of community development.
Values which underpin all work carried out by the agency:

- People are empowered to the extent that they are able to exercise control over their lives.
- Elimination of poverty.
- Facilitation of learning as a non-directive two-way process of dialogue occurring within the parameters of a specific and transparent values agenda.
- Honesty (truthfulness, openness and preparedness to demand accountability of others).
- Promoting social change that is long-term and sustainable.

Strategic aims:

- To develop an organisation which is open to learning, responsive to change and committed to its ongoing development.
- To explore, promote and support the process of community development as a way of working.
- To be a positive force for the elimination of poverty, inequality and social exclusion.

Source: South and Mid West Community Development Support Agency (2010)

community capacity through a process of organisational development. They have been instrumental in identifying opportunities that communities want to grasp and issues that communities want to address. The critical role played by the South and Mid West Community Development Support Agency in organisational development and community empowerment in the region is set out in Table 4.1 overleaf.

Table 4.1. South and Mid West Community Development Support Agency: organisational development and community empowerment strategies

Organisational Development	Policy Work
• *Pre-development* Support the setting up of new community projects as needs arose in the region and assist in the development of community profiles • *Capacity building* Identification of training and development of voluntary management committees Review and evaluation Development of strategic plans Support best practice in recruitment and staff management, running meetings and decision making, roles and responsibilities Conflict resolution Organisational change • *Training* in areas such as strategic planning, facilitation, community development evaluation/review, recruitment, staff support structures, good employment practice Developing appropriate training materials Developing flexible and innovative responses to the training needs of voluntary management committees Provision of training to projects in the development and implementation of equality and anti-racist policies	• Research development and support • Identification of policy lessons and issues emerging from the work of projects • Resource projects on an individual and collective basis in the identification and development of policy • Documentation • Policy training and support • Networking and facilitation • Development of policy submissions • Co-ordinating policy networking at regional level • Supporting the work of project representatives on various forums

CONCLUSION

Empowerment begins with an understanding of how society works – the rules of the game. Community development processes work to improve the capacity of individuals and communities to relate to the world around them as active, critical, engaged citizens capable of changing the rules of the game. The explicitly moral and political nature of community development work finds expression in changing the rules of the game so that needs are met, well-being is promoted and communities are strengthened. As Jordan puts it:

> Because it deals in natural settings and collective action, community work is necessarily concerned with how resources and power are distributed, both within communities themselves, and between them and wider society. It addresses issues of equality, justice, participation and change directly, through collective action which makes claims on mainstream society and the government, as well as in members' dealings with each other. (Jordan 2007:115–16)

The essential distinguishing feature of community development is its concern with real social progress. For those engaged in community development, well-being provides something more than gross domestic product as a measure of progress. Real value is created through the interpersonal economy and community empowerment, is achieved by putting community development values and commitments into action, and can offset some of the risks to people's well-being in recessionary times.

Notes

1   The term 'social capital' refers to social networks based on trust and reciprocity that enable people to collectively resolve common problems and achieve common goals. Essentially, the theory of social capital can be summed up in two words: 'relationships matter'. There are different types of social capital which are important in different situations or moments of people's lives. *Bonding* is based on relationships between people who are similar – friends, family and other close-knit groups. Bonding social capital resides in family and friendship relationships, and in peer groups. *Bridging* is formed from connections between people who have less in common – people from different communities, classes or racial or ethnic backgrounds. It is about creating links with people outside our immediate circles. *Linking* refers to alliances between communities and individuals or groups with formal power, particularly power over resources required for economic and social development.

2   Capacity building is achieved by increasing the personal and collective resources of individuals and communities, to help them develop the skills and knowledge they need to respond to challenges and seize opportunities that come their way.

3   Active citizens get involved with each other to pursue their interests and goals, for example relating to sports, residents' associations, cultural activities and faith groups. Active citizens also get involved in challenging the way things get done – becoming 'awkward' and vocal citizens who challenge systems and structures of governance and power so that they work better for them and their communities.

Achieving Culturally Competent Practice in Community Development Settings

Bernadette Naughton

CHAPTER SUMMARY

This chapter is an introductory text addressing the issue of cultural diversity in Ireland. A short vignette sets out some of the complex issues that are linked to cultural diversity. The chapter defines culturally competent best practice, providing suggestions for enhancing the knowledge and skill base of the reader, as well as highlighting the importance and value of cultural competence in community development work.

INTRODUCTION

The history of cultural diversity in Ireland has been quite distinct in the European context. It is sometimes assumed that 'diversity' is a 'new' challenge for a society that was previously homogeneous. However, Ireland has always been a diverse nation, with a range of ethnic, cultural and faith-based communities whose presence has been of sufficiently long standing to be considered permanent. In the past, immigrants to Ireland came mainly from the UK, the USA and continental Europe. In 2001, people of Chinese descent formed the largest ethnic minority in Ireland; there was also a small but long-established Jewish community and growing Islamic and Asian communities (NCCRI 2003).

Two of the main channels of legal immigration for non-EU migrants are: as work permit holders; and via the asylum system.

Work Permit Holders (Labour Immigrants)

From 1995 to 2007, during Ireland's economic boom known as the Celtic Tiger, unemployment fell drastically and, facing a labour shortage, the government opened its borders to non-Irish nationals in order to meet employers' demand for labour. Most of the new arrivals were young males from Poland and Lithuania, reflecting the accession of these states to the EU in 2004. Many found work in the retail and service sectors and the construction industry (Barrett and McCarthy 2006). By 2008, 14 per cent of the workforce comprised non-Irish nationals. The Irish ethnic landscape had changed dramatically, particularly in Dublin and other large cities – Cork, Limerick and Galway – where immigrants formed a growing proportion of the population (Barrett and McCarthy 2006). Barrett and McCarthy (2006) also noted that Ireland was unusual in terms of the speed with which the non-native national percentage of its population rose.

A second unique feature of immigration into Ireland has been the relatively high levels of education of immigrants. This is in contrast to the experience in the USA, for example, where immigrants are generally less skilled than the native population (Barrett and McCarthy 2006). Relevant studies note that not all non-Irish immigrants are employed in occupations that fully reflect their education levels. McGinnity et al. (2006) found that almost two-thirds of work permit holders they sampled reported being overqualified for their current job. Immigrants, particularly those from non-English-speaking countries, typically suffered a wage penalty, earning less than comparable Irish workers. Hegarty (2007), in her study of black African women's experiences in Ireland, suggests that the main barriers experienced in accessing employment were: lack of recognition of professional qualifications; lack of work experience in Ireland; multiple discrimination based on gender, race and religion; and lack of references from Irish employers. Many women were engaged as domestic workers, a hidden, isolated and largely unregulated sector of employment in which there are high levels of corruption and in which workers are at greater risk of becoming undocumented (Hegarty 2007).

Importantly, linguistic ability is also a factor which determines integration and economic progress for the immigrant worker.

Asylum Seekers

A person seeking asylum, or an 'asylum seeker', is someone who has left their country of origin, has applied for recognition as a refugee in another country, and is awaiting a decision on their application (Migrant Rights Centre Ireland (MRCI) 2008). If their application is successful, they will be given refugee status. Applications for asylum began to build up from a very low base of nine in 1991 to around eight thousand by the end of the 1990s (MRCI 2008). The sharp increase in the number of applications continued into the new century and reached a peak in 2002, though it still represented only a tiny proportion (2 per cent in 2006) (MRCI 2008) of the overall European figure (Office of the Refugee Applications Commissioner 2010). In 2009, the top six nationalities seeking asylum in Ireland were from Nigeria, Pakistan, China, Democratic Republic of Congo, Zimbabwe and Georgia. In 2010, the majority of applicants were men aged 25–34 (Office of the Refugee Applications Commissioner 2010).

The Irish government has always operated a restrictive policy in terms of granting asylum seekers refugee status and the legal privileges associated with refugee status. As a result, most asylum applications in Ireland are unsuccessful. In 2002, of 11,634 applicants for refugee status, only 894 were successful. There were ninety-seven successful applicants in 2009 (Office of the Refugee Applications Commissioner 2010).

The issues which confront people seeking asylum and those with refugee status in Ireland are complex and varied. Asylum applicants may not take up work in Ireland and if they are unable to source accommodation from their own funds, must reside in direct provision centres where all food and board costs are met by the state. This inability to contribute to the economy and to society heightens asylum seekers' feelings of marginalisation and exclusion.

The following vignette is a short illustration of the experiences of one asylum seeker in a school setting. It provides a window into some of the challenges faced by minority groups living in Ireland and their service providers.

Nigerian-born Zola is 9 years old and celebrating her fourth Christmas in Ireland. She arrived with her mum, Victoria, from Nigeria in 2005 seeking asylum status. Zola and her mum are part of the 10 per cent of our island's population who consider themselves non-Irish (CSO 2008).

Zola is generally regarded as a happy child, though she and her mum have experienced difficulties in accessing the state services to which they are entitled as asylum seekers. Like many other migrants, Zola's mum was not aware of how the state's various systems work, what services exist and how they can be accessed.

Zola attends school in the town where she and her mum live. She is playful and occasionally perceived as boisterous. She tends to express her feelings openly and with expansive gesticulations, leading to a perception among some of her indigenous peers that she is 'a bit mad' or 'crazy'.

There are six other children of Nigerian extraction in Zola's class at school. Zola is friendly with some of them, less so with others. Contrary to expectations among some of her teachers, Zola does not share a common first language with the other children of Nigerian extraction in her class, because she comes from a different racial sub-group in Nigeria, and different languages are spoken and different customs followed in each home.

Zola has experienced some difficulties in dealing with authority figures at her school. Although she is not a disruptive child, teachers have noted her tendency to look at the ground when being addressed by an older person. This has led to the mistaken assumption among some that she is untrustworthy, painfully shy and has poor concentration skills.

As illustrated in this example, membership of any ethnic group helps to shape a person's interpretations, responses, attitudes and behaviours. When we overlook culture, or when we do not understand what is normal in the context of a particular culture, we limit our ability to engage children and families and build on their strengths. One of the main challenges facing service providers is communication. This encompasses everything from the need for interpreters to nuances of words in various languages to the significance of non-verbal communication. The lack of awareness about the diversity that exists within similar cultural backgrounds means that Zola and her Nigerian friends are treated as if they were all the same, leading to over-generalisation and stereotyping. Education and training can provide service providers with the knowledge and skills to work effectively with children and families of all backgrounds. Cultural competence can foster a positive cultural identity, promote social contact, combat loneliness and isolation, as well as maintain people as active members of society.

Zola was one of 420,000 non-Irish nationals living in Ireland at the time of the Census in April 2006. They came from 188 different countries (CSO 2006) and have greatly diversified the cultural tapestry of Ireland. Zola and her family are 'ethnic minorities' in Ireland. For the purposes of this chapter, this term refers to all sub-groups of the population not indigenous to Ireland who hold cultural traditions and values derived, at least in part, from their countries of origin. The author deals in the main with families from Africa, Asia and other non-EU countries, Irish-born members of these groups and people of mixed race, in other words the ethnic minorities who have come to comprise 'new communities' in Ireland.

The term 'ethnic minority' refers to groups who are in the minority. The term 'minority' in itself can be confusing and misleading. Non-Caucasians, for example, constitute the majority of the world's population, and the term can rob people of a sense of cultural heritage and cultural identification.

This chapter will now address the meaning of culturally competent practice and its practical implications for community development workers, and will make suggestions for best practice when working with families like Zola's.

DEFINING CULTURAL COMPETENCE

The drive for cultural competence comes from the recognition that Irish society is increasingly becoming a multi-ethnic and multi-faith society.

The definition of culture is central to the study of cultural competence. Culture is defined by Devore and Schlesinger (1999) as a broad, overriding concept that revolves around the view that human groups differ in the way they structure their behaviour, in their world view, in their perspectives on the rhythms and patterns of life, and in how they perceive the essential nature of the human condition on matters such as the relationship between humans, the spirits, and the gods (Schlesinger and Devore 2007). 'Culture' refers to the common experiences that shape the way a group or community understands the world. Culture is often referred to as the totality of ways of being passed on from generation to generation. Culture is therefore reflected in religions, morals, customs, technologies and survival strategies. It affects how we work, parent, love and marry, and how we understand concepts such as health, mental health, wellness, illness, disability and death (Chu and Goode 2009). A definition of culture should be dynamic (McGoldrick and Giordano 1996). A static definition reduces culture to sets of enduring traits. It encourages broad generalisations and stereotypes that do not allow for the constant transformation that people and societies undergo. A fluid definition of culture allows for change and attention to individual differences while recognising the lasting influence of certain experiences (Mederos and Woldeguiorguis 2003).

There is a clear distinction between culture, ethnicity and race, and these terms should not be used interchangeably as they have different meanings. Social scientists often refer to a group of people who share a common set of beliefs, common history, common religion, often similar physical features and a common language as an ethnic group. Yet many cultures and subcultures can exist within a defined ethnic group, though some common history may be shared (Roberts *et al.* 1990). For example, in Nigeria alone, there are over three hundred different cultural patterns evidencing distinct beliefs, values, customs and cultural identity.

A multitude of terms, such as 'cultural awareness', 'cultural sensitivity', 'cultural knowledge' and 'cultural competence' have all been used interchangeably to describe 'best practice' in working with ethnic groups. However, 'cultural competence' is most preferred by those working with ethnic minorities and typically denotes more than simply being 'sensitive' or merely 'knowledgeable' regarding the needs of others. Competence pertains to proficiency in cross-cultural interactions with an emphasis on restructuring attitudes and developing the ability to work effectively across cultures in a way that acknowledges and respects the culture of the person or organisation being served. Competence requires that all practitioners develop a critical mindset that questions frames of reference. This necessitates an explicit awareness of one's own cultural roots and the biases one might hold about those who are culturally different. Competence implies the possession of skills and knowledge that help to translate opinions into appropriate behaviour in the context of daily interaction with service users. Similarly, Green (1995:52) asserts that a culturally competent practitioner is able to conduct his or her 'professional work in a way that is congruent with the behaviour and expectations that members of a distinctive culture recognise as appropriate among themselves'.

Cultural competence is never fully achieved or realised, but is rather a lifelong developmental process of learning and relearning. Individuals and organisations are at various levels of awareness, knowledge and skills, represented by what Mason refers to as the 'cultural competence continuum' (Mason 1993, cited in Hanley 1999). The cultural competence continuum includes five progressive steps: cultural destructiveness, cultural incapacity, cultural blindness, cultural pre-competence and cultural competence (see Figure 5.1).

Figure 5.1. The cultural competence continuum

Cultural Destructiveness	Cultural Incapacity	Cultural Blindness	Cultural Pre-competence	Cultural Competence
The most negative end of the continuum is represented by attitudes, policies, and practices that are destructive to cultures and consequently to the individuals within cultures, e.g. the Anti-Trespass Act 2002, which blocked off traditional camping areas to Travellers and the lack of provision of transient accommodation to facilitate nomadism.	The system or agency does not intentionally seek to be culturally destructive, but rather lacks the capacity to help minority clients or communities, e.g. not providing bilingual personnel when needed.	This is the midpoint in the continuum. The system and its agencies provide services with the expressed intent of being unbiased. They function with the belief that colour or culture make no difference and that all people are the same, e.g. the Melting Pot Theory, which refers to the fusion of all nationalities into one culture and ignores cultural strengths.	Agencies and individuals move toward the positive end of the continuum by recognising cultural differences and making efforts to improve, e.g. making the waiting room more welcoming with pictures, magazines and music that reflect the culture(s) of the community served.	Culturally competent agencies and individuals accept and respect cultural differences, continue self-assessment of cultural awareness, pay careful attention to the dynamics of cultural differences, continually expand their cultural knowledge and resources, and adopt culturally relevant service models in order to better meet the needs of minority populations.

Source: adapted from Hanley 1999.

CULTURALLY COMPETENT BEST PRACTICE

Three essential elements have emerged from the literature as being central to the development of culturally competent best practice:

1 values and attitudes
2 knowledge
3 skills.

(See Figure 5.2.)

How these three elements work to create culturally competent practice is explained below.

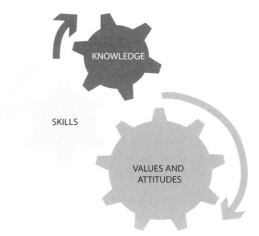

Figure 5.2. Elements central to the development of culturally competent best practice

Values and Attitudes

At the heart of culturally competent practice is the notion of values. Values underlie the interactions that take place in cross-cultural situations (Woodroffe 2007). Values are standards or principles about what is right or wrong expressed by both practitioner and the client in the interaction (Woodroffe 2007). Values are learned. Communication patterns, attitudes and behaviour are influenced by values. Lifestyle choices, education, career, relationships, male/female roles, family structure (who is considered a family member), care of the elderly, childrearing, patterns of attachment, decision-making styles, approaches to completing tasks and approaches to conflict are all influenced by cultural values. Traditional approaches to disciplining children are also influenced by culture. Self-identity is influenced by cultural values.

Values are an inherent part of non-verbal communication. Take, for example, the non-expressed value behind silence. Traditional eastern cultures typically value silence more than western societies. Silence is often seen as a sign of mutual respect, dignity and wisdom, whereas in the USA, for example, silence can be seen to signify lack of attention and lack of initiative.

Typically in western culture, a person must speak to participate, in contrast to the Chinese notion that silence means agreement. In Chinese culture, silence denotes respect, not a fear of communicating (Jandt 2010). Similarly, direct eye contact is often regarded in the west as a sign of listening and respect. In African culture, direct eye contact denotes a lack of respect. Many African children, like Zola, don't look older people in the eye for this reason. This cultural norm can lead to the misinterpretation that Africans are uninterested, less honest, are withholding information and have poor concentration, etc.

Cultural competence challenges the professional to engage appropriately and sensitively with people in order to understand their different values and to attribute correct meaning to their behaviour. This requires the community development worker to adopt a 'style of enquiry', a willingness to listen more and learn from clients, to tolerate silence and have patience. Humility ('the professional does not always know best'), a strong desire for social justice and a willingness to learn from other cultures can ameliorate the community development worker's own personal biases and reactions to persons from different ethnic minorities.

Valuing 'Difference'

Valuing 'difference' is the hallmark of culturally competent practice. Difference itself can connect people, as curiosity can be a spur to ask questions and to listen. Walker (1994) advocates four key principles in valuing difference.

1 People work best when they feel valued.
2 They feel most valued when they believe that their individual and group differences have been taken into account.

3 The ability to learn from people regarded as different is the key to becoming fully empowered.
4 When people feel valued and empowered, they are able to build relationships in which they can work together.

Failure to recognise and acknowledge difference, however well meaning, denies the notion that race influences individuals. 'Cultural blindness' is an expressed philosophy of viewing and treating all people as the same.

By acknowledging differences in each other's racial group, race is no longer a taboo. A culturally competent community development worker expresses genuine respect and tolerance for cultural difference and its value in a pluralistic society. This does not imply a universal or automatic acceptance of all practices of all cultures. For example, some cultures subjugate women, oppress persons on the basis of their sexual orientation, and value the use of corporal punishment and the death penalty (NASW 2001). Valuing difference implies that each cultural group has its own strengths and perspectives, from which all can benefit in solving problems and enriching community life. By valuing strengths, people are empowered.

Self-assessment

Cultural competence often begins with self-assessment and an awareness of the need to examine how one's own cultural values, unexamined constructs and beliefs affect the provision of services and influence relationships with service users. Cultural prejudices operate at both a conscious and unconscious level, at emotional and cognitive levels. The willingness to reflect and articulate those values, assumptions and beliefs is an essential element of culturally competent practice. This process can be aided by a more explicit awareness of one's own cultural background. For example, what does it mean to be Irish? Since the foundation of the state, 'Irishness' and citizenship have been correlated with 'whiteness' and Catholicism, both of which implicitly acted as the measure against which difference was constructed (Haraway 1992), despite the fact that the very concept of 'whiteness' itself hardly constitutes a homogeneous unified entity.

Knowledge

Based on Weaver's (1999) research into culturally competent practice with Native Americans, four areas of knowledge were identified in promoting best practice:

1 diversity
2 culture
3 history
4 contemporary realities.

Knowledge of Diversity

Comprehension of the cultural milieu in which individuals or groups operate will assist the community development worker in understanding the causes and consequences of human behaviour. Although cultural identity is an important determinant of human behaviour, considering an individual or family only in terms of their cultural identity can lead to generalisation and stereotyping. In working with culturally diverse clients, community development workers soon learn that individuals or families from the same country are very different from one another. For example, as discussed above, the very diversity of Nigerian culture is one of its hallmarks. In addition, each person is an individual who *may or may not* have a strong cultural connection to his or her native culture, or may experience that cultural connection differently from another (Weaver 1999). Many migrants assimilate into mainstream culture, while others maintain the lifestyle and cultural values of their ancestral homeland. Those who *assimilate* take on the behaviour, language and practices of the host culture. Yet others adapt to *elements* of the dominant culture while keeping aspects of their own cultural identity. Therefore, each person will have a unique relationship with his or her own culture. The heterogeneity that exists along this continuum is as great as the diversity that exists among individuals generally.

It is important also to recognise that culture is only one aspect of a person's identity. Identity is multifaceted and is influenced by other factors such as age, gender, social class, historical factors and temperament. Equally, elements of a person's identity can vary in significance across time and in different situations. What it means to be Irish may take on greater significance abroad than at home! Culturally competent practice is therefore as much about appreciating cultural differences between individuals in the same ethnic group as it is about understanding the cultural ties that bind ethnic groups together.

Cultural Knowledge

Although diversity and individuality exist in ethnic groups, some common core cultural values exist. The provision of effective and respectful community services must be compatible with these cultural beliefs, practices and languages of the people receiving services. Culturally competent community development workers must go through a developmental process of moving from using their own culture as a benchmark for measuring all behaviour to considering behaviour within a cultural context. This is a conscious, ongoing process requiring the community development worker to have cultural encounters with people from diverse backgrounds, to build relationships, to ask questions, to listen and learn. Indeed, much of what culturally competent community development workers must know and be able to do is therefore learned in relationships with families and communities. Community development workers should work to gain first-hand experience with a culture. They should visit homes, walk in the neighbourhood, converse with families and demonstrate a willingness to break down barriers. (See MRCI (2008) Section 2 for excellent 'engagement' strategies with ethnic minorities.)

Information must be sought from families or other key community informants regarding culture and tradition. For example, the definition of the family is a cultural construct. Within ethnic minorities, often each family member will have specific roles that are not usually the norm in white European families. In general, Nigerian society is strongly patriarchal (particularly so in the Hausa–Fulani ethnic group) (Gannon and Pillai 2010). The status of men and women are often defined by culture, and community development workers need to understand and respect the hierarchy of power within the family. Culture also defines the value given to age: western individualistic societies tend to value youth; conversely, age is valued in many cultures, such as Nigeria, where it is associated with wisdom (Gannon and Pillai 2010).

Culture and ethnicity may influence how individuals express and cope with problems. What is behaviourally appropriate in one culture may seem abnormal in another. Cohen (1988, cited in Robert Smyth Academy 2011) believes that few mental illnesses are reported in India because mental illness is seen as a curse, so sufferers are looked down upon. Similarly, Rack (1982) believes that depression is far more prevalent in Asian culture than the figures would suggest. Asians tend to report physical illness, but mental illness is dealt with within the family to avoid stigmatisation. Goldrick et al. (1996) (cited in Schlesinger and Devore 2007) suggest that ethnic groups' differences become evident in times of crisis as individuals often return to familiar sources of comfort, including ethnic rituals and behaviours. Levels of frankness regarding personal details and what it is appropriate to express, particularly to outsiders, will vary between cultures. Africans tend generally to be quite emotionally expressive ('doing things quietly is not the Nigerian way'), while Asian cultures tend to see controlling one's own emotions and feelings as a sign of maturity (Schlesinger and Devore 2007). Culturally competent community development workers need to be aware of the 'help-seeking behaviours' of different cultures, the resources (informal and formal helping networks) that can be used to assist diverse client groups, and the power relationships within the community and their impact on client groups. Meaningful interventions in community development cannot be effected without insight into how they will be interpreted by targeted individuals and groups.

Religion and spirituality can be for many an important source of emotional support. Culturally competent practice is achieved, for example, when a community development worker takes the trouble to find out the significance of religious and cultural traditions to the client or client's family. Is there a need to accommodate, in some way, non-Christian religious holidays and prayer times? Does an agency show respect for non-Christian traditions, for example wearing the hijab, and specific dietary requirements? As regards community development work, cultures also differ regarding their approaches to completing tasks. Different access to resources, different judgements of the rewards associated with task completion and different notions of time all influence task completion.

When it comes to working together efficiently on a task, cultures differ as regards the importance placed on the development of relationships early in the programme. Asian cultures tend to attach more value to developing relationships at the beginning of a shared project, with more emphasis on task completion towards the end, as compared with Europeans or Americans. Europeans and Americans tend to focus immediately on the task at hand, and let relationships develop as they work on the task. This does not mean that people from any one of these cultural backgrounds are more or less committed to accomplishing the task, or that they value relationships more or less; it means they may pursue these objectives differently.

Similarly, the roles played by individuals in decision-making vary widely from culture to culture. Be aware that an individual's expectations about their own role in shaping a decision may be influenced by their cultural frame of reference.

History

The dramatic and sometimes violent social and political changes in many countries in the former Communist Europe, Africa and Asia during the 1980s and 1990s contributed in no small measure to the greater numbers of asylum seekers and immigrants who fled to Ireland. An awareness of the relevant historical experiences of an ethnic minority is a key element of culturally competent practice. A community development worker should be open to learning about these experiences and their significance to a particular community and individual. These experiences may have led to a sense of oppression, injustice and trauma on the part of the service user, and an awareness of, and sensitivity to, these possible feelings is an important element of culturally competent practice.

Contemporary Realities

A recent report by the EU's Fundamental Rights Agency found that Ireland was among the top five countries in the EU when it came to racial discrimination and abuse (MRCI 2010). Black Africans report a particularly high level of racial harassment on the street and on public transport, relative to other migrants. With few exceptions, they also report more discrimination in shops and restaurants, commercial transactions and in institutions (MRCI 2010). Eastern Europeans report generally lower levels of discrimination than black Africans (MRCI 2010). In a study carried out by Amnesty International in 2002, 44 per cent of respondents believed that asylum seekers were depriving indigenous Irish people of local authority housing; 95 per cent believed that some asylum seekers were in Ireland illegally; 15 per cent believed that asylum seekers could obtain grants to buy cars; while 10 per cent believed that they were given free mobile phones (Amnesty International 2002).

Anti-racism is integral to the value base underpinning culturally competent practice. Any consideration of cultural competence must take into account the specific forms of racism experienced in the local area. The culturally competent community development worker is therefore required to profile the experiences, needs and concerns of local minority ethnic groups. Community development workers must genuinely listen to the *personal experience* of the client with respect to his or her race and perceived difference. This includes his or her experience in school, in the community and with friends, and experience of name calling, etc. What are the consequences of racist attitudes and beliefs on the individual's emotional and psychological self? How has *difference* been handled in the past by systems surrounding the individual?

In addressing anti-racist practices, community development workers must examine the possible privileges afforded them in Irish society. Dillern (1999) and Swigonski (1996), as cited in Dewees (2001), suggest that privilege as an offshoot of oppression is so evasive, especially to those it benefits, that it is often denied. Peggy McIntosh (1988), cited in Dewees (2001), has defined privilege as follows:

- The freedom to associate with members of your own group.
- The level of social acceptance one can presume across varying contexts.
- The ability to see members of your group in a positive light, in the records of history, in texts, in the media and as role models.
- The freedom from stereotyping.
- The ability to be oblivious of other groups.
- The ability to feel at home in the world.

The development of an environment in which community development workers can explore their privileged status is essential in the process of becoming more culturally competent. Community development workers should be prepared for the possibility that those they work with might manifest anger or inhibition because of the internalised effect of majority–minority relations. As community development workers, we must repeatedly affirm our willingness to share power and practise this by seeking suggestions, creating consultative forums and giving space to divergent points of view.

Skills

The skills required for culturally competent practice are not so radically different from generic community development skills (Weaver 1999). Gelman (2004), however, proposes that some modifications of the traditional style of community practice may be required for cultural competence. He suggests that an increased amount of self-disclosure, accepting gifts (often food), and more physical contact (e.g. handshakes, pats on the back), as well as being closer spatially may be required. Active listening to clients is a fundamental part of culturally competent practice. Generally, we need to lower our defence levels and have the courage to risk making mistakes. Genuineness, empathy, warmth and kindness are often lost in the increasingly complex array of skills now required for best practice.

The US National Association of Social Workers (NASW) (2001:20) identifies that the personal attributes of culturally competent workers should include the following skills:

- the capacity to respond flexibly to a range of possible solutions;
- an acceptance of and openness to differences among people;
- a willingness to learn to work with clients of different backgrounds;
- an articulation and clarification of stereotypes and biases and how these may accommodate or conflict with the needs of diverse client groups;
- a personal commitment to alleviate racism, sexism, homophobia, ageism and poverty.

Three more skills are identified by this author as central to culturally competent practice and worthy of separate mention:

1   problem-solving skills
2   communication skills
3   service delivery.

Problem-solving Skills

Any problem-solving process must be based on a definition of the problem from an ethnic minority perspective. Community development workers need the critical skills of asking the right questions, being comfortable with discussing cultural differences, asking clients about what works for them and what is comfortable for them in these discussions (NASW 2001). Glicken (2004) proposes consideration of the following questions in assessing cultural strengths:

- Are the clients' cultural backgrounds positive about the clients and their problems, or do they tend to isolate and condemn clients because of their problems?
- Do cultures strongly oppose the abuse of alcoholism and drugs, and the abuse of spouses and children?
- Do they urge people to seek help for social and emotional problems, or do they have very pejorative views on the need to seek help?

Community development workers must recognise that cultural environments are often rich in opportunities for support, encouragement and assistance. Bowman (2006), as cited in Allen-Meares (2007), suggests that cultural strengths may come in the form of positive protective skills, a focus on the family, or a belief in higher education and achievement. Solutions should also incorporate indigenous supports and strategies (e.g. folk healers) into intervention plans.

Communication Skills

The way people communicate varies widely between, and even within, cultures. One aspect of communication style is language use. According to research carried out by the National University of Ireland Maynooth, there are 167 languages spoken in Ireland today, and 6,912 languages worldwide (*Irish Times* 25 March 2006). For many, language expresses heritage, identity and pride. However, differences in linguistic ability create unequal power relationships. Many ethnic minorities may feel an anxiety about speaking English properly, which may lead them to avoid interactions with English speakers, and so limit their interactions to people who share the same language.

To facilitate participation in community development, there is an obvious need to present information in a participant's primary language. Signage, instructional literature, mission statements and policies should be presented in the service users' language(s) and be consistent with their cultural norms. If a service user's spoken language is unfamiliar to the community development worker, it is essential to find an appropriate and qualified interpreter, keeping in mind that cultural values, social class and gender all influence the interpretation process (Purnell 2008). Family, friends or children should not be used to provide interpretation services (except at the request of the service user). Equally, it should not be assumed that if a person can speak the English language, they are equally proficient in reading and writing.

The importance of non-verbal communication (i.e. 'body language') is heightened when communicating across cultures, as we tend to look for non-verbal cues when verbal messages are unclear or ambiguous. In western culture, we have culturally specific ideas on the norms governing non-verbal communication, such as appropriate gestures, touch, personal space, physical appearance, eye contact, etc. Greeting rituals are an important part of any communication system and are often the first step in developing culturally competent practice. For example, social greetings are of the utmost importance in Nigeria. A handshake and a long list of good wishes for a counterpart's family and good health are expected when meeting someone. This is often true even if you saw that person a short time earlier. Greeting rituals often differ depending on age, gender and social stratification. Becoming culturally competent requires a proficiency in the client's non-verbal system of communication.

Service Delivery

Cultural competence embraces the principles of equal access and non-discriminatory practices in service delivery. A community development worker needs to detect and prevent exclusion of diverse clients from service opportunities within his or her own agency. Levels of participation may be superficial unless the community development worker has an understanding of culturally unique courtesies, customs and expectations. There must be a willingness to make community development services more accessible by taking into consideration the location of ethnic minorities, costs of transportation, lack of childcare facilities, working hours, language and communication needs, financial and environmental circumstances.

Checklist for community providers to ensure culturally competent practice

At service level, all community agencies need to ask the following questions.

- During the planning stage of any programme, is adequate consideration given to the needs of the various cultures in my community/area?
- Does the overall programme offered reflect the cultural make-up of my area?
- Can the programmes offered be readily accessed by those who are culturally different from the mainstream in the community?
- Do people from different cultures actively seek participation in my programmes?
- Are people of different cultures accepted on my programmes?
- Have people from different cultures been invited to serve on key policy-making committees?
- Are leadership roles filled in the programmes by people from different cultures?

At policy level, cultural competence permeates through the hiring of multi-ethnic and multi-racial staff. There should be training for staff regarding cultural issues and the language of the people they serve.

GUIDELINES FOR CULTURALLY COMPETENT PRACTICE

Cultural competence is a developmental process that is active and requires learning and re-learning over time. Figure 5.3 provides a summary guideline to give the reader an overview of culturally competent practice.

Figure 5.3. Summary guidelines for culturally competent practice

Values and attitudes

- Begin with an honest self-assessment and examine your own personal cultural values, beliefs, biases and stereotypes and how they influence relationships with clients
- Question your own frame of reference, expressed attitudes and behaviour grounded in ethnocentric tradition
- Value and celebrate differences in others rather than maintaining an ethnocentric stance
- Engage sensitively with people in order to understand their different values and to attribute correct meaning to their behaviour

Knowledge

- Recognise that culture is only one aspect of a person's identity
- Appreciate differences between individuals within the same ethnic group
- Take every opportunity to acquire specific knowledge about a cultural group's values, beliefs and norms through reading, attending cultural events and festivals, sharing knowledge, visiting other countries. Get to know the community and its families – build relationships, ask questions, listen and learn

Knowledge

- Become aware of the 'help-seeking behaviours' of different cultures, the resources that people draw on, the significance of religion, spirituality and cultural traditions to the service user or service user's family
- Recognise that decision-making styles, task engagement and participation in community development may be influenced by a cultural frame of reference
- Acquire specific knowledge regarding the service user's history, migration story, personal experience of racism and oppression, adjustment styles and socio-economic background to understand and fulfil the client's needs
- The power relationships in the community, agencies or institutions and their impact on diverse service user groups need to be understood

Skills

- General community work skills are required, as well as specific skills, such as listening, patience, kindness, warmth
- Specific reference to communication skills, problem solving and service delivery
- Develop culturally appropriate communication techniques which include effective listening, attentive body language, eye behaviour and clarity in linguistic dialogue. Other specific cultural non-verbal communication may include attention to time, space, distance, modesty, touch, silence, dress, provider gender and other unique cultural patterns and expressions
- Use a strengths-based approach in defining problems and seeking solutions with children and families
- A community development worker needs to detect and prevent exclusion of diverse service users from service opportunities within his or her own agency
- Be cognisant of barriers that could impede a minority individual from using services

CONCLUSION

The period since the 1990s has seen immigration into Ireland of a scale and speed unprecedented in comparable contexts (Barrett and McCarthy 2006). Immigrants in Ireland are a heterogeneous group in terms of nationality, ethnicity, legal status and language skills, although the largest segment comes from the new EU member states (Barrett and McCarthy 2006). These demographic trends provide evidence of the growing importance of culturally competent practice as an essential part of service delivery in modern Ireland. Culturally competent practice obliges the discerning community development worker to examine any possible cultural myopia and develop the ability to integrate cultural knowledge, values and skills for a more effective and culturally appropriate service delivery. Cultural competence builds on the caring profession's valued stance of self-determination and individual dignity and worth, adding inclusion, tolerance and respect for diversity in all its forms (NASW 2001). Community services must promote policies and practices that demonstrate respect for difference, as well as willingness and capability to respond flexibly with culturally appropriate solutions.

6

Community Development, Conflict and Power in the North of Ireland

Féilim Ó hAdhmaill

CHAPTER SUMMARY

The chapter explores the experience of community development as a contested site operating in a conflict zone, using the experiences in the North of Ireland as an example. It starts by describing how both the theoretical conceptualisation and the practical application of community development can be contested sites. It further describes how its linkage to ideas about power, who should have access to it and how much power they should have, can itself lead to conflict. The struggle for empowerment and the right to participate has the potential to challenge Gramscian 'common sense' notions of society, power relations and the status quo.

INTRODUCTION

At a macro level, access to power in the North of Ireland, as in most societies, has been linked to socio-economic factors, gender and other attributes. However, throughout its existence access to power has also been determined by major ethno-religious divisions in the society that have led to conflict. Indeed, the very existence of the entity was a source of ongoing conflict.

The onset of armed conflict from the late 1960s, at a time when community development ideas were coming to the fore, provided both opportunities and challenges. At a macro level the state alternated between viewing community development groups as something positive, providing a mediating role (during the days of the old Community Relations Commission (1969–74)), and as a potential threat (during the political vetting era of the 1980s). Community development groups themselves could view the state and its forces as existing somewhere on a continuum between 'enemy' and 'friend' based on their view of the conflict, time and events. At a micro level, community development groups often had to operate in an arena of conflicting loyalties and agendas and, at times, with different armed groups vying for control.

With the onset of the peace process in the early 1990s, community development became incorporated into state and EU strategy geared towards conflict transformation and peace-building. Ensuing debates around concepts of weak community infrastructure, the promotion of 'good relations' and the pursuit of equality, social justice and human rights nonetheless continue to reflect different ideas about end goals in community development.

As an uncertain 'peace' appears to be emerging, there are questions about the extent to which a genuine grassroots bottom-up approach to community development actually exists any more, and whether community development is becoming more about delivering services to, and placing responsibility for social problems on, more marginalised communities.

COMMUNITY DEVELOPMENT AS A CONTESTED SITE

Both the theoretical conceptualisation and the practical application of community development have historically proved to be contested sites. Ideas about community development have often involved contesting consensus and conflict views about society. These have been reflected in the writings of Alinsky (1971), Freire (1973) and Putnam (2000) and others and show differing approaches to the perceived 'problems' which community development seeks to address, their perceived causes and the presumed solutions. Community development might therefore be viewed from some perspectives as promoting self-help (Thomason 1961) or social cohesion and stability (Putnam 2000), while in others it might be viewed as demanding far-reaching social change (Freire 1973).

Community development is intrinsically linked to concepts of participation in society, empowerment and ultimately democracy. It is not difficult, therefore, to understand why community development can be viewed by those in positions of power as something which could be both positive and threatening.

PROCESS AND END GOAL

Competing consensus views and conflict views of society often influence how community development practitioners view both the process of community development and the end goal. A conflict view, for example, might suggest a need for an Alinskyian-style protest or campaign to force an issue, since the holder of power may not be willing to make concessions.[1] A consensus view might adopt tactics of operating within the system, lobbying or forming partnerships in collaboration with the power elites, in an attempt to promote mutual benefits or efficiencies for all.

While all proponents of community development may argue that 'process' is important when working with local communities and that that process should involve participation through empowerment and capacity building, differences often emerge in terms of scope – how much participation and empowerment and how widespread throughout the community. Differences may also emerge in terms of the perceived end goal of such participation.

The end goal and how to achieve it may in turn be linked to different ideas about what is 'problematic' in society and where the solution is situated – in the individual, his or her local community or in inequalities and injustices in wider society. The end goal may also define where responsibilities lie for the solution of local problems, the provision of local needs and the realisation of rights. A Putnamian view may see the problem as something which the community itself can solve through increased co-operation and pooling resources, for example providing a local community centre themselves, challenging anti-social behaviour, etc. (Putnam 2000).[2] An Alinskyian perspective might view society as unequal, but the end goal could be to achieve small incremental changes which might improve life for the more marginalised in the here and now, for example better housing conditions or lower rents. A Freireian perspective might demand widespread changes in how society is organised, from a top-down to a bottom-up approach, redistributing power from the powerful to all (Freire 1973).

COMMUNITY DEVELOPMENT AND POWER IN SOCIETY

At a macro or societal level, it is clear that ideas about community development, both process and end goal, are intrinsically linked to ideas about power in society – who holds it, who else should have access to it and how much, and what they should do with it. For some, empowerment may be limited to a local community dealing with a local community-based issue themselves, with limited impact on wider power relations in society. However, for others the struggle for empowerment and the right to participate may reflect wider ideas about the greater democratisation of society. It may thus have the potential to challenge Gramscian 'common sense' notions of society, power relations and the status quo.[3] Indeed both process and end goal may challenge existing hierarchies and accepted discourses in society.

Power relations also exist, of course, at micro or community/community group level and community development also has the potential to reinforce and reproduce existing hierarchies of power in local communities or to challenge them. In an Irish setting this might involve, on the one hand, appointing local priests or professionals to the boards of local groups or, on the other, holding open democratic elections.

In some community 'development' projects, for example, 'participation' may involve varying degrees of access to decision-making and agenda-setting power in practice.

A project may have to fulfil certain funding or service provision criteria and this may militate against developing greater involvement from local people in deciding what their needs are and how they can be met. On the other hand, a community group may reflect the 'pet' interests of those involved on the group's committee rather than reflecting the interests of the local community.

Practical or pragmatic factors may influence who actually gets to 'participate'. Sometimes such participation is limited to those who want to participate and their reasons may range from the highly personal to a particular world view (religious, political, etc.) or be based on relationships with others in the project. It may also be the case, where there is diversity or division in a community, that only some section/s of the community feel willing, able or welcome to participate. Questions may then arise about how representative/reflective the project is of the whole community and the project itself might be viewed as a clique or become a contested site among opposing groups/factions.

How different aspects of community group activity are affected by internal divisions and factors external to the local community may of course throw light on what exactly is going on in that particular community and in society in general. Marris (1974), for example, saw research into community groups as a form of 'contemporary political history'. Thus in an Irish setting a move from parish committees appointed by the local priest to community committees elected by local residents might be seen to reflect changes in Irish society – secularisation and democratisation.

Community development is of course dependent on the notion that some form of community – geographical, interest, or whatever – exists in the first place, and this notion itself may be contested.

Some communities are defined more by whom they exclude than by whom they include. Exclusion may be a defining aspect. In a society like the North of Ireland, for example, deeply divided along ethno-political-religious lines, (as well as class, gender, etc.) it is not difficult to see how community membership and community 'rights' can themselves be highly contested sites and can be linked to conflict and challenges over access to power and rights to participation. Likewise, it is not difficult to see how community development itself might be viewed as either positive or a threat to opposing viewpoints.

In the North of Ireland access to power was long a contested site and long before the establishment of Northern Ireland as a statelet.[4] As in most societies, access to power had been linked to socio-economic, gender and other attributes. However, in the North, it had also been determined by major ethno-religious divisions in the society, leading to conflict. When the new Northern Ireland entity was established its very existence had been challenged by a relatively large minority and this in itself was to become a source of ongoing and often violent conflict.

COMMUNITY ORGANISATION IN THE NORTH OF IRELAND: HISTORICAL BACKGROUND

Throughout its existence Northern Ireland has exhibited many of the same attributes linked to community organisation and development in the South. Like the South it inherited many of the structures and practices and the laissez-faire approach to society laid down during direct British rule before 1920. It also inherited the endemic poverty of the rest of Ireland. Throughout its existence and up to the advent of the Northern Ireland peace process in the 1980s and 1990s[5] it remained one of the poorest regions of the UK and, like its counterpart in the South, after EU entry in 1973 it 'enjoyed' for many years EU Priority Status for funding support. However, it also exhibited many distinct differences (Ó hAdhmaill 1990).

Whilst it was still predominantly an agricultural entity, especially west of the Bann, the area to the east around Belfast had witnessed continuing industrialisation and urbanisation since the early nineteenth century, and this continued up to the outbreak of conflict in the late 1960s. Indeed much of its industrialisation, particularly ship-building and engineering, was strategically important to the British Empire, providing it with important markets and wealth-producing capacity (Jones 1960; Beckett and Glasscock 1967).

Unlike the South it was also to be greatly influenced by the advances in the British welfare state, particularly from the end of World War II. This, combined with a subvention from the British Exchequer which was eventually to grow to £9 billion by 2009 (DFPNI 2011), meant that many of the worst effects of poverty were ameliorated to some extent. Despite this, however, on most socio-economic indices Northern Ireland remained worse off than other regions of the UK for much of its existence. (See, for example, Baird Report 1980 and CSO 1987.)

Welfare statism also introduced the notion of state responsibility to provide services and support to its citizens (and a citizen's right to such support), something which has been very slow to develop in the South, and this had a knock-on effect in terms of the role of the voluntary sector. Whereas in the South the influence of the Church, Catholic social teaching, and laissez-faire thinking among politicians situated the voluntary sector as primary providers of welfare, by the late 1970s the state occupied much of that role in the North, particularly in relation to health and social care.[6]

AN 'APARTHEID' SOCIETY

Northern Ireland was/is also a deeply divided entity. The process of colonisation and in particular the Ulster Plantation of 1607 facilitated the extensive transfer of ownership of land from native to 'planter'. By 1704, while the native Irish owned 14 per cent of land in Ireland as a whole, this figure was just 5 per cent in Ulster (Corish 1981:74). However, unlike much of the rest of Ireland, this process also led to a transfer of the occupancy of land. Tenant farmers, not just landlords, from Scotland and England occupied the land, and in large parts of Antrim and Down and other Ulster counties they formed the majority population. The segregated living patterns which continue to exist today were thus laid down during the seventeenth century and frequently refreshed with bouts of rioting, intimidation and expulsions (Boyd 1969; Darby 1986). Also laid down was a categorisation of differential citizenship based on ethno-religious grounds.

By the time of Partition a type of economic, social, cultural and political apartheid had evolved in the North, and while many working-class and rural

Protestants also suffered poverty and deprivation, Catholics tended to occupy a much more disadvantaged position. Partition was to reinforce and reproduce this disadvantage – with the experience of discrimination, gerrymandering,[7] periodic rioting, intimidation and armed conflict (Barritt and Carter 1962; Cameron Commission 1969; Rose 1971; Budge and O'Leary 1973; Darby and Morris 1974; Aunger 1976; Farrell 1976; Buckland 1979; O'Dowd *et al.* 1980; Boal and Douglas 1982; Darby 1986; Whyte 1983; NICRC 1971).

Northern Ireland was established in response to the demands of Irish Unionists and British Conservatives to protect the position of Protestants in the North of Ireland from rule by an overwhelmingly Catholic independent Ireland. (It also served some of the strategic political and military concerns of the British state of the day.) Under the 1920 Government of Ireland Act, and later the Anglo-Irish Treaty of 1921 the North was allowed to secede from the new Free State in the South (and rejoin at a later date if it wished – though this never happened). The six northeastern counties were picked for the new entity, rather than the whole nine counties of Ulster, because it was felt that this would provide a more sustainable two-thirds majority for the Unionist community (Buckland 1979). However, large tracts had Catholic/nationalist[8] majorities, for example the rural areas west of the River Bann, Derry City, Newry and West Belfast in the east. The impact of this is important because in many areas Catholics were actually the majority – not just in Ireland, but in their own locality – yet had a minority group status.[9]

From the outset, northern nationalists/Catholics opposed the new entity, as did the Catholic Church and indeed the new Free State in the South.[10] Northern Catholics reacted by variously boycotting, protesting (sometimes violently) and ignoring the new arrangements. There was little serious co-operation or engagement between Unionist and the Nationalist politicians in the North on a political level during the Stormont years (1921–72).[11] Although the beginnings of some level of rapprochement did start to emerge in the mid-1960s with the visit of Lemass to Stormont and negotiations between Church and State over funding for Catholic education, these were subsumed in the reaction to the emerging civil rights campaign and subsequent thirty years of violent conflict.[12]

Protestants/unionists for their part embraced the new state as their state. The existence of what appeared to be a rebellious Catholic minority in their midst and a Catholic Church-dominated confessional state in the twenty-six counties, appeared to confirm their worst fears and the need to defend their state, their rights and liberties at all costs.[13]

After the establishment of Northern Ireland, the Catholic Church continued to play the role it had had in Ireland throughout the nineteenth century – that of a quasi-state within a state. It provided schools, hospitals, social services, relief from poverty and community organisation, adopting the same principle of subsidiarity.[14] As in the South, it was also linked to the bulk of social and recreational provision for Catholics via parishes, with the establishment of parish halls, and in its involvement in the GAA, Irish language, etc. (Acheson *et al.* 2005; Ó hAdhmaill 1990).

Protestants had a closer connection with the state and with local industry, but they too tended to have social and recreational provision organised by the different Protestant churches. Acheson et al. (2005), for example, note the importance of evangelical Protestant philanthropy in the development of voluntary provision. The Orange Order, a politically and economically strong unifying force for Protestants, also became particularly important as a source of social and recreational activity for many Protestants (Boyd 1995). As a result the emerging voluntary sector in the North tended to mirror the segregated communities.

The state itself adopted a laissez-faire approach to provision, based on the politics of the day. It did, however, establish a state primary school system, moulded in consultation with the Protestant churches and generally not attended by Catholics (Akenson 1973). The extension of the British welfare state to Northern Ireland after World War II – with additional funding from London to provide coverage that was comparable with Britain (Birrell and Williamson 1983:130) – was to have a major impact for both Catholics and Protestants. The provision of free education (albeit organised along religious lines up to the end of secondary school) in 1948 meant that many working-class and poorer rural children could now for the first time get access to a university education – something which has been cited as a factor in the development of the civil rights campaign in the mid-1960s (Darby 1983).

COMMUNITY ACTION IN NORTHERN IRELAND BEFORE THE 'TROUBLES'

Prior to the onset of armed conflict in Northern Ireland in the late 1960s, ideas about community development and community action to promote social change appear to have been generally limited in their impact on local communities. Significant social change through political action was difficult to accomplish, due to the sectarian nature of politics. Therefore, when community action did occur it was largely self-help in nature, drawing on the resources of a strong sense of community identity and the existence of extended family networks. This type of activity is probably best illustrated in the development of local tenants' associations after World War II and the growth of credit unions, housing associations and economic co-operatives in the 1960s (Deane 1981; Lewis 2006; Ó hAdhmaill 1990). In the 1930s, at the time of the Republican Congress[15] (1934–35), republicans had attempted to mobilise some local communities around social issues such as housing conditions and rents, often with opposition from the Catholic Church (Munck et al. 1987). Indeed, for a short time during this period there was an IRA unit made up of Protestants on the Protestant Shankill Road in Belfast (Ó hAdhmaill 1990). There had also been short-lived cross-community campaigning culminating in the Outdoor Relief Riots of 1932 (Devlin 1981). Cross-community collective action for social change, however, was limited since it could be viewed as a challenge to the state and the status quo. The divisions over constitutional issues, which were themselves linked to notions of unequal access to power, put paid to any long-term attempts at joint unionist/nationalist community initiatives. Cross-community self-help activity did, however, occur where it was limited to neighbourly help and was not seen to challenge power relations in the wider society.[16]

CIVIL RIGHTS AND THE OUTBREAK OF ARMED CONFLICT

The failure of the IRA's border campaign in 1956–62, in large part due to its apparent failure to garner support among the North's Catholic community (Bell 1979), was one of a number of factors feeding the growth and development of new types of community action in the 1960s, on a scale never before witnessed. The republican movement moved towards cross-community political agitation rather than armed struggle, while a new group of university-educated Catholics (thanks to the education reforms of 1948) began to emerge to demand a stake in the society, spurred on by the civil rights campaign in the USA and the advent of more accessible television coverage. The emergence of a new, more moderate Unionist leader (Terence O'Neill) also seemed to suggest that reform within Northern Ireland might be possible. A string of campaigns began, some of them, at least initially, cross-community, linked to social housing and then invariably to the contentious issues of civil rights and discrimination in housing, jobs and services practised against the Catholic population.

One such campaign, in 1965, aimed to locate the North's new university in the second largest city, Derry, which was predominantly Catholic, rather than the eventual location of Coleraine, a relatively small provincial town which was predominantly Protestant. The campaign appears to have attracted significant cross-community support among nationalists and unionists in Derry and among both the working class and middle class. However, according to Robson (2000), despite the sectarian undertones of the decision, the campaign was non-confrontational largely because it addressed the relatively non-controversial issue of higher education. It also failed.

Much more controversial were the various civil rights protests and marches. Initially attracting an element of cross-community support, this eventually dwindled away – as the movement became stronger, so too did the state's response. By August 1969, the growing civil strife led to the establishment of no-go areas in parts of Belfast and Derry and the emergence once again of armed conflict.

THE EMERGENCE OF COMMUNITY DEVELOPMENT IN A TIME OF CONFLICT

The many negative aspects of the armed conflict which erupted in the late 1960s are obvious. They included deaths, injuries, loss and destruction. Nearly four thousand people died on all sides/communities and many more were injured

(Sutton 2001; McKittrick *et al.* 2004), while thousands lost their homes (Boyd 1969; NICRC 1971; Darby 1986). Many communities were torn apart and set against one another.

However, the 'Troubles' also coincided with a major upsurge in community action and community group formation in the North, especially in areas, such as Belfast, that were most affected by the conflict (NUU 1975; Rolston 1984; McCready 2001).

A number of these groups were concerned primarily with peace and reconciliation, including some that aimed to promote integrated education as a way out of conflict (Ó hAdhmaill 1983; Dunn 1986; Dunn *et al.* 1989; Collins 1990).

However, much more significant was an upsurge of community activity in the form of community-based responses to the political situation, principally in nationalist/Catholic working-class and rural communities, and in particular in the emerging 'no-go' (to the state) areas (Acheson *et al.* 2005; Ó hAdhmaill 1990; Lewis 2006).[17]

Initially such groups were primarily concerned with the defence of areas, organising vigilantes to protect local areas, catering for incoming refugees and organising the everyday needs of communities: however, as the emergency situation ameliorated, they increasingly developed new foci on existing and new areas of need, drawing on the 'long-standing traditions of self-help within that community' (Acheson *et al.* 2005:198).

Initially community activity took the form in some areas of co-operative developments, such as the rebuilding of burnt-out homes in Bombay Street in West Belfast (1970) and in Ardoyne (1971); the establishment of the Gaeltacht on Shaw's Road in Belfast (1969); the subsequent development of Irish-medium schools (1971 onwards); and eventually the development of a number of social enterprises, notably the 'People's Taxis' in nationalist areas of Derry and Belfast. The significant point here is that most of these developments took place independently of and often in opposition to the state (Ó hAdhmaill 1990). As O'Dowd *et al.* (1980) argued, working-class Catholics, confident that Stormont cared little for their plight, had no hesitation in organising self-help groups (O'Dowd *et al.* 1980:153). For long periods, a political vacuum existed which was filled by politicisation at street level – because that is where political events were being acted out. In times of heightened conflict people were often confined to their own areas, while statutory services were often unable or unwilling to meet needs, leading to the growth of both self-help and campaign groups (Darby and Williamson 1978; Gaffkin 1976). By 1972, direct rule and the reform of local government had also removed much of the power from local politicians and placed it in the hands of direct rule ministers from London and faceless civil servants, making community representation even more important.

The fact that the state appeared to be no longer capable of functioning for much of the 1970s in parts of the North led to a heightened awareness and confidence among many Catholics/nationalists about what they could do themselves. A new consciousness developed based on the belief that everything had changed and there was no going back to the old system (Ó hAdhmaill 1990). According to some researchers, it was clear that, for periods at least, the effect of the Troubles had been to unleash a 'revolution of rising expectations' that had been partially channelled into community action (NUU 1975: 54). How long the 'confidence' of change would last was of course a moot point. Cairns *et al.* (2004), for example, reported, in the wake of the Peace Process, that 'many working class communities, irrespective of whether they were predominantly Catholic or Protestant, were characterised by low morale and by low expectations about their future' (Cairns *et al.* 2004:4).

Whilst people came together for defensive purposes in Protestant/unionist working-class areas at times of emergency, this generally did not expand into other forms of community development activity (Cairns *et al.* 2004), partly because these populations viewed their situation as being supportive of the state. This was also reflected in the political sphere. While republicans saw their role as 'revolutionary' –linked to changing society – the emergent loyalist armed groups saw themselves simply as unofficial 'paramilitary' back-up support for the official forces of the state.[18] As nationalist/Catholic communities increasingly organised independently of, and often in opposition to, the state, Protestant communities tended to remain co-operative and supportive of the state and were less willing to campaign or protest, partly because this is what the Catholics were doing. Weiner (1976, 1978), however, does describe attempts to mobilise Protestants on the Shankill around what was felt to be the depopulation of the area by redevelopment. Indeed, he also points out how easily loyalist paramilitary activity could be used to support community action against road and redevelopment proposals in the inner city in the early 1970s. Whilst some community action, some of it cross-community, emerged in campaigning around redevelopment and housing issues from the 1970s, and later in the 1980s on welfare rights issues, throughout most of the 1970s and 1980s there was an assumption that Protestants were less inclined to become involved in community action and certainly less inclined to be to the forefront in the more radical community group organisations. Certainly, some of the campaigns of the 1980s – based around action on housing issues, welfare rights and community action – did not, with a few notable exceptions (e.g. Rathcoole and Shankill), appear to have been as well supported in Protestant areas as in Catholic areas. Griffiths (1978) felt that a profound difference existed between Protestant and Catholic political ideology and that this had strongly influenced the ways in which each perceived the ruling agencies. Hence the manner of their respective dealings with the latter was very different. Anderson *et al.* (1988) also appeared to find a lack of motivation among working-class Protestants in the Nelson Drive area of Derry. According to them there was 'an almost fatalistic acceptance of situations and problems as unchangeable'.

The apparent lack of involvement in community development among Protestant communities was to lead to a number of research reports in the 1990s and 2000s into why community development was slow to take hold in Protestant areas (CRC 1991; Voluntary Activity Unit 1999; Cairns *et al.* 2004). By the mid-

1990s, funding for community groups to promote the newly emergent peace process in nationalist and unionist communities became available from a number of sources, particularly the Peace Programmes of the EU (Morrow 2000; Acheson and Milofsky 2008). However, concerns began to emerge that Catholic/nationalist community groups were much more likely to apply for such funding than groups in Protestant/unionist areas. The reason identified for this was the lack of community group infrastructure in Protestant/unionist areas. This led to the development of a series of initiatives to try to promote community development activity in such areas and the creation of funding programmes to develop areas of 'weak community infrastructure' (O'Prey and Magowan 2001).

THE COMMUNITY RELATIONS COMMISSION, COMMUNITY DEVELOPMENT AND THE STATE

As the conflict progressed through periodic emergencies – for example internment (1971), the Ulster Workers' Council strike (1974), the hunger strikes (1980–81), etc. – there was an accompanying increase in community activity and participation in many mainly Catholic/nationalist areas.

However, other factors had an influence on such activity, over and above events directly linked to the Troubles. From the late 1960s, for example, community development had been in vogue in Britain and this had a knock-on effect in terms of both discourse and policy in Northern Ireland. For example, the Skeffington Report (1960) argued that government should encourage greater participation by local communities on planning issues; the Maud Report (1967) argued for more active citizen participation; the Seebohm Report (1968) advocated that community development should be part of the new social services department's commitments; and the Calouste Gulbenkian Report (1968) argued for the development of community work. One view was that there could be bottlenecks preventing the government finding out what community needs were, and what a community's views were on a situation. This is where community development came in. If a community organised itself, discovered its own needs and passed this information to the government, it could make the government more aware of people's needs. This view presupposed that the main problem facing a community in its relationship with government was that government did not know what the community's views were, rather than it being a question of competing views over the distribution of scarce resources, etc. Nevertheless, community development became part of British government policy in 1968 with the establishment of Community Development Projects in Britain, and this had a knock-on effect when the new Community Relations Commission was established in the North in October 1969 (Hayes 1972; Griffiths 1974a).[19]

The experience of the Commission is a case study in how the state deals with the empowering implications of community development. Griffiths' (1974a) analysis of the political manoeuvrings which went on makes fascinating reading.

Initially the community development officers employed by the Commission acted in a liaison role between local communities and statutory bodies, at a time when the state was virtually boycotted by many Catholic/nationalist communities. By January 1972, however, the government was trying to change the emphasis of the Commission's work from one of community development to one of community relations. 'Civil representatives' were appointed, civil servants who worked out of Royal Ulster Constabulary (RUC) and British army barracks. They were supposed to co-ordinate community groups in each police/army area and to promote good relations between the community and the security forces and between rival communities. The Commission, much to its annoyance, increasingly came to be seen in some areas as another counter-insurgency tool of government. The chairperson and director resigned in protest in 1973.

In April 1974, the Commission was abolished by Ivan Cooper, the new Minister of Community Relations in the short-lived power-sharing Executive,[20] in what many saw as local politicians attempting to regain control from independent community groups in some local areas. Its community relations role went to local Department of Health and Social Services (DHSS) area boards and local councils. Many local politicians were annoyed at the attention and thus power given by direct rule ministers to local community groups in their areas, some of which they claimed were controlled by their political enemies, when they themselves were supposed to be the community representatives (Ó hAdhmaill 1990). This view was also expressed by some prominent civil servants. One rather colourful quote from a former Permanent Secretary in the Northern Ireland Civil Service during the Stormont regime, John Oliver, should suffice to illustrate the antagonism of many civil servants towards community groups:

> A well meaning but dangerously vague concept of community action is offered as a replacement (to normal party politics). Potentially more dangerous still is the astonishing new growth of community associations, some with dubious connections, but nevertheless intent on imposing their will on housing, roads, redevelopment, community halls, libraries and so on to the virtual exclusion of elected politicians and rational argument, financial considerations, ordered priorities and other realities of public administration. The alternative to elected representative government can only be anarchy or tyranny in the long term. (Oliver, J. (1978), quoted in O'Dowd et al. 1980:166)

While the loss of the Commission had a knock-on effect in terms of the funding of community development, particularly in Belfast, other initiatives such as the establishment of the independent Northern Ireland Voluntary Trust (later called the Community Foundation for Northern Ireland)[21] and the promotion of community development principles by the Northern Ireland Council for Voluntary Action (NICVA),[22] helped promote an independent community development sector.

Funding policies can obviously affect the activities of a group. For example, in the 1970s, government money was available to groups for cross-community ventures, holidays, etc. During the 1980s, much available funding for community groups seemed to be centred on job creation (e.g. Action for Community Employment (ACE) schemes) and environmental clean-up schemes. From the mid-1970s, the increasing professionalisation of community work, coupled with state management mechanisms to control community group activity, impacted on the type of community group activity engaged in (Rolston 1984). The use of financial incentives and then political vetting meant that, while community activity was booming in Catholic/nationalist areas in the late 1980s, a large portion of it was controlled by the Catholic Church and other such bodies, which fitted in with contemporary government ideology on community self-help (Ó hAdhmaill 1990; Political Vetting of Community Work Working Group 1990).

Political vetting illustrated an iron fist approach to community development by the Thatcher government of the day.[23] Concern at the rise in the Sinn Féin vote in nationalist areas of the North and the widespread involvement of Sinn Féin activists in community work in local areas led in 1985 to what became the Hurd Principles. Douglas Hurd, the then Secretary of State for Northern Ireland, announced on 27 June of that year that statutory funding would be denied to any community groups where it was alleged that an individual associated with the group had a close link with a paramilitary organisation. A number of community groups, mostly in nationalist areas, had their funding removed with little or no redress. The result was that Church-run groups were favoured by funding bodies, as being 'safe', while many secular groups went to great lengths to try to prove that they were not associated with Sinn Féin members (Kilmurray 2009; Ó hAdhmaill 1990).

The Hurd Principles stayed in place until 1995, by which time the British government was moving away from excluding republicans to a position of working with them to promote the new peace (Kilmurray 2009). After the signing of the Good Friday Agreement in 1998, money became available through the Irish and British governments and the EU to promote conflict transformation and peace-building initiatives both within and across communities. Former political prisoners' groups were established and government and EU funding was provided to them both to work with ex-prisoners and to help prevent conflict at sectarian interfaces. Victims' groups and a range of human rights and campaign groups also received funding, along with locally based community groups funded to do development work within their own communities and in co-operation with others (Williamson 1995; Graham 2008; McEvoy and Shirlow 2009; Mitchell et al. 2005; Shirlow et al. 2005; CWC 2007).

As the peace process progressed, debates began to emerge around whether community work and funding programmes should be directed more towards promoting 'good relations' between different communities than towards social change and local community development. Indeed, arguments emerged that the promotion of social change at too fast a rate could actually drive the different communities apart. Often such arguments could be seen to reflect different perspectives on the 'end goal' for society and community development (CRC 2003, 2005; CRU 2005; CWC 2007; CAJ 2010).

INTERNAL PRESSURES ON COMMUNITY GROUPS IN A CONFLICT ZONE

The development of community group activity can be said to be a product of the interaction between: a) the desire of people in local communities to become less powerless and to gain greater control over their own lives; b) the needs and wishes of the state and its agencies (e.g. statutory bodies, security forces); and c) the needs and wishes of institutions and interest groups (e.g. churches, political parties and groups) based in the same local communities.

In normal situations, these conflicting interests and influences can have a major impact on local communities and how they organise to obtain their needs and wants. In a near 'war' situation, as existed in parts of the North over the past forty years, the strains placed on community groups were probably that much greater. For much of the 'Troubles' many community development workers trod a thin line between warring (literally) groups, both internal and external to their communities.

Community group activity is often strongly affected by the divisions between different individuals and interest groups within a given community. Conflict between different interest groups in a community – for example established residents/newcomers, Church/independent community activists, conservative/radical – are often played out in the internal politics of the group, thus limiting the political effectiveness of community action (Smith and Anderson 1972). This is even more likely to be the case if some of the internal bodies are armed.

Pressures also occurred for community groups if they came up against or challenged the authority and control of power elites or established institutions in their area. In Catholic/nationalist areas of the North, one very powerful institution which resisted any diminution in its power and influence was the Catholic Church. Because its approach was more conservative than many of the other community groups in the area, it was increasingly patronised by the state, leading to conflict with some community bodies (Ó hAdhmaill 1990).

In areas of the North that were highly politicised, political differences often manifested themselves through community action. Often such groups found themselves in confrontation with local politicians, though this was not unique to the North (Ball 1971). In reaction to this, local elected councillors often accused such groups of being unrepresentative of their communities and of lacking the councillors' mandate. Besides condemning their unrepresentativeness, local politicians often reacted to perceived threats from community groups by challenging the groups' credibility and responsibility (Ó hAdhmaill 1990). It's ironic perhaps to note that many established politicians, and not just in the North, started off as community activists in their own communities.

As for political group involvement in community groups, there is a lot of evidence, particularly dating from the early and mid-1970s, of the involvement of such groups in, or at least their influence on, community groups (NUU 1975; Burton 1978; Griffiths 1975; Ó hAdhmaill 1990). In the North in the 1960s and 1970s it tended to be socialists, SDLP and the old Republican Clubs (later called the Workers' Party) who were to the fore in such activity. In the 1980s it was local community activists affiliated to or supportive of Sinn Féin. However, by that stage many of the working-class and rural communities concerned were also electing Sinn Féin candidates to be their representatives on political forums, and this in turn had an impact on how they and their supporters viewed and related to community groups and how such groups acted in response (Ó hAdhmaill 1990). There is at least anecdotal evidence to show that community groups often tone down their campaigning activities when they feel 'their own' are now in positions of power.

By the time of the peace process, Cairns *et al.* (2004) noted 'a significant degree of fragmentation in Protestant communities' and 'evidence of political rivalries impacting negatively on community development' in some Catholic working-class communities (Cairns *et al.* 2004:4).

CONCLUSION: DIFFERENT PERSPECTIVES ON COMMUNITY DEVELOPMENT IN PEACE BUILDING

The different perspectives on the conflict in the North, its cause and its possible solutions, led to different approaches to community development. For some, the problem lay primarily with prejudice, negative perceptions of 'the other', and the solution required a community relations approach, based on education and contact and people learning about each other. In this perspective the emphasis was therefore on developing joint initiatives between Catholic and Protestant communities and there was an upsurge in state funding for cross-community youth activities, children's holidays, coffee mornings, etc., as well as for anti-prejudice education programmes, particularly from the 1970s until the onset of the peace process in the mid-1990s.

At the other end of the spectrum, however, were those who felt that the conflict reflected endemic structural inequalities and unequal power relationships. In this view the solution to the conflict lay in addressing not just the power relationships between Catholic and Protestant communities but their respective relationships with the Stormont regime and, ultimately, the British state. Community development and community action needed to be focused in that particular direction. After the signing of the Belfast Agreement (1998), Hughes *et al.* (2003) suggested that there were some signs that:

. . . the community relations agenda has shifted from being 'symptom driven' to addressing root causes of conflict. Current practice is less concerned with promoting cross-community contact per se than with promoting cultural, religious and political pluralism, and the equality agenda has begun to define the nature of some community relations activity. (Hughes *et al.* 2003:1)

It is not difficult to see how those who wanted most structural change in society were attracted to the latter perspective and those who wanted least were drawn to the former. Somewhere in between is probably where most community activists/groups found themselves – trying to survive.

How different perspectives about community development can operate in practice can be seen in the debate around 'good community relations' versus 'social change, equality and social justice'. Advocates of the former, for example, might argue that the main aim is to get diverse communities talking, working and ultimately living together. This might necessitate the avoidance of certain controversial issues in the short term (and in the long term, if necessary) in order to build up trust and mutual respect, accepting the current status quo and working to change it through agreement.

An alternative perspective argues that the primary aim must be equality and social justice and from that will stem mutual respect. Often perspectives on the role of community work and community development will exist on a continuum, with each view at opposite ends. Sometimes the differing views held are linked to differing views about what the 'core problem' is. A 'good relations' approach may be related to a view that the problem is linked more to ignorance and prejudice than to power relations or structural inequalities. It might view the solution as everyone accepting one another within a new Northern Ireland. The alternative view might be based on a notion that the 'problem' is linked to structural inequalities and social justice issues and even the very existence of 'Northern Ireland' as an entity. However, views are often not that polarised and community practitioners will often adopt both approaches in their work within and between communities, whatever they might view as the ultimate end goal. Indeed, the end goal will often be more focused at the micro level – the need to stop rioting at the interface every night, or the need for jobs or improved services in the local area. Whatever strategy is perceived to work may be adopted and may be reflected in tactics such as protest or making quieter representations to those able to deliver. Examples of the different perspectives in relation to tactics are seen in the use of negotiation, as opposed to protests, at the interfaces or around unwanted political marches in an area. The negotiations between local Derry residents and the Apprentice Boys[24] over their annual marches is an example of this.[25] This can be compared to the use of protest and riot by loyalists at the Holy Cross Primary School, Belfast in an attempt to prevent Catholics using a school at an interface (Heatley 2004) or by republicans/nationalists at the Ardoyne shops in Belfast, in reaction to Orange marches passing the area (Moriarty and Nihill 2011).

It was not surprising that community development and how it should be used as a tool itself became a contested site in a Northern Ireland gripped by warfare. The outbreak of violent conflict provided opportunities and challenges (depending on perspective) for social change, local communities and the state. At a macro level, the state alternated between viewing community development groups as something positive, providing a mediating role (during the days of the old Community Relations Commission), and as a potential threat (during the political vetting era of the 1980s). Community development groups themselves could view the state and its forces as existing somewhere on a continuum between 'enemy' and 'friend' based on their view of the conflict, the particular time or event. At a micro level, community development groups often had to operate in an arena of conflicting loyalties and agendas and, at times, with different armed groups vying for control. The current uneasy peace, coupled with a rising recession and cutbacks in community funding, make the future seem highly uncertain.

Notes

1 Saul Alinsky (1909–1972), a community organiser and activist, became famous/ infamous for organising communities in the USA to protest and campaign on a range of social issues. His ideas about community activism are outlined in *Reveille for Radicals* (1969) and *Rules for Radicals* (1971). Alinsky believed that competing interests in society often mean that weaker sections of society need to band together to demand concessions from more powerful elements. He did not rule out partnerships and collaborations for mutual benefit, but saw these more in terms of tactics than anything else. Tactics needed to change to suit the situation.

2 Robert Putnam (2000) has argued that many of the social problems in society can be addressed by strengthening social bonds between people living in communities and thus promoting 'social capital'.

3 Antonio Gramsci (1891–1937), in explaining his concept of hegemony, argues that power is reinforced and reproduced in the hands of existing ruling elites not simply via overt force but by the rest of the population being convinced by the ruling elites that existing power relations and the status quo represent the 'common sense' view of looking at the world (see Bocock 1986).

4 While the six northeastern counties of Ireland that became known as Northern Ireland in 1920 were given their own regional parliament, they remained part of the UK state.

5 The peace process emerged from a long series of secret talks starting in the late 1980s which led to the 1994 IRA ceasefire. The uneasy peace which has followed since has meant that most commentators see the process as ongoing. For more on the peace process, see Mallie and McKittrick (1996) or Gilligan and Tonge (1997).

6 The state was also an important employer, with more than 32.3 per cent of total jobs provided by the public sector at the end of 2009 (compared to about 14 per cent in the South). It was also estimated that a further 30 per cent of jobs were state-subsidised jobs in the private sector (DFPNI 2010).

7 Gerrymandering is the unfair redrawing of electoral boundaries to suit one particular political candidate/party. The term originated from the activities of a US politician called Elbridge Gerry: he had one constituency redrawn into what looked like the shape of a salamander and a newspaper dubbed it a 'gerrymander'.

8 When referring to membership of political parties or religions capitals will be used throughout this chapter, e.g. Unionists (party members) or Catholics, etc. When

referring to a community with nationalist or unionist views, lower case letters will be used throughout.

9   According to Kennedy (1986), about two-thirds of the landmass of Northern Ireland had a Catholic/nationalist majority at the time of Partition.

10   Articles 2 and 3 of the 1937 Irish Constitution, for example, laid claim to the other six counties of the 'national territory' until 1998, when the claims were rescinded as part of the Good Friday Agreement.

11   From the establishment of the Northern Ireland Government in May 1921 until it was prorogued in 1972 and subsequently abolished in 1973, it was controlled by one party, the Ulster Unionist Party. The various Nationalist politicians only ever succeeded in getting one Act passed – the Wild Birds Protection Act (1931). The Parliament moved to a new purpose-built building at Stormont in 1932 (Farrell 1976).

12   In 1962, the Catholic Church appointed a Catholic Chaplain to Stormont for the first time in its history, and this had helped to further set the scene. In 1965 there were for the first time ever exchange visits between the southern Taoiseach, Lemass, and the northern Prime Minister, O'Neill. This directly influenced the Nationalist Party to become the first official opposition party in Stormont in 1966 – although they withdrew again in 1968. By 1967 the Catholic Church had, again for the first time, reached agreement with the State to give it some control over its schools in return for greater grant aid (Ó hAdhmaill 1990).

13   'They still boast of Southern Ireland being a Catholic State. All I boast is that we are a Protestant Parliament and Protestant State.' Sir James Craig, Unionist Party, first Prime Minister of Northern Ireland, 24 April 1934, reported in Parliamentary Debates, Northern Ireland House of Commons, Vol. XVI, Cols. 1091–95.

14   The principle of subsidiarity, articulated in the 1891 Papal encyclical *Rerum Novarum* (Leo XIII), rejected state intervention in the family.

15   Set up by IRA members in 1934 to pursue a more clearly defined socialist agenda, it soon clashed with the IRA leadership and was moribund by 1936. Some of its former members went off to fight for the Republican side in the Spanish Civil War (1936–39).

16   See, for example, Harris's (1972) study of neighbourly co-operation in a 'mixed' rural community in the North in the early 1950s.

17   For example, according to Paddy Docherty, a community activist in Derry, the Bogside Community Association umbrella group was established as a result of the growth in community action concurrent with Free Derry (lecture given by Paddy Docherty at Ulster People's College, Belfast, 23 January 1985).

18   It was the use of the term 'paramilitary' by groups such as the Ulster Defence Association (UDA) which led to it being used in the media to describe all the unofficial armed groups in the North during the conflict. Whilst loyalists were content with the term, republican groups tended to reject it because of its mono-dimensional aspects (Ó hAdhmaill 1990).

19   The Community Relations Commission was set up in October 1969 in Northern Ireland, followed by a newly established Community Relations Ministry, mainly as a state response to the Troubles. There was also a recognition of the rapid growth of community group activity already taking place in Northern Ireland and a desire to try to channel such activity in a 'positive' way. Its aim was to foster harmony in Northern Ireland and it initially set about this task, under its chairperson Maurice Hayes and director Hywel Griffiths, by promoting community development in local communities in much the same way as community development was being promoted as a concept in Britain at this time.

20   The power-sharing Executive lasted from 1 January to 28 May 1974, when it was brought down by the Ulster Workers' Council strike. It involved moderate Unionist and Nationalist politicians but was opposed by most Protestant/unionists and by the IRA.

Except for these few months the North experienced direct rule from Westminster from 1972 until December 1999, when a new power-sharing Executive was established. Fraught with disagreement and periodic suspensions, the latter finally collapsed in October 2002. It was re-established in May 2007.

21 The NIVT was set up in Northern Ireland in 1979 as an independent grant-making trust for community groups.

22 The NICVA is an independent umbrella organisation for the voluntary/community sector in the North. It changed its name in 1986 from the Northern Ireland Council of Social Services (which had been set up in 1938).

23 Margaret Thatcher was the Prime Minister of the Conservative Government at Westminster from 1979 to 1990.

24 A Protestant organisation established in the nineteenth century to commemorate the closing of the gates of the walled city of Derry in 1689 to prevent its capture by the Catholic King James during the Williamite War (1688–91). Its marches around Derry were viewed by Catholics in the city as triumphalist reminders of the dominance of Protestants over the Catholics in the North, and this often led to protests and violent clashes. One such clash in August 1969 led to what became known as the Battle of the Bogside, when nationalist residents battled with the RUC and was followed by the establishment of the Derry 'no-go' area. For more about the Battle of the Bogside, see McCann (1973).

25 For more about these negotiations see, for example, Kelly (1998).

7

What is Family Support Anyway?

The story of how a family support project was set up and implemented using core community development principles

Gerard Phillips

CHAPTER SUMMARY

This chapter describes how an intensive family support project was set up in two areas that suffered from sustained poverty and disadvantage. The chapter hopes to provide a unique insight into how a project is set up and implemented from the very beginning. Consequently it is hoped that it will benefit practitioners and those who reflect on practice. Regular examples from practice are used to illustrate points and provide the reader with a sense of context.

The focus is on how resilience can be developed in communities through a variety of means, including: individual one-to-one support to vulnerable children and parents; targeted and specific group work support to at risk or very isolated groups of people; and whole-community initiatives that strengthen and enhance communities. The rationale for adopting this strategy and clear examples of each strand of the strategy (individual support, targeted group work and community support) will be outlined. To begin it may be helpful to interrogate the meaning of the phrase 'family support'.

INTRODUCTION

'What exactly is family support anyway?' A spirited elderly woman posed this question on a cold morning early in the life of the Springboard family support project. As the recently appointed Springboard project manager I faced this question with a sense of discomfort and apprehension. This was an experienced woman who had witnessed many changes in her local community and knew her community much more comprehensively than I did. This woman would not be misled by practised jargon or sophisticated language and terminology.

'But this is not new,' she said as I endeavoured to convey that this was a fresh, innovative approach. This intense investigation of my motives and methods coming so early in the life of the project provided a sterner test than any of the presentations that I have subsequently given to professionals and agencies. I later grew to know and respect this elderly woman; she taught me to be clear and precise in what I mean by family support, and to be able to translate that meaning to a local setting.

I left our encounter chastened and challenged to obtain clarity and precision as to what is really meant by 'family support'. Of course practitioners, researchers and academics have defined family support (see Canavan *et al.* 2000; Dolan *et al.* 2006; O'Doherty 2007; Gilligan 2000, among many others). Dolan *et al.* (2006:11) state: 'Family support practitioners . . . continue to work without a common view as to its meaning. That lack of clarity is a shared challenge to all of us involved with family support.'

'Family support' seems such an innocent and innocuous phrase: of course we should support families, and all families need and deserve support. But what is a family, how do we define it, and which families need support? Are all families, or only some, in need of support? Who decides, and how? What happens when the family is detrimental to children and parents? How does family support work then?

And what of 'support'? What do we mean by support? Is it financial, emotional, physical, psychological, communitarian or some blend of all of these elements? Quinton (2004) points out that being supported requires both a giver and a receiver and also a lot of activity on the part of parents (Quinton 2004, cited in Sandbaek 2007:75).

Ghate and Hazel (2002), in a UK national survey of parents living in poor circumstances, assessed the types of informal as well as formal help that parents received. They point out that strong relationships between people lie at the heart of support. They also introduce the concept of 'negative support', highlighting parents' fears around lack of privacy, and the fine line between help, interference and losing control of one's life. Parents considered these factors as possible consequences of receiving support (Ghate and Hazel 2002, cited in Sandbaek 2007:78–80).

Example from Practice

The Springboard project confirmed some of these findings in one of the initiatives that it undertook. This took place under the 'Community' strand of the project's strategy. Springboard conducted a joint piece of research with a community health project, the Northside Community Health Initiative (NICHE). This research focused on the experiences of local residents in relation to helping agencies and professionals. The research examined the residents' experience of a wide variety of disciplines, including social welfare, health, and statutory and non-statutory agencies. In general, many of the residents' experiences with helping agencies were not good. They were often treated judgementally and sometimes in a derogatory way. To be treated with respect, courtesy, and to be included in decision-making were among the most important values cited by parents (NICHE Springboard 2007).

To define family support with clarity and precision is not easy; one is quickly drawn into areas of governance, policy, equality, legislation and practice. It is an even more difficult task to clearly outline how, to whom, and in what circumstances family support is to be delivered.

Therefore the seemingly simple phrase 'family support' turns out to be a rather complex and overpopulated space, which eludes simple definition and elucidation. Furthermore, as Katz and Pinkerton (2003) point out, it is an area that is influenced by the impact of social, political and cultural events (Katz and Pinkerton 2003:318–19).

The Springboard project put in place a specific programme of family support for vulnerable families, and also offered a generic programme to all residents living in both areas for which it was responsible. The latter programme included interventions such as street theatre, art, and general community health and well-being programmes.

CONTEXT AND BACKGROUND OF THE SPRINGBOARD PROJECT

The Department of Health and Children established the Springboard Family Support Project for Children at Risk in 1998. This was in response to a perceived need at the time for community-based family support. At the outset fifteen projects were established countrywide on a pilot basis. McKeown *et al.* (2001) produced an evaluation of participating children and parents in Springboard and found that they experienced improvements in well-being which they attributed to the support they received from Springboard.

The Springboard Project in Farranree and Knocknaheeny is located in two communities, geographically close to each other, on the Northside of Cork City. The project is part of a general strategy by the Irish government to provide increased supports for families who are experiencing difficulties. The communities are also part of the government's Revitalising Areas by Planning and Integrated Development (RAPID) programme, a policy initiative that promotes partnership at local levels in communities with a history of disadvantage.

A study by O Toole (2002) concluded that both areas experienced social, economic and infrastructural disadvantages. However, these communities also have a rich history in culture, art, sport, writing and folklore. Furthermore, as Ungar (2005) posits, such communities are part of an unheralded good news story, in that these histories of art, culture, fortitude and resilience are less often referred to in the media and in society. 'What we fail to understand in a media awash with worry is that interventions and a widening social safety net are having the effect we anticipated' (Ungar 2005:xx).

Nevertheless, both communities had higher than average levels of unemployment, early school leaving, antisocial behaviour and crime rates (O Toole 2002). The communities also suffered from poor-quality housing, and a transient population in certain areas. The need for a targeted family support project was put forward by O Toole (2002) and supported by the local RAPID inter-agency groups. The project was championed and driven by the local child care manager and principal community worker, and other statutory, non-governmental and community representatives. Springboard has a staff complement of four project workers from multidisciplinary backgrounds, and a project manager. The professional backgrounds of the staff include social work, community work, childcare and counselling.

Thus the Springboard Project for Farranree and Knocknaheeny was approved by the Department of Health and Children and established in 2003. The project was set up under the aegis of the Health Service Executive (HSE) in Cork City and placed under the management of the child care manager for the area.

WHAT IS A 'FAMILY'?

In a comprehensive social history of the family, Luepnitz (1988) suggests that the closely bonded nuclear family of the contemporary period is not a constant in history. The rise of capitalism in the eighteenth and nineteenth centuries changed the family from a unit of production to a unit of consumption. The transformation from an agrarian to an urban economy led to profound changes in the roles of parents and children. Men were removed from the home to separate places of work, such as the factory or the office, which required long hours of work and separation from family. Women were required to devote themselves entirely to childcare and housework, 'a category of work that became socially invisible' (Luepnitz 1988:144).

Children were placed under the care and control of their parents, with no rights of their own. The so-called 'nuclear family' would fuel and maintain an entire economic system and would dwarf in legislative terms alternative forms of family, such as same-sex couples or single-parent families. The dominance of this type of family structure would dictate policy in relation to the family, especially in Ireland up to the early 1990s.

POLICY INITIATIVES IN RELATION TO THE FAMILY

The term 'family policy' took a long time to mature and was relatively unused until the mid-1970s. Family policy started small and was quite contentious (Daly and Clavero 2002:34). In Ireland, the principal architects were the state and the Church, with the influence of the Church waning from the 1970s on.

In general, family policy comprised monetary contributions in the form of child benefits, tax allowances for children and maternity benefits. Until the 1990s, family policy in Ireland was underpinned by a number of underlying principles and assumptions, which included the following.

- Families should, in the main, take responsibility for their own welfare.
- Policies focused on cash support rather than the provision of services.

- Support was for families founded on marriage in the traditional sense of defined roles: father as breadwinner and sole earner; and mother as homemaker and principal carer of the children (Daly and Clavero 2002:28–33).

Until the 1990s a picture of minimal state involvement in the family emerged in Ireland, with a selective rather than a universal approach to assisting families. This contrasted with many European countries that adopted a universal approach to family policy that assisted all families.

In Europe, family policy has been on the agenda since the Council of Europe's first Conference of Ministers Responsible for Family Affairs, held in Vienna in 1959. 'Family policy measures in Europe attempt to address the determinants of parenting albeit to different degrees and not always in a coherent and co-ordinated manner' (Sandbaek 2007:60). Daly and Clavero (2002:40) point out that support for the family was very limited in Ireland compared to other European countries.

In EU member states the reduction in population growth and demographic ageing were associated with longer life expectancy, the postponement of marriage, an increasing number of consensual unions, a growing rate of divorce, longer cohabitation of children with parents, and large increases in the number of women entering the labour market (Hantrais and Letablier 1996:174).

Significant changes took place in Ireland in relation to family policy during the 1990s. These included the Commission on the Family in 1996, large increases in child benefit, and more childcare places. The decade also saw the development of services to support families. This took the form of a strategy to support families in need, especially in areas of disadvantage. Another strategy focused on providing counselling and mediation for couples experiencing difficulties (Daly and Clavero 2002).

A clear vision in relation to family support was contained in the final report of the Commission on the Family in 1998, which recommended an approach (to family support) 'which is empowering of individuals, builds on family strengths, enhances self esteem and engenders a sense of being able to influence events in one's life, has significant potential as a primary preventative strategy for all families facing the ordinary challenges of day-to-day living, and has a particular relevance in communities that are coping in a stressful environment' (Commission on the Family Final Report, cited in McKeown *et al.* 2001:5).

Of course these policy initiatives were responses to huge changes in the structure and composition of the family in Ireland and also in Europe around that time. These included greater diversity in types of family (Fahey and Russell 2001) and a large increase in the employment of women, which became a hugely important social factor in Ireland. This was especially true in relation to mothers: between 1988 and 1998 the number of women working outside the home increased by 60 per cent (Daly and Clavero 2002:12).

The traditional family unit of father as main earner, mother as homemaker, and two children was no longer the norm; in the USA, for instance, this arrangement accounted for less than 5 per cent of family units (*International Social Security Review* 1994, cited in Daly and Clavero 2002:11).

In Ireland, rates of separation and divorce (which was introduced in 1997) increased (Canavan and O Brien 2005:17–18). The number of lone parents also increased.

Canavan and O Brien (2005) chart other policy and legislative developments reflecting a family support orientation, which include the following.

- The Children Act 2001 provided the HSE with the legislation and responsibility to meet the needs of young people whose behaviour posed a risk to themselves and others. This Act adopted family support measures to meet the needs of such young people and their families.
- The National Children's Strategy (2000), which stressed the importance of family and community in the lives of children.
- The Family Support Act 2001 provided a statutory basis for the family resource centre programme.
- Other policy initiatives included the Health Strategy (2001), which emphasised the importance of environmental, social and economic factors for health and well-being, and the National Anti-Poverty Strategy (1997), which set policy goals in relation to the alleviation of child and family poverty. (See Canavan and O Brien 2005:24–5.)

The principal framing legislation with regard to the care and protection of children is the Child Care Act 1991. This aimed to promote the welfare of children, especially those not receiving adequate care and protection, and to strengthen the capacity of the state to provide childcare and family support services. 'However only in the late 1990s did the potential of the act in relation to family support begin to be realised nationally, with the establishment of the Springboard programme' (Canavan and O Brien 2005:24). Other policy developments included: the National Development Plan (2000–2006), committed to funding childcare, family support and community services; and the National Children's Strategy (2000), which laid out a ten-year plan for children. The National Children's Office was established in 2002 and the Ombudsman for Children took up office in 2004. The issue of children's rights has also been prominent in the discourse around child welfare, with a national referendum on establishing children's rights promised by the government.

DEFINING FAMILY SUPPORT

The UK Audit Commission defined family support simply as 'any activity or facility aimed at providing advice and support to parents in bringing up their children' (Audit Commission (UK) 1994).

Gilligan (2000) envisaged family support as falling into three main categories.

1   Developmental family support seeks to strengthen the social supports and coping mechanisms of children and adults in their families and communities.
2   Compensatory family support seeks to compensate children and parents for the disabling effects of disadvantage and adversity.
3   Protective family support seeks to strengthen the capacities and coping mechanisms of children and adults against identified risks and threats in individual families (Gilligan 2000:15).

Dolan *et al.* (2006) use social support theory in a predominantly Irish context on which to base their definition of family support. They state:

> Family support is recognised as both a style of work and a set of activities that reinforce positive informal social networks through integrated programmes. These programmes combine statutory, voluntary, community and private services and are generally provided to families within their own homes and communities. The primary focus of these services is on early intervention aiming to promote and protect the health, well-being and rights of all children, young people and their families. At the same time particular attention is given to those who are vulnerable or at risk. (Dolan *et al.* 2006:16)

This definition includes the diverse range of activities that family support can cover, and also calls it a 'style of work'. It also includes the generic and specific orientations of the approach.

McKeown *et al.* (2001), who conducted an independent evaluation on the first fourteen Springboard projects, described family support as an umbrella term that covers a wide range of interventions: 'This diversity indicates that family support is not a homogenous activity but a diverse range of interventions' (McKeown *et al.* 2001:3).

From these and other definitions of family support one gains a picture of a diverse range of interventions and strategies aimed at addressing a complex set of needs for children and families. Of course one must also consider the dimension of power relations when considering any childcare intervention and any strategy that involves the statutory delivery of a service to children and families.

Parton (1991) discusses the nature of power in relation to childcare, child protection and the family. He draws on some concepts developed by Foucault, in particular the idea of 'discourse'. Foucault saw discourse as a key element in the creation of power in society: 'Discourses are structures of knowledge through which we understand, explain and decide things' (Parton 1991:3).

The discourse of the family is different from the discourse of a sports club or an academic institution, for example. However, the discourse of a profession or a government department carries a great deal of power: take, for example, the complex terminology associated with medicine or the legal profession. One consequence of this is that it allows members of the profession to communicate with each other. However, it also excludes the patient or 'client' from understanding the nature and meaning of the discourse.

The professional in this instance can take decisions, draw conclusions or recommend treatments without anyone other than another member of the profession being able to challenge their authority and judgements. Discourse can thus be associated with power and the ability to exercise that power (Oliver 2010:29). Writing directly about the power of the family support worker, Warren (1997) writes:

> For example, the power you have as counsellor or mentor, the power vested in the facilitator in the group-joining phase, the powerful knowledge of the experienced networker, the power of the educator and so on. It seems to me that what is important turns on how such power is negotiated. (Warren 1997:116)

The concluding sentence points to the most important aspect in the analysis of power in relation to family support: how we negotiate power with the people we work with. Sandbaek (2007) states that two overarching principles are central for programmes that support parenting: a focus on protective factors as well as risk factors; and treating parents and children as agents in their own lives (Sandbaek 2007:70). These principles were central to the strategy that Springboard developed.

HOW THE SPRINGBOARD INTERVENTION WAS DELIVERED

This chapter began with the apparently simple question, 'What is family support?' The question has been unpacked in terms of history, policy, definition and power relations. These features were all present when the springboard project was launched. So how did Springboard go about finding answers to these complex questions? In the beginning the project started in the usual places, doing a good deal of background reading, visiting and talking with other Springboard workers. We* also engaged in an apparently simple activity: we went out on the streets and started conversing with, and – more important – listening to, local people.

Gill and Jack stress the importance of listening to children and parents: not a form of selective hearing based on the requirements, procedures and service arrangements of agencies (Gill and Jack 2007:53). They stress the importance of listening regardless of theoretical approach or professional background. Of course, such principles lie at the heart of good community development practice.

However, this was not an easy task in the beginning: the residents of the areas did not know who we were, and had no history of family support. Naturally there was a degree of suspicion since some residents had in the past had negative experiences with statutory services. Were we from the social welfare spying on people, were we gathering information on how children were being reared? Who

---

* In this passage 'we' is used as a convenient term to represent the workers of Springboard.

in fact were we, and what were we about? We dressed in different clothes, spoke a different professional language and had little knowledge of the culture and customs of the communities we were entering. It is little wonder that we were met with some suspicion.

Gradually, as we continued to come back each day and listen to the concerns and needs of people, we experienced a guarded sense of acceptance – at least we were persistent and did appear to listen without judgement. We would be judged by our actions and how we followed up on concerns raised.

Springboard encountered a wide range of needs and concerns, none of which would fit into a neat box or could be dealt with easily. For example, the broad description of Springboard projects stipulates that the projects work in the main with children aged 0–12 years (see McKeown *et al.* 2001).

Example from Practice

During the first week of the project a very distressed mother and her teenage child, who was upset and disturbed, approached the project for assistance. The age of this child placed them outside the age category for Springboard. Accessibility brought responsibility, and in this and other cases, it would have been difficult, if not impossible, to close our doors and plead lack of ability or resources. What we could do, we would try to do, and if we could not provide the service ourselves, we would advocate to obtain the service needed.

The range of need and concerns impelled the project to seek out an anchoring set of principles or theoretical framework. The workers came from a variety of backgrounds: social work, childcare, counselling/psychotherapy and community work. The work could be classified under a number of theories; for example ecological practice, as described by Gill and Jack (2007), or social support theory, as described by Dolan *et al.* (2006), would be appropriate theoretical frameworks for the project.

The project also looked at research that was done in the United States on prevention work that assists children and young people (see Weissberg *et al.* 2003). Arising from this review of the literature and from ongoing dialogue and discussions with people at street level, three different but related sets of needs emerged. These needs emerged around: a) the individual one-to-one level; b) the targeted group level; and c) the broader community or universal level. Concomitantly a strategy was formed to meet these needs.

STANCE AND ORIENTATION OF THE SPRINGBOARD WORKER: BUILDING A COMMUNITY DEVELOPMENT APPROACH INTO FAMILY SUPPORT

Before the strategy is outlined, it is necessary to explain the stance or orientation of the workers. This stance or style of work is influenced by community development principles. Furthermore, because this is a practice-led model, it means that the theoretical and empirical are held in constant dialogue; theory affects practice and practice affects and shapes the evolution of new theory.

This orientation also incorporates structural, historical, social and political factors. Therefore people are not blamed for being poor, or for being single parents or because they are recipients of social welfare. Rather, structural and political factors are taken into consideration when considering the reasons for poverty, and how poverty, dependency and isolation are maintained. To quote Mullaly, 'we need a political analysis that distinguishes the causes and the consequences of social problems. We need a vision of a humanized society to give us direction in our efforts . . . and we need a commitment to carry out the difficult task of social transformation' (Mullaly 2007:362).

In relation to social and political factors, Garrett (2009) urges us to be suspicious and wary of the dominance of 'neo-liberalism' in the provision of children's services. Fredric Jameson urges his readers to 'do the impossible, namely to try and think positively and negatively all at once; to achieve . . . a type of thinking that would be capable of grasping the demonstrably baleful features of capitalism along with its extraordinary and liberating dynamism simultaneously' (Jameson 2000:225–6, cited in Garrett 2009:152).

Taking account of these analyses the staff at Springboard adopted an 'emic' perspective in relation to their dealings with parents and children (see Westoby 2008). This is an anthropological term, which privileges the insider perspectives of parents and children, in contrast to 'etic' or outsider definitions and perspectives. This does not mean that professional perspectives are disregarded or ignored; rather it means that the perspective of the parents and children are put centre stage, in a needs-based assessment that considers and values all perspectives. In the case of a conflict of definition of need (among professionals or parents), decisions are taken with the best interests of the child as the primary focus, whereby the child is treated as an active subject, and adults do not speak for children.

Adopting an emic perspective involves taking time to step back and re-engage with people as they define their own needs. Within this community development approach, the worker takes an elicitive stance oriented toward facilitation and discovery (Westoby 2008; Lederach 1995). An elicitive stance of facilitation sees the primary focus of work as a mutual journey of discovery between the worker and the parent, child, family or community that they work with (see Westoby 2008:492).

The orientation of this stance is also in keeping with participatory and collaborative practice (see D'Cruz and Stagnitti 2008). Adopting this type of elicitive approach has also been found to foster resilience. Ann Buchanan, citing research from two national studies in the UK, states, 'Exciting new research on resilience suggests that we need to get into young people's heads, or to perceive the world as they see it if we want to help them' (Buchanan 2002:261).

The Practice Model Outlined

Arising from this elicitive process of identifying needs with parents and children in the target areas, a number of distinctive but interrelated sets of needs began to emerge. These needs could be grouped into: a) intensive individual one-to-one work with parents and children; b) targeted group interventions; and c) community interventions aimed at the broader community level.

First there was a need for family support at the individual level or 'indicated preventive interventions' (see Weissberg *et al.* 2003:426–7). These interventions involved providing support to individual families who were extremely vulnerable and at high risk. Early childhood interventions targeted at the most disadvantaged children have a proven effectiveness rate (Danziger and Waldfogel 2000, quoted in Daly and Leonard 2002).

The nature of this support meant regular home visitation (always undertaken with the family's permission), at least once per week, sometimes more if needed. At the upper end of the support spectrum the work could involve child protection, or mental health, addiction or behavioural difficulties in the family. Some of this work involved situations where parenting had broken down or was detrimental and harmful to children. The work required honesty and clarity, and was guided by the best interests of the child, as expressed by the child themselves – if they could safely do so. The need to speak to and observe children in situations where there is neglect in families was highlighted by the Roscommon Child Care Case Report, which recommended the following:

> Contact with children should appear on the agenda for every professional supervision meeting and form part of every report for a Case Conference. Where there is more than one child in a family, the needs, wishes and feelings of each child must be considered and reported on as well as the totality of the family situation. (HSE 2010:87)

The second area that emerged was the need for targeted or specific group work programmes, or 'selective preventive interventions' (see Weissberg *et al.* 2003:426–7). These groups did not replace existing groups in the community. Rather, the need for such groups arose from the individual one-to-one interventions. Examples included support groups for parents, and targeted behavioural groups for children who were diagnosed with conduct disorders or attention deficit disorder. Another example was a group that helped with the speech and language needs of pre-school children.

The third area of need that emerged was the need to work at a broad community level or 'universal preventive interventions' (see Weissberg *et al.* 2003:426–7). For example, this could mean working on broad issues that affect the community, such as poor housing or playground facilities; or population health issues, such as infant health and parental well-being.

Home-Start International (2005) brought attention to the need for social and community support for parents. This research, carried out in a number of European countries including Ireland, found that, in addition to sufficient income and adequate purchasing power, personal and community relationships are protective factors for preventing exclusion and maintaining mental health (Home-Start International 2005, quoted in Sandbaek 2007:73).

The project decided to apply this approach in its day-to-day operations. At the individual level each worker carried a caseload of approximately twelve individual cases, some of which were at the higher end of the support spectrum (e.g. children on the verge of entering statutory care or returning from residential care).

Each worker also facilitated or co-facilitated a targeted group; the need for such a group was assessed at the individual or community level. For example, a cluster of parents who had a child on the autistic spectrum were engaged with individually. The project decided to form a support group for these parents. The parents were doing an invaluable service for their children, and for society in general, with a tremendous focus on the needs of the children. However, the needs of the parents were often at the bottom of the agenda. The group approach enhanced the individual work and vice versa.

Each worker also became actively involved in community activism as part of local networks and committees. Issues addressed included the production of a video, involving local residents, on car crime. The research conducted with NICHE (referred to earlier) on residents' experience of the helping professions is another example. This research was launched and published with the residents themselves involved in the entire process. This was extremely rewarding for them, and they could also see a definite outcome to the research, in that they were not just involved as passive recipients of information about their lives.

Advantages and Disadvantages of the Approach

In the beginning the implementation of this model – to work at three distinct but interconnected levels – appeared a daunting task. There were risks that the project and the workers could become overstretched. How would the levels interact and would the most vulnerable people become marginalised yet again?

In fact the opposite began to emerge as the model was introduced and developed. It offered the workers and the project two key qualities: flexibility and adaptability. Because the project offered a range of interventions – individual, group and community – it was a much more flexible response to needs in the target areas. Daly states that family support services should be multi-focused and flexible, taking account of the uniqueness of each family and the complexity of the problems that they face (Daly 2007:120).

Another advantage of the model employed by Springboard is that it operated as an extremely effective caseload management instrument, thus minimising the need for long waiting lists or undue delays in responding to requests for help.

For example, the project worked with some sixty to seventy families on the one-to-one, individual level at any one time, a comparatively high number for the size and nature of the project. It also facilitated or co-facilitated some eleven to thirteen targeted groups at a time, which enabled the project to reach a large number of people collectively. (The average group size ranged from six to eight individuals.) Finally, the project worked on a large number of community issues, including improved housing, childcare facilities, and improved nutrition and diet.

People could begin at the individual, one-to-one level, and move perhaps to a targeted group or to greater community involvement. This built their social capital in some of the ways O'Doherty (2007) has outlined. Furthermore, it increased the protective factors of resilience among residents (see Phillips 2008).

Example from Practice

A working example of this process is the garden project. Springboard took over a vacant council house when it first moved into one of the target areas. This house had been vacant for some years, and had a back garden that had been used as a local dumping ground and was very unkempt.

As part of its community strand, Springboard undertook a clean-up and replanting of the garden. In time this proved very successful, both in terms of introducing the project to the area, and through the involvement of children and parents in the project. Some of these children and parents were quietly and confidentially involved in direct one-to-one work with project workers.

Gradually some of the parents took over the management and day-to-day running of the garden project. They organised Christmas celebrations and other events in the garden, which proved to be very successful in involving local parents. Some of these parents later joined the management board of a newly established childcare facility that had come into the area.

This example shows a real progression among people who at the beginning were quite isolated and not involved in their local neighbourhood. It is an example of how the model works in practice and how the three areas of individual, group and community work are interrelated. A professional from another agency stared in amazement one late winter evening as a local woman whom she had known for many years was solving a problem in the garden. The professional worker could not believe it was the same person, and how transformed she was in this setting.

Daly states, 'scholarship is increasingly moving towards a holistic conception of parenting and its influences in which the parent and child are at the centre of a process that has multiple influences and outcomes' (Daly 2007:114). These values lie at the very core of the Springboard model outlined here.

SUMMARY: DATA ANALYSIS OF FAMILY SUPPORT INTERVENTIONS BY SPRINGBOARD

The following data was collected following one-to-one individual work that was completed by Springboard workers with 103 families. This work was completed over a twelve-month period and the data begins at referral stage to Springboard. The information may be useful for appreciating the scale of problems that are referred to family support projects.

In the vast majority (62 per cent) of families the mother was the primary carer of the children (see Table 7.1). The next highest category was mother and father parental relationship (30 per cent). The data confirms the vitally important role of mothers in the most vulnerable families and the concomitant need to provide support to these families. Ironically, however, single-parent households are often among the first to be financially affected in an economic recession. This data confirms the importance of nourishing and supporting women in the vitally important roles they play in their families and in society in general. This support relates not only to child rearing but also to support in accessing educational and employment opportunities.

Table 7.1. Family composition

	Number	Percentage of total
Mother lone parent	64	62.1
Mother and father parental relationship	31	30.1
Father lone parent	3	2.9
Parents separated – shared care	4	3.9
Grandparent caring for child	1	1.0
Total	103	100.0

Source (Tables 7.1–7.4): SPSS data analysis of the Springboard Project conducted by the author.

The main form of housing for the 103 families was city council rented accommodation (82.5 per cent). Only 3.9 per cent of families lived in a mortgaged property. The data confirms high levels of dependency on statutory provided housing.

Table 7.2. Type of accommodation

	Number	Percentage of total
City council rented house	85	82.5
Privately rented house	14	13.6
Mortgaged property	4	3.9
Total	103	100.0

The principal reason for referral to the project contained on the referral form to Springboard was either: a) behavioural difficulties with a child under 7 years (26 per cent); or b) parental difficulties (also 26 per cent). In this instance a parental difficulty might refer to a relationship difficulty or a struggle to cope financially or emotionally.

Table 7.3. Presenting problem at referral

	Number	Percentage of total
Behavioural difficulty with child > 7	27	26.2
Behavioural difficulty with child 7+	21	20.4
Parental difficulty	27	26.2
Housing issue	9	8.7
School issue	8	7.8
Child with special needs	11	10.7
Total	**103**	**100.0**

The primary category with regard to income source for the 103 families was, not surprisingly, 'mother dependent on social welfare' (61 per cent): see Table 7.4. The next highest category was 'father and mother dependent on social welfare' (26 per cent). Only 1.9 per cent of mothers and 1.9 per cent of fathers were working full

Table 7.4. Primary income source of family

	Number	Percentage
Mother dependent on social welfare	63	61.2
Mother and father dependent on social welfare	27	26.2
Father dependent on social welfare	3	2.9
Mother working full time	2	1.9
Mother working part time	1	1.0
Father working full time	2	1.9
Mother dependent on social welfare; father working part time	3	2.9
Father dependent on social welfare; mother working part time	1	1.0
Grandparent dependent on social welfare	1	1.0
Total	**103**	**100.0**

time. These statistics indicate the high degree of disadvantage and dependency that families endure along with existing difficulties such as rearing a child with autism or other behavioural difficulties. The figures are a stark reminder of the high needs of vulnerable families and the responsibility of a caring society to cherish its most vulnerable citizens and children.

CONCLUSION

This chapter has attempted to provide an analysis of how a family support project was set up and delivered to two communities with histories of disadvantage. The chapter has shown how the work of the Springboard project fits into the context of family policy in Ireland and outlined some of the ways that the project established itself with residents, parents and children. The overarching stance or style of work was described and outlined, along with the system of working at three distinct but interrelated levels of need: the intensive individual level; the targeted group level; and the community or universal level.

8

Nurturing Collaborative Relationships and Developing Local Communities: An Irish Case Study

Delores Crerar

CHAPTER SUMMARY

Collaborative working is widely accepted to be a cost-effective method of working with families and local communities. International and national literature in relation to collaborative working recognises that this approach requires time, investment and commitment by all stakeholders involved in the process (Atkinson *et al.* 2002; Darlington *et al.* 2005; McInnes 2007). This chapter is concerned with identifying best practice in relation to collaborative working and exploring the impact the international collaborative model of co-location has had on community development practice nationally. The first section of this chapter will discuss existing literature, highlighting various definitions and models of collaborative working. Strategies for informing collaborative working will then be explored.

The second section of the chapter will discuss one particular collaborative approach, identified in the literature as the co-location model of collaborative working. An Irish case study will be presented which explores a newly developed co-location centre for young people and families. The case study will highlight examples of the strengths, challenges and outcomes of this collaborative partnership. The chapter concludes with a summary of the main points presented.

UNDERSTANDING COLLABORATIVE WORKING: DEFINITIONS, TERMINOLOGIES AND MODELS OF PRACTICE

When attempting to provide a definition for collaborative working, one enters into a 'terminological quagmire' (Lloyd *et al.* 2001:3). There *is* currently no universally accepted definition, leading to the emergence of competing definitions seeking to highlight the various forms and address the professional practices associated with collaborative working. This form of working is therefore often referred to as 'inter-agency working', 'partnership', 'multi-disciplinary work' and 'collaborative working'. A useful definition of this form of work is presented by Mattessich and

Monsey (as cited in Townsend and Shelly 2008:102): 'Collaboration is a mutually beneficial and well defined relationship entered into by two or more organisations to achieve common goals. This relationship includes a commitment to mutual relationships and goal, a jointly developed structure and shared responsibility; mutual authority and accountability for success; and sharing of resources and rewards.'

Various alternative definitions have been created for those terms frequently utilised to refer to the many forms of collaborative working present in the not-for-profit and community development sector (Lloyd *et al.* 2001):

- *Inter-agency working* – more than one agency working together in a planned and formal way that can be at operational or strategic level.
- *Joint working* – professionals from more than one agency working together on a project or initiative.
- *Multi-agency working* – more than one agency working with young people, families or communities, but not necessarily in a co-ordinated partnership.

A detailed study of thirty inter-agency collaborations conducted by Atkinson *et al.* (2002) identified that not only do competing definitions present, but competing models also emerge. Such models include:

- *Consultation and training groups* – expertise and knowledge from one agency provided to another in the form of training and consultation opportunities.
- *Decision-making groups* – forums for different agencies and services to meet and make decisions together.
- *Centre-based delivery* – developing and delivering comprehensive professional services in one central location.
- *Co-ordinated delivery* – occurring within centres, or communities, advanced by a co-ordinator who is responsible for the cohesion of different services.
- *Operational team delivery* – professionals from different agencies working together to form an integrated team delivering services directly to service users. (Atkinson *et al.* 2002)

Therefore, it can be argued that 'collaboration' occurs across a continuum presenting different forms and levels of partnership between stakeholders.

DEVELOPING CAPACITY TO ENGAGE IN COLLABORATIVE WORKING

Collaborative working relationships will differ in terms of form and purpose within partnerships. Variations are likely to occur due to the lifespan of a relationship (e.g. pilot project, one-off initiative, ongoing activity). Individual collaborations will also present alternative degrees of risk and commitment, or strive for specific outcomes. To assess the potential for collaboration, agencies must reflect on their individual position to determine whether a partnership with additional agencies is actually required or beneficial. Where collaborations are created between agencies these may occur for a variety of reasons (Walsh *et al.* 2006), which include:

- forming consortia to undertake a one-off project or event;
- forming partnerships to undertake a series of work or a long-term project;
- developing procedures in relation to how one organisation will interact with another when conducting separate services, or activities in local communities (e.g. referral protocols);
- agreeing the sharing of resources, expertise and premises (e.g. when several agencies agree to operate a co-location model of service provision);
- merging two or more agencies for economic, mainstreaming and restructuring purposes.

Figure 8.1. Continuum of collaborative practice

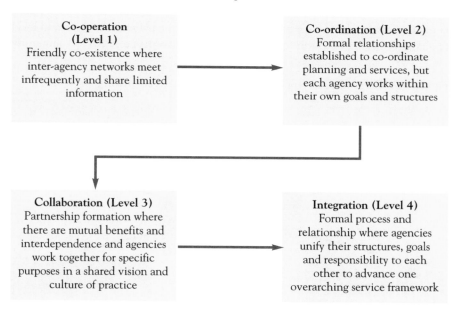

Where the potential for collaborative relationships exists, the capacity of those involved in the process must in turn be developed. Harris *et al.* (2007) (cited in Cheminais 2009:31) have identified four developmental stages essential for building capacity when engaged in collaborative working:

1   Create internal conditions and structures within one's own agency that will facilitate collaborative working. This will include the development of an

internal agency policy on collaborative working that highlights a 'can do' ethos for this method of practice.

2   Create an understanding of the ethos, culture, moral purpose, leadership, decision-making and communication structures which will exist between agencies who are involved in collaborative working.

3   Develop structures for enhancing and extending community support and involvement. This will entail establishing youth groups, parents' groups, community groups, co-location centres and opportunities for the community to engage with other agencies.

4   Secure additional external support and additional funding to sustain the activities of the collaborative partnership. This will entail gaining support from local schools and business, as well as securing sponsorship, ring-fenced funding and additional resources.

A variety of relationships and formal ties will exist between agencies and communities in daily practice. Some collaborative relationships will be easily identified, while others may be more subtle and require nurturing. Community mapping assists agencies new to collaborative working to assess the type and level of relationship they hold with other services (Butterworth *et al.* 2001). Community

Figure 8.2. Community mapping tool for collaborative working

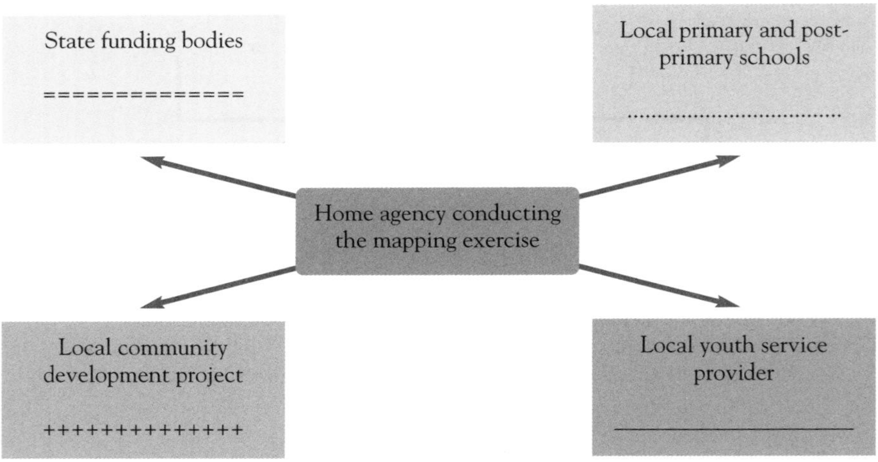

Nature of the relationship	Purpose
Co-operating ————————	Steering group committee member for project
Co-ordinating	Highlights home agencies services to students
Collaborating ================	Funder of project and requires ongoing reports
Integrating +++++++++++++++++	Intends to amalgamate with home agency

Source: adapted from Butterworth *et al.* 2001.

mapping can take many forms, but for the purpose of collaborative working this approach refers to an 'abstract' graphic presentation of the relationships which exist between agencies (Melcher 1999). This visual presentation of relationships is also referred to in literature as 'eco-mapping' (Hartman 1995). The tool enables an organisation to identify the type of relationship entered into with other services across the four continuums of co-ordinated working: co-operating; co-ordinating; collaborating; and integrating.

The community mapping tool is useful as it can assist agencies to identify where there is overlap with other services, where gaps in capacity exist and how links and collaborations with other agencies can be improved. Once an organisation has identified the type of relationships it already holds with additional services, it can then assess the potential for developing new collaborative relationships or strengthening existing ones. Successful agreements between agencies can then be reached which clarify the nature, purpose and vision of the collaboration; who owns the agreement; which stakeholders are involved in the process; what boundaries have been reached between agencies; and how the agreement will lead to action. Topics contained in such agreements should include the following.

- Background or introductory information that sets the context for the agreement.
- Purpose of the collaboration, including aims, objectives, vision and purpose.
- A list of agencies involved in the collaborative working process, to include the roles and responsibilities of each agency.
- The guiding principles that inform the agreement and practice, such as open communication, power-sharing.
- Legal implications for the work, if relevant, to include tenancy agreements.
- A clear implementation plan which will advance service provision.
- Arrangements for monitoring and evaluation of the existing collaborative agreement.
- Procedures for responding to grievances, conflict and the dissolution of the working relationship.
- Appendices to include forms, checklists, legislation and contact details for the designated person of each agency responsible for contributing to the process (Atkinson *et al.* 2002; Darlington *et al.* 2005; Metcalfe *et al.* 2007).

STRATEGIES FOR FACILITATING EFFECTIVE COLLABORATIVE WORKING

It has been recognised that collaborative initiatives are easy to establish but hard to sustain long term (Butterworth *et al.* 2001). For collaborative working to be successful it must be underpinned by a variety of principles and strategies which include the following.

Creating Effective Communication Structures

This must become the responsibility of not only the workers but also the agencies involved in collaborative working (Cunningham-Smith 2004; Darlington and Feeney 2008; Ervin 2004). It has been argued that for effective communication to occur the individual worker must be willing to engage in self-reflection and be open to new working practices (Darlington and Feeney 2008; Darlington *et al.* 2005; Dolan *et al.* 2006). It has been identified that appointing a 'contact person' to ensure that regular collaborative meetings take place (Harlow and Shardlow 2006; Metcalfe *et al.* 2007) and having space to 'unpack and discuss entrenched differences' (Head 2008:744) can assist in creating effective communication processes which strengthen collaborative working between agencies.

Fostering a Shared Culture of Practice and Learning

Many commentators have recognised that in order to develop a shared culture, commitment to the collaboration must be displayed by agencies involved in the process (Atkinson *et al.* 2002; Darlington *et al.* 2005; Henderson 2004; Head 2008). For collaborative relationships to be successful, they must be built on trust between agencies. Ongoing capacity building and staff training must occur to ensure that a shared culture emerges and that the collaborative relationship remains sustainable. Strategies should be developed to ensure that staff can engage in joint training and development opportunities (Atkinson *et al.* 2002; Frost 2005). Tomlinson (2003) suggests that a variety of resource tools should be utilised to engage staff in this process. Examples include shadowing between agencies, case studies, role play and experimental placements.

Understanding and Planning for Conflict

Several publications highlight the challenges involved in preventing, managing and resolving disputes (Fine *et al.* 2005; Hopkin 2006; NSW DCS 2005). There are a variety of reasons why conflict may arise during collaborative activities. Understanding the driving forces which fuel a conflict situation can help agencies to better manage the collaborative relationship and move forward. The distribution of power, status and perceived inequalities are perhaps the most frequently perceived underlying forces which contribute to conflict arising. Fine *et al.* (2005:6) state that 'conflict is particularly likely to be evident in any arrangement involving proposals for budget-holding and/or transfer of authority'. Conflict that arises from such power struggles or imbalances is also known as 'relative deprivation' and may intensify when concessions are made between agencies (Walker 2010). Often there may present numerous sources of conflict, which may converge, leading to complex disputes between agencies. Such disputes may arise due to differences relating to power sharing or ideological perspectives relating to beliefs, whether cultural or value-related.

Where conflict is not successfully managed there can be a direct impact on the sustainability of the collaboration. For these situations to be handled successfully an agreed strategy for resolving conflict must be utilised by all partners involved in the collaborative process. This will require agencies to enter into negotiations that are respectful and that will ideally produce win/win situations for all stakeholders. Situations may present where an 'impasse' has developed between agencies. Impasses may arise amongst stakeholders during the distribution of resources as part of the collaborative process, particularly in situations where some members are unlikely to benefit from the process (e.g. the allocation of funding, employment positions or service provision). In such situations it may be beneficial to identify a skilled outside person who can act as a mediator or facilitator: a third party can have the ability to move the process forward and create a successful outcome. However, for this to succeed all stakeholders must have a desire to compromise where necessary in order to achieve an advantageous outcome. All collaborations should be supported by agreed written documentation containing a section on conflict negotiation and dispute resolution techniques to be implemented by the group when competing agendas surface among stakeholders.

Developing Ongoing Evaluation Structures

Monitoring and evaluation are key elements of operational practice and provide clarity with regard to the performance and effectiveness of the collaborative process. Creating regular monitoring checkpoints over the lifespan of the relationship enables reflection, appraisal and review of agreed protocols and goals to take place. In turn, this provides an opportunity to re-examine previous agreements, discuss issues which are creating conflict and, where necessary, make the necessary amendments to strengthen the collaborative relationship. Evaluation also provides a method of assessing the effectiveness of the collaborative relationship and service provision. Results from such processes can be used to justify programme expenditure, harness support for securing funding from additional funding sources and leverage additional resources for the community.

Enhancing and Extending Community Support and Involvement

Developing support and creating community involvement requires agencies involved in collaborative working to develop effective participatory structures working from a bottom-up approach with local communities. It has been recognised that 'being involved in a process is not equivalent to having a voice' or being meaningfully consulted (Cornwall 2008:280). Community support can only be brought about by creating opportunities for community involvement (Simpson et al. 2003), which ensures that members of the community are aware of what their role in a collaborative relationship will be and which activities or stages they will be involved in (Cornwall 2008:280). Ultimately, for collaborative working to be successful in harnessing community support and involvement, the relationship 'should contribute toward bringing about social change' and tangible outcomes for local communities (CWC 2008).

IDENTIFYING THE BENEFITS OF COLLABORATIVE WORKING

Collaboration does present increased benefits and outcomes for professionals, and for agencies that would otherwise compete for access to private and statutory funding. In addition, the benefits and outcomes of such work with regard to young people, families and local communities has been well documented in the literature (see Bertram *et al.* 2002; Mackinnon Partnership 2005; Townsley *et al.* 2003). McInnes (2007) documents such benefits across three distinct fields: youth and families; professionals; and agencies.

Table 8.1. Benefits of collaborative working

Young people, families and communities	Professionals and practice	Agencies
• Positive outcomes in the lives of young people, families and communities (Townsley *et al.* 2003; Valentine *et al.* 2006; Browne *et al.* 2004) • Reduction of behavioural problems and truancy in adolescence (Halsey *et al.* 2005; Lloyd *et al.* 2001) • Enhanced social, intellectual and emotional well-being (Friedman *et al.* 2007; Sylva *et al.* 2003; Sloper 2004) • Reduced stigma associated with accessing services (Whyte 1997)	• Better links and understanding of differing professional practices (Atkinson *et al.* 2002) • Rapid and appropriate support provided to families (McInnes 2007) • Workers no longer operate in isolation and can share risk (McInnes 2007, Atkinson *et al.* 2002; Metcalfe *et al.* 2007; Darlington and Feeney 2008) • Creates innovative thinking, self-reflection and joint training opportunities (Atkinson *et al.* 2002; Darlington and Feeney 2008)	• Greater efficiency and less duplication of services (Atkinson *et al.* 2002; Whyte 1997; Costongs and Springett 1997; Richardson and Asthana 2006) • Access to additional resources through sharing resources (Hultberg *et al.* 2005) • Improved co-ordination across agencies, with better pathways and referral systems (Green *et al.* 2008) • Capacity building within the process and between agencies (McTernan and Godfrey 2006).

Source: McInnes 2007.

However, there are potential challenges to this form of work. For agencies and professionals lacking experience of engaging in collaborative working, uncertainty with regard to what the process actually entails can present. Forming effective collaborations demands investment in capacity building and developing trust among agencies, which requires time (Costongs and Springett 1997). Collaborative working can therefore present greater workloads for staff (Costongs and Springett 1997; McInnes 2007), challenge mainstream culture and practice within organisations (Costongs and Springett 1997; McInnes 2007; Richardson and Asthana 2006) and lead to extensive organisational change in response to the collaborative process (Butterworth *et al.* 2001).

UTILISING A CO-LOCATION MODEL OF COLLABORATIVE WORKING TO DEVELOP MULTI-TENANCY CENTRES

'Co-location refers to individual organisations with separate legal identities and governance structures choosing to operate from one facility or service outlet' (Butterworth *et al.* 2001).

The co-location model of collaborative working has already been successfully adopted by various organisations in Australia, the USA and the UK. Successful examples of this model include the childcare and family support hubs established by the Department of Families in Australia, and the emergence of childcare centres under the Every Child Matters Strategy (2006) in the UK. Operational activities and services reflect community development and family support principles.

Recent studies have recognised that co-location services have been found to have a positive impact on collaborative working (see Katz and Hetherington 2006; Lennie 2006). Gray (1989) and Fine *et al.* (2005:41) state that upon entering into any collaboration there is a risk to those involved as 'the process is unfamiliar and outcomes uncertain and threatening to autonomy and accountability of the participating organisations'. However, research conducted by Tasmanian Communities Online (Norris 2005) has identified that the co-location model can be considered as one that can contribute to the sustainability of small and medium-scale community projects which would otherwise face resource depletion in times of economic difficulty and crisis. In addition, such premises can facilitate opportunities to develop a highly visible and unified presence in a community (Katz and Hetherington 2006).

However, there are recognised challenges in developing and implementing such services centres. The major challenges identified by Lennie (2007) are:

1   Concern or uncertainty about co-location of services, or entering collaborative relationships.
2   Fostering staff and community ownership of the initiative.
3   The significant time and workload involved in creating the service.
4   The costs and time required for capacity building of the local community, staff and agencies involved in the process.
5   The initial financial costs involved and securing funding to develop the service.
6   Developing a shared vision and purpose among agencies involved in the collaborative venture.
7   The increased complexity of collaboration, linkage systems and management and administrative arrangements.

8 Managing the change process and overcoming organisational and cultural differences.
9 Identifying and implementing successful strategies for dealing with conflict.
10 Technology, privacy and confidentiality issues that may arise from joint administration processes within the service.
11 Marketing the new service, so that it becomes a focal point within the local community.

Few practice examples exist of successful collaborative approaches which have created tangible co-location service centres. The following case study therefore seeks to familiarise the reader with a current collaborative working partnership that has successfully gained funding and support to establish a co-location centre for young people and families in a local community in Ireland, which will be the first of its kind in the Midlands region.

CASE STUDY: THE GATEWAY PROJECT AND YOUTH BOOTH CAFÉ SERVICES

A co-ordinated co-location community centre established for young people and families.

Summary

The Gateway Project was established in 2009 by Athlone Community Taskforce. The need for the service was first identified by a core group of eight young people who conducted a feasibility study with five hundred of their peers to identify an appropriate response to the lack of flexible youth service provision in the community. As a direct response to the findings of the feasibility study, an inter-agency collaboration between thirteen statutory, non-statutory, voluntary and community groups took place. The members of this collaboration worked towards the development of the first co-ordinated co-location family centre and youth café facility in the Midlands region of Ireland.

Partner Agencies

There are a host of partners and programmes co-located within the Gateway Project Youth Café and Family Centre, including:

• An office for the Minister for Children and Youth Affairs and Foróige-funded project co-ordinator to oversee the strategic development of the project.
• An office for the Minister for Children and Youth Affairs and Athlone Community Taskforce-funded youth worker to implement family and educational support service provision.

- A Big Brother Big Sister project co-ordinator to oversee the implementation of the Big Brother Big Sister peer mentoring project for young people.
- An education/training development worker employed by Athlone Community Taskforce and funded by the Office for the Minister of Children and Youth Affairs to support young people in the second-level education system.
- A women's equality worker funded by Westmeath Community Development Ltd (partnership company) to oversee the development of women's groups that create education, training and employment opportunities for the women in the local community.
- A volunteer tutor panel of secondary school teachers to offer educational support services to young people at risk of educational disadvantage and early school leaving.
- A volunteer panel of youth workers to offer support to the core youth work staff working in generic youth work services operating from within the service.
- A free and confidential counselling service for young people and families experiencing crisis, the effects of addiction, bereavement and domestic violence.

Other groups/organisations that utilise the Gateway Project Centre include:

- St Mary's Youth Ministry and Parish Services;
- the Athlone branch of the Society of St Vincent de Paul and the Ren Club;
- community groups involved in Community Games, Special Olympics and performing arts initiatives;
- Lissywollen asylum-seeker accommodation centre youth group;
- People with Disabilities Ireland (PWDI) weekly social group;
- Athlone Martial Arts Karate Club.

Historical Development of the Gateway Project

Athlone Community Taskforce (ACT) was established in 1992 to create employment and enterprise opportunities, and measures leading to these, in consultation with the Athlone community and statutory agencies. Through effective collaboration with local community groups, statutory bodies and social partners, key measures were established to combat unemployment and undertake effective initiatives to counter disadvantage in the community. In 1996, ACT was successful in securing funding under the Local Development Programme (1997–99) to deliver a host of projects, some of which included:

- after-school projects;
- food and health projects;
- training for employment initiatives;
- business and enterprise initiatives.

In 2001, ACT implemented the successor to the Local Development Programme – the Local Development Social Inclusion Programme (LDSIP) to support its aims. Under the National Cohesion Programme (2007–2013), ACT successfully transferred these projects, and others, to Westmeath Community Development Ltd.

In 2005, ACT reviewed its policies on employment projects and subsequently established the Educational Action Research Project. This project aimed to be an effective strategy for combating unemployment in adulthood by addressing educational disadvantage and early school leaving in adolescence. From 2006 to the end of 2008, young people aged 11–17 years participated in thirteen different initiatives designed by young people for young people to alleviate the pressures associated with the transition from primary to post-primary school.

Situation that Triggered the Development of the Collaboration

A core group of young people who had participated in the previous activities of the Educational Action Research Project approached the project manager employed by ACT and highlighted that there was a lack of services and facilities for young people in the community. While a number of neighbourhood youth projects did operate in several locations in the locality, these young people argued that there was a lack of flexible youth service provision operating from a central location, and opening late in the evenings, at weekends and coinciding with school holidays and mid-term breaks. The project manager supported these young people to develop and administer a youth feasibility survey, which would identify whether an actual gap in service provision existed for young people in the community. The study was conducted in March 2009 and five hundred young people participated in the process.

The findings of the youth-led feasibility study identified that there was an evidence-based need to develop a central youth service provision, and it acted as the catalyst for change in the community. In April 2009, statutory, non-statutory, voluntary and community groups entered into a collaborative working relationship with ACT to respond to the need for a central youth service provision, as had been identified by the young people. The partnership established between these agencies is formally known as the Gateway Project Steering Group. Members of the steering group are mutually responsible for and directly oversee the development of the service to date.

Location and Description of the Gateway Project

The Gateway Project Youth Café and Family Centre is located in a three-storey building which once housed the Athlone workhouse. This workhouse was one of over a hundred Irish workhouses constructed in the 1840s under the Poor Law Act. It was designed to accommodate eight hundred desolate families; however, anticipated capacity was greatly exceeded during the Great Famine and auxiliary workhouses were used to accommodate the overflow.

The property is owned by the Diocese of Ardagh and Clonmacnoise and had been infrequently utilised by a small number of community groups in previous years. In 2009, representatives from the Gateway Project Steering Group Committee approached the bishop of the diocese to negotiate the possibility of upgrading the existing facilities to develop a co-location centre and establish a dedicated youth café and family service. Permission was granted for the Gateway Project to house its service in the premises by a long-term leasehold arrangement.

Gateway Project Service Provision Framework and Practice Principles

The Gateway Project utilises the Hardiker model as a framework for service planning and delivery. This model is widely recognised internationally as a robust and flexible framework for planning services to meet needs (McTernan and Godfrey 2006). The framework demonstrates actions which occur across four levels and highlights the interdependency which presents between levels.

- Level 1 represents universal service provision for mainstream services (e.g. youth, education, family support).
- Level 2 represents targeted supports which are provided to children and families who are vulnerable.
- Level 3 represents support extended to children and families where there are serious problems. Services are often provided by a host of agencies, but not necessarily in a collaborative manner.
- Level 4 represents support to children and families where breakdown has occurred temporarily or permanently. State bodies are crucial to the delivery of services at this level and may include social services, prison services, in-patient care, or rehabilitation services.

The Gateway Project operates three distinct service provision strands which are designed and implemented in line with the Hardiker framework. Services are operated across youth work, family support and educational support strands, and are aligned with three of the four Hardiker model levels.

The project operates from community development and family support principles which build the capacity of individuals while engaging with the local community and wider society. These principles include:

- Creating multi-referral and multi-access points in the community which act as gateways to service provision and support.
- Working in partnership with young people and the community to ensure a needs-led response to local issues.
- Promotion of social inclusion and addressing inequality, disadvantage and issues such as disability, rural isolation and ethnicity.

Table 8.2. Examples of Gateway project service provision aligned to the Hardiker framework

Hardiker level	Example of service provision	Aim of service	Target population
Level one	Youth Café and Drop-in Centre	• To provide a flexible service provision for all young people residing in local urban and rural communities	• 10–21-year-olds residing in local urban and rural communities
Level two	Educational Support Programme	• To lessen the effects of educational disadvantage • To act as a protective factor against early school leaving	• Youth residing in RAPID communities • Those at risk of early school leaving and educational disadvantage • Those requiring additional educational supports as identified through education assessment
Level three	Counselling and Mentoring Services	• To provide opportunities for young people to engage with positive adult role models with similar interests • To provide a private and confidential counselling service for families and family members experiencing difficulties and/or crisis	• Young people referred to the project by statutory, non-statutory, voluntary and community agencies • Young people already accessing the project's services • Families referred to the project by statutory, non-statutory, voluntary and community agencies • People who are already, or have family members who are already, accessing the project's services
Level four	Services do not at present operate at this level in the Gateway Project. The project does, however, interact with statutory agencies to support families and young people at this level through referral to lower-level services and interventions.		

- Advancing engagement strategies based on participatory process and structures which include and empower marginalised, excluded families and communities within society.
- Service delivery is accessible and flexible in respect of location, timing, setting and changing needs.
- Monitoring and evaluation measures are routinely built into service provision to facilitate ongoing support for quality services based on best practice.

How the Collaboration and Co-Location Centre was Achieved

There were a number of strategies advanced to progress the development of the service, including:

- Developing appropriate communication structures between partner agencies. The steering group meet every month to discuss the development and progress of the project.
- Developing a shared vision, purpose and strategic plan to contribute to the development and sustainability of the Gateway Project.
- Identifying suitable premises which would accommodate the needs of the agencies, young people and local community.
- Providing regular information with regard to the status and development phase of the project to each agency and the local community.
- Providing opportunities for young people and the community to engage in the planning and development of the project (e.g. focus groups, youth forums, community meetings).

Tools and Strategies for Effective Collaboration

The Gateway Project Centre is characterised by:

- The alignment of organisational goals and values based on the purpose, expectations and principles of the collaboration.
- The co-location and augmenting of services in a central location in the community that provides a focal point for youth and community activity.
- Strong communication networks with surrounding neighbourhoods and communities in the locality to raise the profile of the project.
- Developing appropriate participatory structures to ensure that the voices of young people and the local community are heard and, importantly, reflected in the development of the service.
- Creating diverse opportunities for young people and the community to engage in service provision operating from the centre.

Outcomes for Agencies, Young People and the Community

The development of the Gateway Project collaboration has resulted in a variety of outcomes for individual agencies, families and the community.

- The established partnership enables greater sharing of resources, expertise and information between the partner agencies, leading to less overlap in services.
- The development of a focal point for youth activity in the locality which provides opportunities for personal growth and development

- A cost-effective way for the local community to access multi-disciplinary services, general resources and administration.

Gateway Project's Success Factors

The success of the collaborative approach adopted by the Gateway Project has been due to a number of factors.

- Commitment by the partner agencies to developing effective management and partnership structures to oversee the project's implementation and sustainability.
- Encouragement and support from statutory funding bodies, including the Office of the Minister for Children and Youth Affairs, Young People's Facilities and Services Fund, Midland Regional Drug Taskforce and Pobal Dormant Accounts Youth Café Funding stream.
- The participatory processes implemented to encourage youth and community ownership of the project's development has resulted in 402 young people actively engaging in a range of service provision during 2010.
- Development of an adult volunteer model to advance elements of the youth and educational support services in line with best practice (Garda vetting, induction training, supervision, ongoing development opportunities).
- Acknowledgement by the community, service providers and funding bodies that the project can be recognised as a model of good practice and a centre of excellence which other communities can replicate.

Challenges the Project has Encountered

While the project has experienced high levels of success, there have been challenges, in particular:

- Encouraging agencies that would traditionally work in isolation to engage in the collaboration process and contribute to the Gateway Project Steering Group committee.
- Developing a mutually beneficial relationship between collaborating agencies to ensure that expectations, resources and responsibility are shared equally.
- Identifying appropriate funding streams to upgrade the existing facility to comply with health and safety, conservation and disability-proofing standards.
- Identifying appropriate funding streams to employ core staff to advance service provision across youth, family support and educational support strands.

The Future of the Gateway Project

The Gateway Project has recently developed a five-year strategic plan which will assist the co-location centre in aligning its operations to a future management model that partner agencies are supportive of, and committed to achieving. The future of the service will require the collaborating agencies to develop best practice approaches through strong service delivery and inter-agency collaboration, in partnership with young people and the local community, to ensure that the project is a sustainable feature in the community. This will require building indicators for success into daily practice and engaging in ongoing monitoring and evaluation processes.

CONCLUSION

Given the current economic climate and its impact on the community development sector, collaborative working and co-location models of practice could indeed shape the manner in which community development practice is conducted in the future and provide alternative solutions to the issues faced by the sector and local communities. Co-location as a method of collaboration is a relatively new concept in community development practice. Arrangements can be labour-intensive to establish and require careful negotiation to adopt protocols and agreements prior to commencing service provision. Ensuring the sustainability of such approaches requires a commitment by agencies to develop and adopt appropriate communication, negotiation, conflict resolution and evaluation strategies.

The co-location model of collaboration can present an opportunity for community development groups willing to explore innovative practice, or those seeking to ensure sustainability and to mobilise within their sector. In turn, the development of well-resourced facilities with shared office infrastructure could begin to emerge: this would alleviate the strain of securing annual operational and administrative funding and contribute towards the strengthening of local communities.

9

Volunteers as Managers of Family Resource Centres: The Experiences of Voluntary Management Committee Members

Patricia Neville

CHAPTER SUMMARY

This chapter is concerned with one of the major additions to the community development sector in Ireland over the past two decades, namely the family resource centre (FRC). Currently over one hundred FRCs deliver a range of community-based supports and services to families in their locality. As government funding of this sector comes increasingly under pressure from capital restrictions it is timely to consider the contribution that local community members play in the administration of these FRCs.

This chapter introduces primary research undertaken with a number of voluntary members of an FRC to reveal and discuss the time, energy and inputs that such voluntary commitments make to the successful running of these centres on behalf of their local community, as well as community development practice in Ireland.

INTRODUCTION

In this chapter, we look at the ways in which community members participate in the management of their local FRCs. We address five central questions:

1   What role do FRCs play in contemporary Irish society?
2   How can we understand the term 'volunteer'?
3   Who are voluntary management committee members and what do they do?
4   What is the relationship between voluntary management and the overall running of FRCs?
5   Is being a voluntary management committee member in our local FRC important to our identity and our understanding of our local community?

In order to answer these questions we need to consider the following issues:

- Why do people volunteer in their local communities?
- What roles and responsibilities do voluntary managers adopt in their local FRC?
- What significance should we attach to their contributions to the FRC and their local community as a whole?

Over the course of this chapter we will examine the role of volunteerism in the FRC sector. Volunteerism has historically played a major part in community development work in Ireland and we will see that this trend has continued in the recent development of FRCs in Ireland. We consider the impact that the professionalisation of community development work and other policy and governmental changes have had on the contribution of volunteerism in local FRCs. These social, economic, political and policy changes have contributed to the emergence of a new type of volunteer – the voluntary management committee member. A case study of Riverside FRC (not its real name) is included, and taking as a starting point research conducted with six voluntary management members we will discuss and examine some of the personal, community and social outcomes of volunteering at local FRCs.

PROFESSIONALISATION OF COMMUNITY DEVELOPMENT AND VOLUNTEERISM

Historically, Irish society has a long-standing tradition of voluntary community work – from the development of *meitheal* or self-help activities of local communities in rural Ireland to the role that religious orders had in developing the voluntary social services sector (Faughnan and Kelleher 1993; Hayes 1990, 1996; Lee (in press); Powell and Guerin 1997, all cited in Donnelly-Cox *et al.* 2001:196). Many of these voluntary initiatives were established in response to pressing local needs and so were examples of grassroots community activism. However, since the 1990s the work of community development has become increasingly subjected to a 'programme approach' (Lee 2003:54), being directly funded, co-ordinated and administered by a national Community Development Programme and Local Development Social Inclusion Programme. While many commentators have critiqued this state involvement with community development as an example of 'community action from above' (Varley 1999:390) rather than 'from below', the net effect has been that community development in Ireland is increasingly moving towards 'professionalism, managerialism and accountability' (Hager and Brudney 2004; Lewis 1993; Nichols and King 1998; Nichols *et al.* 2000; Russell and Scott 1997, all cited in Cuskelly *et al.* 2006:144). This professionalism can be seen in the role now played by volunteers working in the voluntary and community sector.

The notion of volunteers and volunteerism are commonly used in everyday life and in the media, but their meanings are rarely discussed.

Activity

> Think about the terms 'volunteer' and 'volunteerism'. What do they mean to you? Jot down the first things that come to mind. What character traits do you associate with volunteers?

When we take time to investigate what the term 'volunteer' means, we quickly realise the preconceived assumptions that we, as individuals and as a society, make about volunteers. There has been a long-standing tradition of conceptualising volunteers as emblems of caring and 'goodness' (Donnelly-Cox and Jaffro 1999, cited in Connelly 2006:141) in an increasingly individualistic world. As a result, volunteers are perceived to be energetic, committed and civic-minded individuals. In addition, the construction of volunteers as 'good' people who are eager to 'help out' others is interpreted as a sign of a healthy community: the more volunteers present in a local community, the more community spirit and activism there is in that community. By extension, it can be inferred that a community where very few people volunteer is a fragmented and polarised community (e.g. Brown 1999; Reid and Selbee 2001; Wilson and Musick 2000, all cited in Milligan and Fyfe 2005:417). In this respect, volunteers are assumed to be selfless individuals who, through their duty to others, strengthen the community of which they are members.

This idealisation of volunteers as 'do-gooders' is also reinforced by government and policy documents. The 1996 Taskforce on Active Citizenship presents active citizenship as 'accepting a responsibility to help others and being happy to improve the quality of life of those less fortunate than ourselves' (Bertie Ahern, quoted in Gaynor 2009:2). One of the main aims of this taskforce was to encourage local communities to 'volunteer and help out' (Task Force 2007a, cited in Gaynor 2009:2). In this respect, it argued that volunteers are 'active' individuals who show their commitment to their local community by spending time on community projects. Consequently, local volunteers are increasingly seen as 'inputs' of the non-profit or community organisation, who need to be managed, controlled and retained in order to ensure the successful and efficient running of the organisation (Forsyth 1999:40; Hager and Brudney 2004:1). This bureaucratic response to volunteers involves drafting volunteering policies, developing volunteer programmes for the induction and training of volunteers (Hager and Brudney 2004:3) as well as registering volunteers with the Garda Vetting Unit. Each of these measures is assumed to safeguard the professionalism of the community development project and the accountability of the professional staff who manage the services, as well as ensuring a successful placement for the volunteer.

However, it is worth mentioning that some have contended that the formalisation of the role and contribution of volunteers to community development in Ireland has also contributed to a restricting of the role played by the local volunteer. For instance, Gaynor (2009) is critical of the way the Taskforce on Active Citizenship presents a limited conceptualisation of volunteers as people whose only motivation in volunteering is the fact that they have free time on their hands. Indeed, the amount of time available for volunteering is presented and discussed at length in the document as the only barrier to becoming an 'active citizen' in Ireland (Task Force 2007a, cited in Gaynor 2009:5). By 'narrowingly equating active citizenship with volunteering and "helping out"' in local communities (Gaynor 2009:2), the notion of both active citizenship and volunteering are depoliticised. Clearly, this policy document downgrades the role of volunteers to that of a reserve army of labour and fails to consider that people may choose to volunteer for more altruistic or civic-minded reasons.

Others have brought to our attention the dearth of research literature on volunteerism in Ireland. In direct contrast with many other countries, such as the UK, the USA and Australia, there has been little room given to debating the role and place of volunteerism in Ireland today (O'Ferrall 2000, cited in Donnelly-Cox *et al.* 2001:196). Such a debate has become increasingly timely considering the foreseeable structural changes in the community development sector in Ireland: the decline in core funding, reduction in paid staff levels in FRC projects (FSA 2009) and the closure of community development projects in 2009. As a result, the Irish community sector is currently experiencing serious contraction in staffing levels and service provision. One implication of this contraction is the erosion of the once-lauded professionalism of the sector. Furthermore, in December 2010 the Minister for Social Protection Éamon Ó Cuív TD announced the establishment of a Tús work placement scheme. This work placement scheme will enable people who have been unemployed for more than twelve months to take up a job placement in a community or voluntary organisation for twelve months while receiving their Jobseekers Allowance. With its initial commitment of €30 million in the form of 5,000 work placement opportunities, the Tús scheme appears to be using the unemployed as a reserve army of labour to support the delivery of services in the community and voluntary sector (Department of Social Protection 2010). In this way, the assumption is being made that community work can be easily performed by most people. Such a strategy also underestimates the motivations and impact that volunteering and community development work has on the participant, but also fails to consider the social and political impact of this type of work has on a local community.

Clearly, there is a sense of urgency in initiating a discussion about the present and future prospects of the community and voluntary sector in Ireland. While this section has highlighted the existence of this debate, it is not the purpose of this chapter to discuss it in more detail or to offer recommendations. Other chapters in this book address this question more directly. Rather, the purpose of this chapter is to investigate the volunteering experiences of people who volunteer in their local FRC. Interestingly, very little research has been conducted on volunteering in the Irish community development sector (Connolly 2006:139). While some statistical data is available on how many people volunteer, very little qualitative research has been conducted that we can refer to. Though Connolly (2006) offers us an insight into managerial practices in voluntary organisations in Ireland, there is little research, to the author's knowledge, on the experiences of people who volunteer in the community development sector in Ireland. Why do people volunteer in local community development projects and what impact does it have on them? The rest of the chapter aims to rectify this lacuna in information and to furnish some information for such a discussion.

BACKGROUND TO FRCs

FRCs were first established in 1994 to mark the International Year of the Family in response to the claims that there was a lack of 'statutory support for community development activities focused on support for families and tackling child poverty' (FSA 2007a:1). Initially ten FRCs were funded on a pilot basis for three years. After their evaluation in 1997 the programme was rolled out and funded by the Department of Family and Community Services. Since then the programme has grown considerably to include 107 FRCs in 2009 (FSA 2009). In 2003 the Family Support Agency (FSA) was established by the then Department of Social and Family Affairs to help bring together all the family services and programmes introduced by the government. Since then, through the provision of staff, capital and once-off grant funding, the FSA has helped FRCs provide locally based support to local families.

Table 9.1. Total operating funding of FRCs

Year	Euros (millions)
2004	16.2
2007	32.0
2009	35.4

Source (Tables 9.1–9.5): FSA 2007a, 2007b, 2008, 2009.

However, the future of the FSA has recently been called into question, with the McCarthy Report of 2009 recommending the closure of the FSA. This has thrown the FRC sector into a period of uncertainty as to the short- to mid-term future of this community development service (e.g. FRC National Forum 2009a, 2009b).

THE PURPOSE OF FRCs

FRCs have many aims, some very specific to the community in which they are found and the problems it faces (e.g. unemployment, social exclusion, etc.), others more general.

General aims of FRCs

- To help combat disadvantage by supporting families.
- To be actively involved in anti-poverty initiatives and social inclusion projects.
- To attempt to encourage local people to participate in the centre and its work – from designing and planning an FRC to its actual establishment, and by acting as volunteers – thereby creating the opportunity for community involvement and activism.
- To 'empower and facilitate groups or individuals experiencing exclusion to take control of their own lives and address their needs' (FRC National Forum 2006:10) through community development.
- To build relationships and social networks within communities (FRC National Forum 2006:10). In this way FRCs can facilitate positive working relationships between the voluntary sector and statutory agencies in their particular area, for example through setting up new community groups or influencing social policy (FSA 2007b:1).
- To enhance the self-esteem of individuals in the community, which in turn will help increase the potential for change within a community.

Specific services offered by FRCs

FRCs contribute vital services to their local community:

- They identify gaps in existing services.
- They lobby for the development of adequate services in the community.
- They offer referral services and information to the community.
- They often act as an outreach office for other services, e.g. Money and Budgeting Advice Service (MABS), Citizens Information Service (CIS).
- They should target families in situations of disadvantage and should outreach or make links out into the community and the most marginalised there.
- They are expected to provide a mix of developmental activities (e.g. adult education classes, parenting classes, arts and crafts classes) and access to services (e.g. affordable childcare and after-school services) at a local level for the local community.

HOW ARE FRCs RUN?

FRCs are 'community based organisations who take a proactive and innovative approach in identifying the needs of families and providing community based supports' (FRC National Forum 2006:4). In keeping with the 2000 *White Paper on Supporting Voluntary Activity*, in which the relationship between the state and the third sector was formalised (Broaderick 2002:105), a code of best practice was established for the community and voluntary sector. Consequently, the relationship between the state and the community and voluntary sector has become formalised, with local community projects having to register and comply with the Companies Registration Office and to apply for charitable status. For this reason, all community, voluntary and charitable organisations must adhere to codes of conduct and articles of association. The articles of association of both community development projects (CDPs) and FRCs require that local community members sit as officers of the limited company and assume overall accountability for the successful running of the community project. Moreover, it is stipulated that voluntary management committees of CDPs and FRCs should be made up of representatives of the local community and target groups within the community (e.g. elderly people, unemployed people, young people, etc.). This ensures that CDPs and FRCs retain a local community focus and commitment. The management committee oversees the overall running of the FRC. All FRCs employ a full-time co-ordinator and administrator who oversee the day-to-day running of the centre.

VOLUNTEER HUMAN RESOURCES OF FRCs

Since 2004 the FSA has published the yearly findings of its evaluation of the FRC sector. Entitled SPEAK (Strategic Planning, Evaluation and Knowledge Networking), this computer-based evaluation program requires all staff, volunteers and management committee members of FRCs to input required information on the project's activities, outcomes and impacts for the previous year. Information provided by each FRC through SPEAK is collated into a national database which is then published as a yearly report. While not every FRC in the programme is contributing to SPEAK (FSA 2007b:2) (because different FRCs are at different project development stages), this annual report offers us the clearest insight yet into the financial, local and human resources that FRCs generate, demand and create each year.

Table 9.2. Number of FRCs participating in SPEAK (2004–2009)

Year	Number of FRCs included in SPEAK
2004	62
2005	64
2006	68
2007	83
2008	96
2009	104

Close examination of the SPEAK database offers us an interesting opportunity to explore the data on volunteers with FRCs. First, it gives us an indication of the number of people who volunteer in their local FRC. As mentioned previously, there are two groups of volunteers working in the FRC sector, namely volunteers and voluntary management committee members. According to this data we find two distinct trends emerging. The data reveals that while there is a steady increase in the number of people volunteering in FRCs, the number of people volunteering as voluntary management committee members shows a less uniform pattern. The data shows a strong increase between 2007 and 2008, from 904 to 1,006 people. However, the following year's figures reveal what might be the beginnings of a slight decline. In fact, it is clear from the table below that twice as many people work as volunteers in FRCs than become directors of FRCs. While the FSA (2009) report attributes the continued rise in volunteers to the increase in the number of unemployed workers available for volunteer work, such an evaluation cannot be offered to explain the slight decline in numbers of voluntary management committee members.

Table 9.3. Number of voluntary management committee members compared with volunteers in FRCs

Year	Total number of voluntary management committee members	Total number of volunteers participating in FRCs
2007	904	1,623
2008	1,006	2,222
2009	985	2,744

One possible way of explaining the difference in volunteer to voluntary manager ratio would be to look more closely at the types of work that voluntary managers perform. Here again the SPEAK database offers us some findings to consider.

Table 9.4. Number of voluntary management committee members in FRCs

Year	Number of FRCs included in SPEAK evaluation	Average number of directors/ voluntary management per FRC	Actual number of voluntary management committee members in SPEAK evaluation	Hours given by directors/voluntary management committee members to the project
2004	62	12	1368	n/a
2005	64	n/a	n/a	n/a
2006	68	17	n/a	n/a
2007	83	16	904	17,700
2008	96	11	1,006	40,478
2009	104	9	985	42,480

Despite the fact that some evaluation data is missing from the final reports published by the FSA, we can again identify a number of trends pertaining to voluntary management committee members. First we can observe an initial growth and then decline in the size of management committees. In 2004, among the sixty-two participating FRCs there was an average of twelve people sitting on the board of management. Since an increase to an average size of seventeen people in 2006, the number of committee management members fell to a mere nine people in 2009. Interestingly, this finding is matched by a substantial increase in the number of hours given by voluntary management committee members to the project from 2007, jumping from 17,700 hours to 42,480 overall in 2009. The extraordinary time commitment that is made by these individuals is quite exceptional, especially when you consider that this work is being done in people's free time.

In terms of understanding more about the types of people who make this type of commitment to their local FRC, the SPEAK database reveals that it is predominantly women and older people who make up these voluntary management committees (FSA 2007b:13, 2008:8, 2009:8).

Table 9.5: Gender ratio of voluntary management committee members

Year	Women	Men
2006	67%	33%
2007	71%	29%
2008	72%	28%
2009	71%	29%

In addition to this gender ratio, the data also reveals that, in keeping with the FRC requirements/stipulations, voluntary management committees must be made up from various target groups from the local community, in addition to representations from statutory agencies such as the Health Service Executive (HSE). While there has been an increase in representation on management committees among lone parents, the unemployed, people with disabilities, men and family units, there has been a decline in representation from people from the Traveller community, the gay and lesbian community and drug users (FSA 2007b:13, FSA 2008:8, FSA 2009:8).

The evaluation data from the SPEAK database provides us with an opportunity to create a demographic profile of people who volunteer in FRCs. Accordingly, we find that people who are voluntary managers are predominately women and older people who give large amounts of time to the project. In addition, we find that the number of people volunteering to join voluntary management committees is falling. However, due to the quantitative nature of this data we are restricted from understanding a number of important issues:

- Why do people become voluntary managers of FRCs?
- What impact and effects does this have on their personal and social lives?
- Why do people decide not to become voluntary management committee members or to resign from such positions?

The next section of the chapter describes a case study which in some way helps shed some light on possible answers to these questions.

VOLUNTEERING IN FRCs: A CASE STUDY

In order to answer these questions this section includes research conducted with six voluntary management committee members of an FRC in Ireland. This small-scale qualitative research was undertaken from July to September 2010 with the voluntary management committee of the Riverside (not its real name) FRC.

Riverside is a town of approximately 12,000 people. It is a predominately urban area with a rural hinterland. After a number of years of pre-development work initiated by a group of local volunteers, Riverside FRC opened its doors to the public in 2003. Since then it has offered an affordable childcare and after-school service, as well as adult education classes to the families of Riverside. In addition, it acts as a meeting place for a number of community groups in the locality and operates eleven months of the year.

In July 2010 I approached the chairperson of the Riverside FRC with a request to present my research proposal at their next management meeting. This was granted, and when I attended the management committee meeting I explained the purpose and aims of the research and answered any questions the members had about the research proposal. I invited them to participate in the project but made it clear that they were under no obligation to do so and were free to withdraw from the research at any time. I also stressed that all information would be held in the strictest confidence and that since the questionnaires were anonymous the identity of the contributor would be neither known nor disclosed by the researcher.

Qualitative questionnaires were used for a number of reasons. First, the researcher was well acquainted with most of the individual committee members and so an anonymous questionnaire was thought to be the best way of avoiding interviewer bias and subject bias influencing the collection and interpretation of the data. Second, the researcher was mindful of how little free time these individuals have and how difficult it might be to organise an interview at a time that was convenient for them.

The questionnaire was divided into eight sections, each focusing on a different aspect of the role of voluntary management committee members. These included: an explanation of the background of their involvement with the FRC; a discussion about their roles and responsibilities as voluntary management committee members; training received; team working and group relations; working relations in the project; work/life balance; and personal reflections on their involvement with the project. In all, eleven questionnaires were brought to the management committee meeting, of which six were returned by the specified completion date using the stamped self-addressed envelopes. This represents a response rate of 54.54 per cent, which is representative for this research sample. A reminder notice was sent to the chairperson to read out at their next meeting. This did not improve the response rate.

Research Findings

Profile and Motivations of Volunteers to Riverside FRC

International research reveals the persistence of a particular profile of volunteers along gender, age, family and work commitment lines. In general, more women than men volunteer (Wymer 1990; Davis Smith 1999; Roks 1986, all cited in Bussell and Forbes 2002:248); and those in their middle age volunteer (Wymer 1998; Tschirhart 1998, both cited in Bussell and Forbes 2002:248). This trend was also replicated among this sample of community development volunteers: the majority of the respondents were in the 40–59 age group, all were female and married. Two were employed outside the home; the rest worked in the domestic sphere. All six participants involved in this study had spent a minimum of two years with Riverside FRC. One participant claimed to have been a volunteer with the project for twelve years. In all, the average length of involvement with the FRC was seven years. These individuals are clearly committed to the project, as shown by the lengthy duration of their voluntary commitment. In fact, two of the respondents mentioned that they had been part of the original working group that set about the pre-development work for the establishment of Riverside FRC.

Clearly, every member of the voluntary management committee has made a long-term commitment to the project. In this respect, it is interesting to investigate the motives behind their joining Riverside FRC as volunteers. Two main reasons were offered by this sample. First, the volunteers joined as a result of being asked to join by a friend. In this situation, the reason to volunteer is made in response to a 'social-adjustive motive' (Okun and Eisenberg 1992, cited in Bussell and Forbes 2002:250). This approach is found to be a particularly effective way of recruiting volunteers, partly because personal contact 'reduced the perceived social risk that deterred some from volunteering' (Riecken, Babukus and Yavas 1994, cited in Bussell and Forbes 2002:250). Second, it was found that the respondents openly expressed a desire to make a difference in their local community: 'I had a great interest in providing a resource centre for our community and wanted to be proactive in bringing it about.'

Such an interest in helping others is a commonly cited reason for volunteering in the literature (Unger 1991; Nichols and King 1999; Thippayanurukiakul 1989; Okun 1994, all cited in Bussell and Forbes 2002:249). On these grounds it is clear to see that the demographic profile and motivations of these volunteers complement the existing literature on volunteering, thereby validating the sample findings.

Joining the Management Committee

It was outlined above that the volunteers joined Riverside FRC as a result of personal requests as well as a desire to help others. However, what motivated them to progress to the voluntary management committee? Interestingly, we again find the situation where the majority (four = 66.6 per cent) of the respondents joined the management committee as a result of an invitation by the management committee. The remaining two members (33.3 per cent) were voted on to the board because they had some particular expertise that would benefit the group. All of the management committee members had spent at least a year on a sub-committee of the centre before joining the management committee; this is stipulated in the articles of association of Riverside FRC and, as we can see, the stipulation has been adhered to.

The Purpose of the Management Committee

Though one respondent abstained from answering this question, the remaining five contributors were very clear about what they considered to be the role of the management committee. First, there was a strong commitment made in their responses to a set of values. These values included 'fairness', 'equality', 'well-being' and 'support'. This deference to a set of values is commonplace in not-for-profit organisations. Organisational research reveals that non-profit organisations are values-based and driven, 'with members displaying a high degree of self-selection based on values affiliation' (Fenwick 2005, cited in Cuskelly *et al.* 2006:144). In this respect, the voluntary managers would appear to be inspired and driven by the ethos and mission statement of their project.

In addition to this strong sense of values, the contributors also displayed a realistic understanding of their work, to offer a service that 'plays a prominent and positive role in the lives of those whom it aims to help'. With this specific task comes a new range of responsibilities. The respondents saw their role as encompassing five sets of responsibilities and roles – to the project as a whole, to their staff, to their service users, to their legal obligations and to their local community. As a result, the importance of operating such a service for one's local community was matched by a strong sense of professionalism about what they did, highlighting that they 'follow a three-year plan', use 'good business practices', 'comply with our legal obligations with regard to staff, health and safety and financial governance', in order to ensure the 'efficiency' and 'stability' of the project. Clearly, these voluntary management committee members display a rounded understanding of their role, one that is inspired by a set of values, but with a clear understanding of the professionalism to which they must adhere.

Specific Roles within the Voluntary Management Committee

The management committee of Riverside FRC is made up of eleven people who have been nominated or elected to the committee. The composition of this committee follows a set structure, with three posts given specific responsibilities within the committee as well as to the project. The chairperson is nominated by the committee to act as the head of the committee; the secretary's main responsibility is to take minutes at each meeting; and the finance director oversees the administration of the committee's finances. Ordinary committee members also play their part in bringing to the committee issues for consideration and debate. While not disregarding the contribution played by ordinary members of the voluntary management committee, this section will document in more detail the nature of the roles and responsibilities of the chairperson, the secretary and the finance director in terms of the management of the project.

In response to the question about the general duties involved in their position, the chairperson of Riverside FRC included an extra sheet of paper outlining a twelve-point breakdown of the duties of the chairperson as she saw them. These included:

> . . . attending management and sub-group meetings, acting as a spokesperson for the project, consulting and liaising with management members and project co-ordinator frequently, recruiting and interviewing of staff, staff contracts, staff appraisals and reviews, dealing with staff problems, legal matters – consulting legal advisers, ensuring that the project is run in a proper manner with regard to our legal and corporate duties, building maintenance issues, attending training and identifying and encouraging training for management members, conflict resolution, liaising with support agencies to the project, driving the project forward with a view to developing services further and encouraging new members to join.

Such an itemised list reveals the extent and the breadth of duties involved in being chairperson. It also reveals that volunteering at this level goes far beyond merely 'helping out' the project. Rather it exposes the professionalism demanded by such a volunteer position and the very real managerial tasks that occupy volunteers' time. Clearly, the chairperson is a very important to the running of the project. However, all of these duties are undertaken in her own time and at no financial cost to the project.

> At times over the years I often gave up my lunch hour to meet re centre business, and many times drove directly from work to meetings, sometimes two or three consecutive meetings, before getting home at all. I found it difficult when I had to attend weekend training sessions, which took up very valuable family times, e.g. all day Saturday, and in the early years particularly I felt very guilty as I have a child with special needs and I probably over-burdened my husband and other two children at those times.

Considering such a workload it is astounding to discover that this person has been in this role for eight years. No doubt the longer the person is in the position the more skills they acquire and develop for the post. Such tenure obviously ensures a degree of consistency for the project and brings stability to the committee. However, as this quote suggests, there are many moments when FRC and family commitments can be in direct opposition. The personal implications of becoming a volunteer manager and the type of work/life balance that they have to negotiate will be discussed in a later section.

The other officers of the project also have impressive responsibilities. The finance director and the secretary of Riverside FRC have spent four and three years respectively in these positions. For the finance director this involves attending finance meetings, approving the payment of invoices, wages, large purchases and maintenance bills. This post also involves working closely with the centre's administrator. The secretary is responsible for maintaining and updating the centre's records of the project, including minuted meetings, changing and amending articles of membership records, preparing reports for meetings, etc.

It is clear that officers of the committee have very specific jobs to perform and specific functions in the committee. This strict division of labour plays an important part in the effective running of the project. However, how do these individuals respond to the level of responsibility that is attached to their role? In response to this query all stated that they dealt well with the responsibility that came with the position.

For the secretary it was revealed that 'time' helped her to feel comfortable about her level of responsibility. Both the chairperson and the finance director mentioned how supportive the staff and fellow committee members were to them as they went about their duties: 'but without the support of a strong and committed group of voluntary management this would be extremely difficult'.

This focus on people again reiterates the people-centred nature of the work performed by voluntary and community development workers and the collegiate nature of the voluntary management committee. The majority of the contributors also commented on the camaraderie of the group and the strong supportive bond that exists between the members.

Working Relations with Agencies, Funders and Staff

At the time of the research, the group rated positively their working relationship with state agencies and funders. However, the comments of one particular respondent threw an interesting light on how the working relationship with state agencies and funders had gone through a number of stages over the history of the centre. In relation to state agencies, there were strong intimations that this relationship was previously a source of stress and uncertainty for volunteers: 'We have got to know how everything works to a large extent and no longer panic like we used to!'

Such a statement indicates the lack of knowledge and confidence that this volunteer initially felt when meeting with and responding to statutory requirements and requests. Under these conditions it would be fair to postulate that the inexperience of the voluntary management member might have led to their feeling overwhelmed and disempowered by the whole experience. This sense of unease about being an inexperienced voluntary manager in such a professional context was also reinforced by the way in which the statutory bodies reacted to the voluntary management committee.

> The attitude I perceive sometimes is that the funders, and their representatives, pay 'lip service' to the voluntary management, always starting out with how much they appreciate all we do, and then proceeding to lay down the law in no uncertain terms!

According to this voluntary management committee member, the relational rhetoric of the statutory agencies can mask a more deliberate and at times inflexible working style. The prescriptive nature of their working relationship with this voluntary management committee can on occasion create more difficulties for the management committee by reiterating the lay–professional divide with which they have become all too familiar.

> The level of professionalism expected of us, in my personal opinion, is taken for granted. They can be quick to point out what we are expected to do, and while of course that is what we do to the best of our ability, I know for a fact that many of us did not realise what we signed up for! It can be very daunting at times for many volunteers, most of whom have never been employers, or interviewed anyone, or disciplined anyone, or even fired someone.

Both of these quotes indicate the ambiguities that voluntary managers face during the course of their work. As lay individuals they struggle to conduct their duties in as professional a manner as possible. Time, experience and training can help increase the skills and knowledge base of these voluntary managers. While company law makes them legally responsible for the running of their community project it would appear that statutory agencies do not see the voluntary management committee as equal partners.

While some statutory agencies might have on occasions second-guessed the professionalism of the Riverside FRC in their dealings with them, the professionalism of the voluntary management committee becomes very clear when they discuss their working relationship with their staff. Overall, the group rated their working relationship with the staff very positively. This was qualified with reference to their development of internal staff practices such as staff appraisals and reviews, and the establishment of a staff liaison officer whose job is to bring staff queries to the management. While it was not within the remit of this research to test whether this is an accurate representation of the nature of the voluntary management–staff relationship the respondents did present a positive image of their staff in their responses. Such endorsements focused on the fact that staff members have volunteered to undertake certain tasks in addition to their work duties (e.g. to facilitate late opening of the centre or to participate in centre open days and special events) as well as offering representation on the board.

Work/Life Balance

It would appear that the amount of time that voluntary managers give to their community project varies depending on the position they occupy on the committee. Ordinary voluntary management committee members were vague in their calculations, stating 'not sure' or 'less than before'. The chairperson, the secretary and finance director were more explicit. Both the secretary and finance director remarked that on average they might spend two to three hours a week on centre issues, more if there was a meeting scheduled. This time commitment rose dramatically for the chairperson, who stated a commitment of twelve hours a week, excluding meetings. This is quite a lot of time to devote to the project and represents how time-consuming being a voluntary management committee member can be. Despite these individual differences, the group were unanimous in their opinion that attending meetings was the most time-consuming aspect of being a voluntary management committee member.

In this respect we could anticipate that voluntary managers, because of their heavy work commitment, might struggle to maintain a healthy work/life balance. Interestingly, every respondent expressed the opinion that they managed their personal and centre commitments well. Half of the respondents attributed this to the fact that their children were adults. However, for one respondent, whose children are young, meeting the demands of family and centre needs can on occasion be testing: 'Depends on whether the centre's requirements clash with domestic requirements'. For two contributors there had been times in the past where work life and personal life were in competition with each other:

> Just sometimes there just aren't enough hours in the day to get round to both. Just have to decide which one is more important at any particular time.

> With difficulty at times, but as my children have now grown up it is considerably easier.

The individual volunteer is aware of the continuous struggle of dividing their time and energy between their family and Riverside FRC. Whether they have a young family or not, all reflected in some way on how having a family can make their volunteering challenging. All remarked that their family were supportive of their involvement with the centre. Some family members were described as actively 'encouraging' them to be involved with the centre. For one respondent, this support was offered in recognition of her own particular values and interests: 'My husband also knows this is part of me.' Support and encouragement come not only from those outside the centre, but also from fellow committee members. The research data revealed that the group received a lot of support from each other. This support was shown through 'good communication' and offering mutual encouragement and regard for one another.

Personal and Professional Development

For all contributors, the experience of being a community volunteer had offered them a new insight into their lives as well as an opportunity for personal growth and development. Some respondents stated that their involvement with the centre encouraged them to develop a new set of personal skills and qualities which they previously thought they could never acquire, i.e. 'higher levels of confidence', 'decision making skills', and 'patience'. In this respect, being a member of the voluntary management committee presented a very real personal challenge to some of the committee members. Others commented upon the sense of pride and accomplishment that comes with seeing a community project up and running after many years of planning and development.

In addition to these personal achievements, many commented on how their understanding of their local community has undergone a transformation as a result of their involvement with the project. Every respondent offered their own interpretation as to what the biggest challenge facing their local community was at the present moment. For some, the problem of social isolation demands more attention, as does the lack of affordable quality childcare in the community. Other issues included the difficulty of getting people to volunteer and the need for community change and empowerment at an individual and community level. It is therefore clear that these volunteers have developed an insight into the needs and challenges facing their local community. However, this awakened critical consciousness is not solely discursive. On the contrary, in all their responses each volunteer identified that Riverside FRC could take an active role in addressing these needs and implementing community change.

While the respondents offered different interpretations of the purpose of community development work, every one was in agreement that if they work together people can make a change, both in their own lives as well as for the community they live in. In recognising the importance of community development work, some respondents did feel that community development work is under-estimated and does not receive the recognition that it deserves.

> Takes up a lot of time! If people are given direction and something to aim for they will come together to make it happen – again, takes time to motivate people!

> I think that the main thing is that community work is challenging and therefore always a challenge.

The two respondents who were part of the original development group offer their own estimation of the significance of their volunteer work in the community:

> To get it up and running successfully and get a building procured.

> Getting to the point where we are at now was quite hard work, and stressful at times; but I am so proud of what we have achieved together, and I so admire all our volunteers.

While these long-standing volunteers can appreciate the fruits of their volunteer work, there is still a sense of modesty about the role that the other voluntary management committee members play in the community as a whole.

> Helping out where I can . . . How every decision you make can affect a member of the wider community – hopefully for the better.

> Being a member and contributing something (small) to my local community (parentheses in original).

CONCLUDING THOUGHTS

It is clear from the above discussion that the voluntary managers of Riverside FRC provide an important community service to their local community. These individuals are not the clichéd 'do-gooders' that would appear to dominate public perception of volunteers. Rather we find individuals committed to 'doing good' in their community in relation to the wider needs reflected in their community. Motivated by this desire to bring about change at the local level, these women face many barriers – a lack of project management skills, feelings of personal inadequacy, the struggle to maintain their family life – as they attempt, in conjunction with their staff and project co-ordinator, to offer an accessible and relevant community service for their locality.

Recommendations for Practice

* This research reveals the utility of the SPEAK evaluation database in shedding light on the FRC sector in Ireland. Clearly, researchers as well as practitioners should make more use of this resource.
* This case study highlights the need for more public as well as sectoral awareness and recognition of the commitments and contributions that volunteers make to FRCs in general as well as at the level of management. This recognition should include the rolling out of more supports – e.g. training (The Wheel 2005) – for the women and men who sit as directors of FRCs.
* The research presented here reveals the personal and political impact that volunteering has on the individual. In this respect, more of an effort needs to

be made to include the viewpoints and experiences of FRC volunteers in the development of volunteer policies in individual FRCs. By involving volunteers in the drafting of volunteer policies, community development workers would help reduce the power imbalance that can exist between paid and unpaid staff. Equally, by collaborating more with volunteers, community development workers are acknowledging that volunteers give more than 'time' to their local community and FRC. In these ways, a more informed, respectful and mutually beneficial working relationship will emerge between volunteers and community development workers, to the betterment of the FRC and the local community as a whole.

10

Family Resource Centres, Community Development and Restorative Justice: Compatible Endeavours?

Steve McNamara

CHAPTER SUMMARY

This chapter looks at community development in the context of family resource centres (FRCs) and at restorative justice initiatives as they are practised in the Republic of Ireland. It will offer the experience of a research project, conducted in 2009, which explored the perceptions of members of management committees and staff of five FRCs of the compatibility of the principles and practices of community development, as they practise it, with restorative justice initiatives currently operating in the Republic of Ireland.

Importantly, the chapter will draw some conclusions as to the compatibility of community development and restorative justice in principle and practice, as well as making some recommendations as to how practice might be developed.

INTRODUCTION

A key challenge facing FRCs and other local community projects in Ireland, which they are attempting to address through community development work, is that of crime and antisocial behaviour (Meagher 2006; FSA 2008b:10, 2008c:8). In 2007, community development projects (CDPs) and FRCs in the South-West Region established a working group on antisocial behaviour, whose discussions have yet to conclude (SMWCDSA 2007, 2008).

The National Commission on Restorative Justice (NCRJ) was announced in 2007 and a community focus to restorative justice was recognised in its establishment (DJELR 2007). However, apart from a general public invitation to submit views (NCRJ 2008:7), there is little evidence of a concerted effort to consult with or involve community organisations in its deliberations.

The research reported on in this chapter explored whether one model of community development organisation – the FRCs – might provide that community focus. It did this through creating the opportunity for those charged with the design, planning and delivery of the organisations' work – FRC management committee members and staff – to discuss the issue.

FRCs AND COMMUNITY DEVELOPMENT

Community development presents difficulties of definition: Powell and Geoghegan (2004:18) tell us that, 'like the camel, [community development] is easier to describe than to define'. However, definitions of community development are offered by the Federation of Community Work Training Groups (FCWTG 2001:10), the Community Development Exchange (CDX) (CDX 2009), the National Occupational Standards for Community Development Work (PAULO 2003:1), and the Budapest Declaration (Craig et al. 2004:2), among many others. All identify key characteristics, which include the following:

Key Characteristics of Community Development

- Community development is a process: it describes a way of working, rather than being an end in itself.
- It focuses on collectivity – on groups of people working together.
- It seeks change – social change and social justice – through influencing power structures and policy- and decision-making processes in society.
- It is based on empowerment and participation – developing people's capacity to work together and to become involved in identifying their needs and taking action to meet those needs.
- It is based on core principles and values.

In 1994, to mark the International Year of the Family, ten FRCs, with management committees comprised of volunteers, were allocated funding by the then Department of Social Welfare on a three-year pilot basis to support community development activities with a focus on supporting families and tackling child poverty.

The Family Support Agency (FSA), established in 2003, brought together programmes offering family mediation services, relationship counselling, and the Family and Community Services Resource Centre Programme (FCSRCP), including FRCs.

The aim of FRCs is to combat disadvantage and improve the functioning of the family unit (FSA 2008a). They emphasise involving communities in developing approaches to tackling their problems and creating partnerships with statutory agencies in their areas.

The FCSRCP offers the following definition of community development:

Definition of Community Development

> 'Community development is about people working together for social change which will improve the quality of their lives, the communities in which they live and/or the society of which they are a part. It stresses the importance of how change is achieved as well as what is achieved. It helps people identify their needs, gives them the confidence to speak out and influence decision-making and structures that affect their lives.' (FSA 2007:11)

The work of FRCs upholds the ethos and principles of community development, which include inclusiveness, promoting the empowerment of people through collective action and emphasising the importance of the process of working as well as the task (FSA 2008a). An integrated approach is taken, acknowledging the interdependence of economic, social and cultural issues. Creativity in ways of working are important, and key values are equality, challenging discrimination, openness and inclusion (FSA 2007:11).

This work includes community needs identification and capacity building, and provision of information, advice, support and practical assistance to community groups. Education courses and training opportunities, childcare facilities, counselling, mediation and advocacy services are provided in the community (Bon 2007:24; FSA 2008a).

RESTORATIVE JUSTICE

As with community development, defining restorative justice is not easy (Johnstone 2003; Zernova and Wright 2007); in fact, it is argued that it is questionable as to whether a definition is useful at all (Zehr 2002). Indeed, the most widely accepted definition emerged as the result of a failure to produce consensus on defining restorative justice (McCold 1998:20).

The process identified by McCold resulted in the acceptance of the following definition as 'the most acceptable working definition' (McCold 1998). This is also the definition used in the Irish context (see Oireachtas 2007; NCRJ 2008):

Definition of Restorative Justice

> Restorative justice is '. . . a process whereby all the parties with a stake in a particular offence come together to resolve collectively how to deal with the aftermath of the offence and its implications for the future'. (Marshall 1996:37)

The principles of restorative justice are explored by Umbreit (1999), Zehr and Mika (1998), Graef (2001), Van Ness (2002), Johnstone (2003), Johnstone and Van Ness (2007b) and Zehr (2002, 2005).

Three fundamental principles are identified by Zehr and Mika (1998):

Principles of Restorative Justice

1 Crime is fundamentally a violation of people and interpersonal relationships.
2 Such violations create obligations and liabilities to make things as right as possible.
3 Restorative justice seeks to put right the wrongs, providing a framework within which the victim is kept safe and empowered, and can seek recovery and healing.

Anslow (2001:98) also identifies inclusion, empowerment, accountability, responsibility and reintegration as key principles of restorative justice. Graef (2001:18), Keeley (2001a:16,17) and Wallis and Tudor (2008:22) further emphasise that voluntariness of participation is crucial. This is contested, however (Levant *et al.* 1999; Ashworth 2002; Zehr 2002; Van Ness 2003). Zehr (2005:198) contends that offenders can be required to make right their wrongs, though full responsibility is not possible without 'some degree of voluntarism'.

It is clear that restorative justice in Ireland is not widespread. It is practised in four initiatives: the Garda Juvenile Diversion Programme (GJDP); Court-Referred Family Conferences for Juvenile Offenders; the Nenagh Community Reparation Project (NCRP); and the Tallaght Restorative Justice Services (TRJS) (Oireachtas 2007; NCRJ 2008; Haverty 2009).

Furthermore, restorative justice in the Republic of Ireland operates in line with two models identified by Raye and Roberts (2007:211): victim–offender mediation (VOM); and conferencing.

VOM is used in the GJDP (through a process called restorative cautioning: Oireachtas 2007:24) and TRJS (NCRJ 2008:30–1). The prototypical VOM involves one victim, one offender and one or more mediators, but can be expanded to include more than one victim, more than one offender, and possibly family members and supporters. The participation of the victim is essential for prototypical VOM to happen. Facilitators' or mediators' roles are to create safety and guide the process (Raye and Roberts 2007:212).

All four initiatives offer elements of the conferencing model. In this model, families of victims and offenders and other supporters, including community members, are brought together, with facilitation, to find their own solutions to conflicts (Raye and Roberts 2007:213).

In all of the processes above, the voluntariness of participation is contestable, given that, with the exception of the GJDP, failure to reach or comply agreement can result in a return before the courts, which raises the question of coercion.

McCold and Wachtel (1998), Johnstone (2002), McCold (2004), Zehr (2005) and Schiff (2007) stress the importance of the role and responsibilities of the community in restorative justice. Schiff (2007:235–8) says that the community should provide a safe forum to talk about the crime and its resolution, include community members, and communicate on the impact of crime. Support to victims and offenders through the processes and on to reintegration are further identified.

COMPATIBLE ENDEAVOURS?

Restorative justice and community development, as described above, clearly share elements of principle and practice.

Both operate from principles of inclusion and voluntariness (Graef 2001; Van Ness 2002; Raye and Roberts 2007:217; Henderson and Salmon 2001; Lee 2006; FSA 2007). While the needs addressed may be different, empowerment is at the heart of how those needs are addressed (Zehr and Mika 1998; Zehr 2002; Ledwith 2005; Lee 2006; CWC 2008). It is seen as important to bring people together to arrive at resolutions collectively, voluntarily and by consensus (Graef 2001:18; Raye and Roberts 2007:217; Ledwith 2005:1; Motherway 2006:7; CWC 2008:10–11). Practices in restorative justice and community development are both adaptable and adapted in multiple ways around needs, while maintaining their goals and values (Raye and Roberts 2007:217; Powell and Geoghegan 2004:163).

The NCRP and the TRJS in particular have much in common, on the surface at least, with community development practice, such as that seen in FRCs. All are heavily dependent upon volunteer involvement (Oireachtas 2007:32; NCRJ 2008:30; FSA 2007; Bon 2007); they seek participation, consensus and collective decision-making (Oireachtas 2007:30–1; FSA 2007:7–11); and they are process-based (NCRP 2008; NCRJ 2008: 30; FSA 2007).

With elements such as these in common, the question arises as to whether the initiatives are compatible in principle and practice. The remainder of this chapter explores this issue with the people who are primarily responsible for the planning and delivery of the work of FRCs – their staff and management committees.

THE RESEARCH PROJECT

Methods

The data used in this chapter came from a qualitative study conducted in the southwest of Ireland between May and July 2009. The method chosen was the focus group, as it is particularly appropriate to allow participants explore issues which are important to them in their own language, following their own priorities, potentially enabling them to become part of the analysis process, and to develop their own perspectives as a result of their interaction with people who have similar experiences (Kitzinger 1995: 299). Extracts are offered in support of the findings rather than as empirical proof.

Results

Similarities and Differences in Principle and Practice

Common principles were identified across all groups in the research. Empowerment, participation and inclusiveness were the strongest themes to emerge, while equality and anti-discrimination, inclusion and volunteer participation were also identified. Similar practices were also highlighted in terms of target groups, collective action, partnership and responsibility. Also identified were inter-agency work, giving voice to victims, and links with current FRC work:

> PH 2: But then, it does say like 'promoting the empowerment of people through working together', that would be the collective action, for the community side. And it says 'All parties should be involved in the response to crime if they so wish'. So there is a partnership, if it works . . . (Group H, p. 2 para. 9)

Differences in principle and practice were also identified across all groups. The lack of voluntary engagement, the narrower focus on crime, perpetrators and the institutions which deal with it, and the pre-designed processes and the different systems of restorative justice were contrasted with the voluntarism, community focus and organic nature of community development.

> PL 2: I mean if we were to be working with a particular target group then we would be looking at the needs of the target group and inviting the target group to participate fully in the development of the process. I think that the way this is laid out, is the process would be designed, and then the individual would be brought into that if they fit into the process. (Group L, p. 14 para. 113)

All groups described the principles of restorative justice and community development as compatible.

Advantages, Disadvantages, Benefits, Concerns

Participants across all groups saw potential advantages and benefits of restorative justice – for victims, offenders, the community and the FRC. These included healing, closure and reintegration into the community, with offenders avoiding the stigma of prison, the community being brought closer together through the process, and enhancement of the position of the FRC in the community.

> PS 5: Because, you know, if you can bring closure to both of them, not just, you know, the victim, but also the perpetrator, it may help him, the perpetrator, to think, 'Well, I can move on from it.' (Group S, p. 6 para. 40)

Disadvantages and concerns were also identified across all groups. Perceptions that restorative justice is an easy way out for offenders, and that the FRC might suffer loss of credibility by being seen to take sides, or do more harm than good through lack of knowledge and expertise, were key themes.

PB 5: . . . I definitely don't know enough information to really comment on it, while there's a little bit of comparison in different . . . you know in ways that you deal with things, but what I would be afraid of . . . the approach that we would use, would we use the right approach, could we end up doing more . . . harm than good. (Group B, p. 9 paras 76–8)

Some groups expressed concerns about an 'onus' being placed on victims to act when they had done no wrong, and on the community to take on the policing role. Fear of intimidation – of victims and community people – was expressed in four groups.

Role, Structures, Supports, Barriers

All groups identified potential roles for their FRCs in restorative justice initiatives, and, indeed, a duty to be involved. Providing a safe, neutral venue, supporting victims, offenders, families and communities, and participating in inter-agency work were the key themes.

PH 1: Yeah, I think we would be involved in putting a plan together for the offender and the victim, both of them. You know, like, we have a centre here where people could come and meet. (Group H, p. 28 para. 299)

Supports needed for such roles were identified, with barriers largely described as their absence. Structures were not specifically identified, participants citing a lack of knowledge preventing this. However, the need for adequate resources, in terms of staffing, training, expertise and information was identified, and the need for inter-agency structures was a key theme across all groups, with the involvement of other partners.

PM 2: And you'd need very good connections with other partners, you would be aware of that you know, even very good connections with agencies let's say like the HSE [Health Service Executive] or the guards, that kind of thing. (Group M, p. 21 para. 203)

Discussion

Compatibility – Principle and Practice

Participants expressed a lack of knowledge of restorative justice, which impacted on their ability to discuss comparisons. Nonetheless, based on the information provided to them as part of this study, participants identified compatibility in principle between the endeavours, along with similarities in practice – notwithstanding that there are also differences.

The lack of knowledge is unsurprising. Only four restorative justice initiatives in the Republic of Ireland are identified in the earlier review of the sparse existing literature (cf. Oireachtas 2007; NCRJ 2008; Haverty 2009). The fact that two programmes are based in specific geographic localities may not be conducive to widespread knowledge of their principles and practices. An apparently low rate of use of the restorative justice options that involve the participation of community participants/representatives (NCRJ 2008:26) may also be a factor.

These commonalities of principle and practice are borne out by the literature. Empowerment, inclusiveness, participation and voluntariness all feature in the literature of restorative justice (Zehr and Mika 1998; Anslow 2001; Graef 2001; Zehr 2002; Van Ness 2002, 2003; Raye and Roberts 2007) and community development (Henderson and Salmon 2001; Ledwith 2005; Lee, 2006; FSA 2007; CWC 2008).

These advantages and benefits described by participants are also consistent with the findings of the literature review, broadly mirroring Umbreit's (1999) description of the creation of opportunities for dialogue and Van Ness's (2002) postulation of the key values of restorative justice of inclusion and reintegration. Healing and restoration were also key themes in the literature (Zehr and Mika 1998; Zehr 2002); and the desirability of community involvement through community development programmes, and of support to families – a core function of FRCs – are stressed by Johnstone (2002), McCold (2004) and Schiff (2007).

The concerns expressed in all groups should be recognised. The possibility of damage to the credibility and standing of their FRCs, coupled with expressions of lack of skills, resources and expertise in restorative justice, and a fear of the potential to do more harm than good, reflect Schiff's (2007:239–40) calls for government recognition of the capacities of communities to engage in restorative justice, and highlight a role for government in providing resources and structure. Johnstone's (2002:14) acknowledgement of the eradication of community spirit resonates strongly in the issue of fear among communities, which arose in most focus groups.

Nonetheless, participants felt that there was compatibility in principle, and the possibility of a role for FRCs in restorative justice.

Role, Structures, Supports, Barriers

The roles identified by participants for their FRCs are consistent with findings from the literature review on the roles and responsibilities which the community would need to take in restorative justice initiatives, outlined in Johnstone's (2002:14) contention that the community must be prepared to get involved in resolving conflicts, supporting victims and offenders, and to generate pressure for a settlement, while echoing McCold's (2004:169) emphasis on the importance of valuing the family, and Schiff's (2007:235–8) description of the responsibilities of the community in restorative justice processes. This would suggest that for participants in FRCs, a putative role in restorative justice is not a huge leap into entirely unfamiliar territory.

Nonetheless, as participants pointed out, FRCs may have some distance to travel before being capable of fulfilling the roles and responsibilities described by Schiff (2007:235–8).

CONCLUSION

Lack of knowledge and unresolved concerns expressed by management committees and staff of the FRCs who participated in this research means that they would be unwilling to commit their FRCs to participation at this time. However, the belief expressed across all groups that the principles of restorative justice, as evident in initiatives in the Republic of Ireland (Keeley 2001b), are compatible with the principles of community development as described in their own national programme gives grounds for further exploration of how their working practices might fit with those of restorative justice in practice. Indeed, members of voluntary management committees and staff of the FRCs involved in this study believe that there are potential roles for their FRCs, which they would feel a duty to explore, in participating in the delivery of such initiatives. Key supports of inter-agency and partnership working, resources, information, training, adequate staffing and expertise would need to be present in any structures for the delivery of restorative justice initiatives in which their FRCs could be involved.

A key conclusion that may be drawn from the findings is not that restorative justice and community development are entirely compatible, but rather that, in principle, the management committees and staff of the FRCs who participated in this research believe that the principles of restorative justice, as followed by some restorative justice initiatives in the Republic of Ireland, and as identified in Keeley (2001b), are compatible with the principles of community development as described in their own national programme.

Community development is, by its very nature, a diverse and adaptable discipline. It is perhaps not surprising that it might have much in common with other disciplines occupying the same space and time.

Greater awareness is needed among FRC management committee members and staff of restorative justice principles and practices as a potential response to issues of crime and anti-social behaviour in communities. This study is a beginning on that road, and might usefully be extended to explore with FRCs nationally the potential for the FCSRCP to become involved in the delivery of restorative justice initiatives.

11

Education: A Tool for Community Development

Tom Farrelly and Andrew Loxley

CHAPTER SUMMARY

While it is always difficult to attribute a causal link between positive social outcomes and education, one can certainly attribute a positive relationship between education and the creation of conditions that enhance community development. This chapter assumes little or no in-depth knowledge of education theories, agencies, initiatives or provision, and is intended to be read as an introductory text.

The chapter will introduce the reader to a number of critical theories as they pertain to adult and community education. The reader will be encouraged to consider how these theories can be viewed as complementary to the community development process. This chapter will provide the reader with a broad canvas of a range of policies, legislation and initiatives, stakeholders, groups and providers in the area of adult and community education. Finally, the reader will be provided with a set of critical thinking tools that can be incorporated into future practice.

INTRODUCTION

While we acknowledge the role that community development education has played in facilitating and encouraging community development, we wish to take a broader view in exploring the role that education (in a number of other forms, i.e. adult education, literacy provision, lifelong learning and higher education) can play in facilitating and encouraging community development. Camilla Fitzsimons (2010:53) notes that 'although community development and adult education are sometimes presented as separate disciplines, there is a lengthy history that connects the two'. Broadly speaking, there are four possible areas of interest in terms of education and its relationship with community development: first, those courses that explicitly teach community development; second, the adult and further education sector; third, the community education sector; and finally, the third-level sector. Our central argument is that community development can also be encouraged by participation in the education process even where community development is not the central aim of the programme; consequently we focus primarily on the community education and to a lesser extent on the adult/further education sectors.

The Community Workers' Co-operative's *Towards Standards for Quality Community Work* (CWC 2008:19) states that in 'order to meet criteria for good community work practice there are essential knowledge, skills and qualities that practitioners must be able to demonstrate'. The document goes on to state that combining these qualities, skills and knowledge should enable the community worker (among others) to: 'facilitate the personal, social and political development and education of communities' (CWC 2008:21). While we cannot make any claims about this chapter's ability to engender personal qualities, our aim is to provide the reader with sufficient knowledge and discussions that can help to both inform and encourage critical practice. The chapter begins with a brief introduction to a number of critical education theories before moving on to an exploration of a range of policies, initiatives, providers and groups involved in community and adult education. The next section explores how these theories of education can be mapped through an exploration of emancipatory and conservative approaches to community development. The final section draws the preceding sections together by providing a summary framework that practitioners may consider incorporating into their practice.

A LITTLE BIT OF THEORY

A focus on the benefits of engaging in the *process* of education, rather than the *product* of education, has many advocates, particularly in the arena of community development. However, one cannot articulate this position without referring to the work of Paulo Freire (1917–1980), the noted South American educationalist. Freire was concerned about the huge economic inequalities that beset his native Brazil, arguing that access to education (particularly basic literacy provision), or rather the lack of it, was used as a tool of oppression. From his perspective he was essentially asking: If people cannot read, how can they be exposed to new, radical ideas? How can they organise? Quite simply, how can they stand up for themselves in a cohesive manner if they cannot read and write? Thus, if people learn to read and write, if they engage in education, they are in effect engaging in a political act. Community education is clearly underscored by Freire's (1970, 1973) concepts of 'praxis' and 'conscientisation', where marginalised people are encouraged to reflect and in turn act in order to transform their situation (praxis) and to engage in consciousness raising (conscientisation) in order that they might view themselves in terms other than what has been 'handed down' to them.

While he was not, strictly speaking, an educationalist or educational philosopher, the work of the German philosopher Jürgen Habermas has, particularly over the past twenty years, gained prominence, providing as it does a critical theoretical framework against which the role and purpose of education, notably adult and higher education, can be analysed (Morrow and Torres 2002). Through his theoretical framework Habermas provides a useful starting point from which to analyse the relationship between society and education (Englund 2006).

Habermas (1985, 1989), in his analysis of the problems that beset modern society, identifies two main issues. The first is that there is an unhealthily close relationship between the state and the economy. The second is the fact that this relationship has resulted in the functional imperatives of the state and the economy becoming so interrelated that civil society has effectively become subservient to meeting these functional imperatives. Thus, from this viewpoint the various components of civil society (including education) become tools to support the realisation of economic and state imperatives. One way of challenging this hegemony is to engage in an education process that seeks to encourage individuals and communities to become critical and empowered. Proponents of adult and, in particular, community education would argue that their form/s of education can provide this catalyst.

Ted Fleming argues that by adopting a humanist transformative approach, 'education would be redefined as an exercise in democracy, teaching democracy and aiming to instil democracy in classrooms, communities, the workplace and in society' (Fleming 2008:15). Thus, learning becomes more than a transactional exercise; it becomes a vehicle for partnership, change, emancipation and empowerment. The consequence of this empowerment is that the education of adults becomes a political as well as an educational exercise that 'mandates participatory democracy as both the means and social goal' (Mezirow 1996:66).

POLICIES, INITIATIVES AND STAKEHOLDERS

It would be impossible in this chapter to cover every policy and initiative that has influenced and driven the provision of adult and community education in Ireland. Like any quick tour of diverse subjects, this overview will unfortunately be selective and partial. However, our intention is to simply articulate some of the key features and trends as we see them in order to provide a backdrop to the rest of the chapter. Additionally we would also argue that contemporary forms of adult and community education do not exist in a historical vacuum, but owe their shape, form and function to the work of these historical groups and organisations, whether or not they still exist. But it is also important to note that these groups and organisations are themselves products of broader social, political, cultural and economic metaphorical 'forces' and 'currents' prevalent in any given historical period.

For the purposes of this chapter, we begin in the 1960s, although it is important to acknowledge the importance of organisations such as the mechanics' institutes,[1] the Irish Countrywomen's Association (ICA)[2] and Muintir Na Tíre[3] (founded in 1937), and of course the establishment of Vocational Education Committees (VECs) under the terms of the Vocational Education Act in 1930.[4]

Policies 1960s–1980s

We should also bear in mind a number of developments – external to the VECs – which have had an impact not only on their work, but on the terrain of adult and community education more generally. The most important of these developments were four major government documents:[5]

1   *Investment in Education* (Department of Education 1966).[6]
2   *Report of the Commission on Higher Education* (Department of Education 1967).[7]
3   *Adult Education in Ireland* (the Murphy Report) (Murphy 1973).
4   *Report of the Commission on Adult Education* (the Kenny Report) (Kenny 1983).

For the purposes of this chapter, we will comment on the Murphy (1973) and Kenny (1983) reports.

The Murphy Report was published at a time when Ireland was just about to join the then European Economic Community (now referred to as the European Union) and was slowly engaging in a process of social and economic modernisation. The report traversed a wide range of areas, from the nature and role of education per se to the mechanics of how to reorganise adult education in Ireland; though unsurprisingly this was pretty much the same terrain as covered by the subsequent Kenny Report (1983) and the *Learning for Life* White Paper (Department of Education and Science 2000). However, it introduced into the adult education lexicon, via the 1972 UNESCO Faure Report (Faure 1972), the idea of lifelong learning; the notion that education is an activity which does not stop when we have completed our compulsory (Leaving Certificate) or post-compulsory (primary degree) learning, but continues on in numerous shapes and forms. Underpinning this model of learning, the report articulated what it saw as a more fundamental view of what adult education should be:

> A philosophy of adult education must reflect Irish beliefs, values and culture . . . it must provide for social betterment and enriched community living so as to further basic Christian values of our society, the continuous flowering of our culture . . . and a keenness and vitality to be involved in the establishment of a true European and World community. (Murphy 1973:22)

As we will show below, this statement of philosophy is quite different from that of *Learning for Life* and many other contemporary documents that prioritise the development of human capital over that of human beings per se and their communities. Indeed, the Murphy Report goes on to characterise adult education in Ireland 'as a "movement" and "instrument" . . . for community development' (Murphy 1973:26).

The *Report of the Commission on Adult Education* (Kenny 1983), more colloquially known as the Kenny Report, whilst no less enthusiastic about the role and position of adult education in Ireland in a similarly humanistic and democratic vein, nonetheless had a pragmatic orientation. There was a recognition in the report of the economic importance of adult education (Ireland was at the time experiencing a serious recession), but, as with the Murphy Report, this was not treated as the dominant rationale as to why adult education should be a major component of Irish social and cultural life. In short, the Commission's brief was to set out the state of adult education in Ireland at that point in time and to recommend any changes (managerial, organisational, financial, etc.) that it deemed necessary. This was done in part by soliciting views from interested organisations and individuals, as well as a national survey of participation in and attitudes towards adult education.[8]

However, it is worth briefly noting some of the developments in the 1970s and early 1980s which are highlighted in the report. From the perspective of the VECs, they were in 1979 authorised to employ 'adult education organisers' (fifty in total) as well as to set up specific sub-committees to deal with adult education issues. Next was the setting up of community and comprehensive schools, which had as part of their remit a responsibility to provide adult education facilities and to make them available to community groups and voluntary organisations. This was seen as an extension of what had been common practice in the VEC sector more generally. In addition to this, the report listed over seven pages a range of organisations which it considered to be 'providers of adult education'. These included the VECs, the universities, trade unions, RTÉ, public libraries, the National Association of Adult Education, the National Adult Literacy Agency (NALA), the ICA, the National Council for Travelling People, and a plethora of (unfortunately unnamed) non-formal education groups, from women's study groups and local history groups to amateur dramatic societies. Despite this 'busy-ness', the world of adult education in the early 1980s was not altogether a coherent one, as the Commission, via its research, was to report.

1990s–Present

If there is one term that has come to dominate education policy in Ireland, particularly as it impacts on adult and community education, it is 'lifelong learning'. In Ireland, lifelong learning 'emerged' as a central theme in the Report of the Commission on Adult Education (Government of Ireland 1984). However, given the financial constraints on the economy in the 1980s, this document remained little more than an aspirational statement. No doubt the startling results in the OECD's *International Adult Literacy Survey* (1997) influenced policy makers to take action. This notable publication advanced the cause of lifelong learning in Ireland, highlighting that the Irish data showed 25 per cent of the Irish adult population scoring at Level 1[9] (the lowest level on the scale). This concern was echoed by the International Adult Literacy Survey (IALS) report itself, which stated: 'it is a matter of great concern that those people involved whose literacy skills were weakest were least likely to be involved in any education and training'

(Morgan *et al.* 1997:99–100). For a country that had long prided itself on possessing a well-educated workforce, and in fact had used this as a strong selling point to potential investors, the impact of these findings cannot be overstated.

The 1995 White Paper on Education, *Charting Our Education Future* (Government of Ireland 1995), referred to the need to promote 'Lifelong Learning and continuous retraining and updating of skills' (p. 79). The theme of lifelong learning was further advanced by the 1998 Green Paper, *Adult Education in an Era of Lifelong Learning* (Department of Education and Science 1998), and reached fruition as full government policy with the publication in 2000 of the White Paper on Adult Education, which sets out very clear objectives for promoting education for life. These objectives are to improve learning, from basic literacy ability to improved access to third-level education. The 2000 White Paper advocated a programme of adult education within an overall framework of lifelong learning, a framework that consisted of six priority areas: consciousness raising, citizenship, cohesion, competitiveness, cultural development and community building. In attempting to address these priority areas a number of policies and strategies have been implemented since the late 1990s:

- *Opportunities, Challenges and Capacities for Choice* (Department of the Taoiseach 1999a)
- Qualifications (Education and Training) Act (Government of Ireland 1999a)
- National Development Plan 2000–2006 (Government of Ireland 1999b)
- Programme for Prosperity and Fairness (Department of the Taoiseach 1999b)
- The establishment of the Taskforce on Lifelong Learning[10] in 2000
- Report of the Action Group on Access to Third Level Education (2001)
- The establishment of the National Adult Learning Council (NALC) in 2002
- The ten-year social partnership plan Towards 2016 (Government of Ireland 2007a)
- The National Development Plan 2007–2013 (Government of Ireland 2007b)
- National Plan for Equity of Access to Higher Education 2008–2013 (HEA 2008).

Given the huge range of policies and initiatives developed and launched since 1999, one might be forgiven for thinking that the place of adult, continuing and community education had been firmly put on the map. For example, the establishment of the NALC in 2002 apparently heralded an era in which adult and community education would be supported and represented to a hitherto unparalleled degree. However, its suspension a year later raised and continues to raise doubts about the degree of seriousness with which adult learning is regarded by the government, and adult and community education still lacks cohesion and co-ordination.

In terms of specific provision there are currently a range of services that target a wide spectrum of groups,[11] the vast majority of which are provided by the VECs

(Bailey 2009). With regard to adult and community education programmes funded by the Department of Education and Skills in 2010, the three largest (in terms of student numbers[12]) were:

- Back to Education Initiative (BTEI)[13] – 27,959
- adult literacy programmes – 54,288
- community education – 55,953.

However, while it occupies a central role, as discussed in the next section, the Department of Education and Skills is not the sole funder or provider in the adult and community education arena.

AGENCIES AND PROVIDERS

Adult education in its various guises and forms is operated by, provided in and funded by a range of settings and organisations that are diverse in terms of their functions, roles and theoretical underpinnings. Jarvis and Griffin (2003:2) argue that 'adult education emerged not so much as an institutional form of education but as an educational social movement, functioning in a wide variety of sectors'. However, rather than viewing this as a problem they see plurality as a positive because 'had it been institutionalised, it would have been constrained from providing learning opportunities in so many contexts' (Jarvis and Griffin 2003:2). Nonetheless, it would be misleading to characterise each stakeholder as having equal status and power; their roles range from voluntary, statutory, advocacy, representational to provider, and hence vary in terms of such things as their underpinning rationale and access to funding. In such a short chapter it is impossible to provide a detailed, comprehensive outline of the primary stakeholders in adult and community education, therefore Table 11.1 is intended only to provide a very brief snapshot. It is expected that you will seek further information from the relevant bodies, which have a plethora of information in the form of journals, annual reports, statistical returns, policy documents and research outputs.

The difficulty with presenting a number of groups in such a manner is that there will be groups not indicated, and with over a thousand community education projects (Kavanagh 2007) it is impossible to outline all the parties. In addition to the aforementioned agencies there is a vast range of groups and agencies that are engaged in different forms of educative activities that could to a greater or lesser extent be classified as community education initiatives. Although funding is generally (though not always) provided by the Department of Education and Skills and administered by the VECs, it is often the local groups that provide and facilitate recruitment of students, trainers and locations in consultation. Examples of these providers/organisations include:

- groups supporting various sectors of society, e.g. people with a disability, Travellers, refugees, older people; and women's and men's groups;

- the ICA;[14]
- the trade union movement;
- community development groups and organisations;
- Macra Na Feírme.

Table 11.1. Organisations and agencies

Name	Role	Website
AONTAS (Irish National Adult Learning Organisation)	Incorporates individuals, voluntary and statutory sector organisations involved in or interested in adult and community education.[15] Representation, lobbying, policy development, organisation of networking opportunities, research and information referral.	www.aontas.com
Department of Education and Skills[16]	Execution of government policy in education and training – provision and administration of various initiatives, funding and statistical returns.	www.education.ie
Further Education and Training Awards Council (FETAC)	Statutory awarding body for further education and training in Ireland. Issues awards from Level 1 to Level 6 on the National Framework of Qualifications (NFQ).[17]	www.fetac.ie
Higher Education Authority (HEA)	The statutory planning and development body for higher education and research in Ireland.	www.hea.ie
National Centre for Guidance in Education (NCGE)	Main roles are to support and develop guidance practice in all areas of education and to inform the policy of the Department in the field of guidance. In terms of adult education it is the lead agency responsible for co-ordinating the Department's Adult Educational Guidance Initiative (AEGI).	http://www.ncge.ie/adult_guidance.htm
Irish Vocational Education Association (IVEA)	National representative association for Ireland's VECs. Promotion, representation and protection of vocational education and training sector.	www.ivea.ie
National Adult Literacy Agency (NALA)	Founded in the 1970s, this social justice-based charity is involved in representation, research, policy making and training issues associated with adult literacy provision.	www.nala.ie
Vocational Education Committees (VECs)	The 33 VECs[18] are the largest provider of adult and community education through a range of programmes.	Link to the various VECs on www.ivea.ie

This by no means an exhaustive list is merely intended to give a flavour of the range of groups and organisations involved in adult and community education. Suffice to say that practitioners in community development and community education can find potential partners among a very diverse set of groups and organisations.

CONSERVATIVE AND EMANCIPATORY APPROACHES TO COMMUNITY EDUCATION

It is not the intention of this chapter to fully explore the theoretical debates regarding the nature and purpose of community development; this debate is discussed and explored at length in the other chapters in this book. Nonetheless it is important to acknowledge the debate and to consider how it impacts on educational provision. This debate can best be conceptualised in terms of the seemingly dichotomous relationship between conservative and emancipatory approaches (van der Veen 2003). However, in pursuing this line we are aware of the danger of presenting approaches in such a polemic manner; we therefore acknowledge that practitioners often operate somewhere along a continuum between these two points, adopting a pragmatic rather than an ideological position.

Lovett et al. (2003) provide a very elegant and informative way of conceptualising this continuum with their exposition of four community education models (summarised in Table 11.2).

A recent large-scale study into the outcomes and impact of Department of Education and Skills-funded community education undertaken by AONTAS (2011) noted (perhaps not surprisingly) that a less than radical type of community education model was evident in Irish community education provision:

> The models of community education most strongly evidenced in the DES funded community education reflect that it is about bringing learning to people in their local areas as a response to the area's needs. It is less about, as described in an action model, learners engaging in local or social action to address structural disadvantage. (AONTAS 2011:10)

The adoption of one position in preference to another has implications in terms of such factors as the choice of pedagogies employed, the role of participants and the degree to which the focus of the programme is to effect individual and/or collective change.

In identifying the characteristics of the conservative approach, van der Veen (2003:582–3) contends that: 'there are also approaches that follow this conservative idea that traditional community should be restored. Such an approach tries to develop professional methods and techniques to support this restoration movement.'

Table 11.2. Four community education models

Model	People/groups involved	Processes	Focus/aim
Community organisation/ education	Education is for all members of the community regardless of social class.	'Entails concentrating on the effective co-ordination and delivery of the wide variety of educational resources available to meet local needs and interests. Appointment of out-reach workers – community education tutors – to work outside institutions in local communities.'	An extension of the liberal tradition with its emphasis on individual rather than community development.
Community development/ education	Education is for all members of the community regardless of social class. Additionally, courses provided for 'police, planners, social workers, professional community workers, etc. as well as professional community workers and local working class leaders.'	'Adult educators operate in local communities . . . providing information, resources, advice . . . systematic learning and training in specific skills and techniques . . . educate the institutions and organisations concerned with the provision of services and resources for the local community.'	An extension of the liberal/reform tradition. 'Concentrates on a mixture of community work and community development.'
Community action/ education	'Adult educators to identify with, and commit themselves to, local working class communities and the groups and organisations found in such communities.'	Community action is in itself an educational process. Less emphasis on systematic formal learning and a greater emphasis 'on "culture" in its widest sense. Community art, community media . . . provide the imaginative material created by people for their own education.'	In line with Freire's pedagogy that engagement in community action 'offers opportunities for consciousness raising'.
Social action/ education Working class education	Role of educators is to 'act in solidarity with local people, aligning themselves with local community action, seeking to provide specific forms of educational support which illuminate the problems which local people seek to resolve.'	In comparison to previous model, 'education must be more structured and systematic . . . [this process] is not to be done through informal dialogue and discussion but by strengthening motivation so that working class adults are prepared to undertake such a hard intellectual effort.'	This model stresses the location 'through education, the origins of local community problems in the larger social, economic and political structures in society'.

Source: adapted from Lovett *et al.* 2003:228–32.

Thus, the role of community development (including education initiatives) is about maintaining stability and cohesion within society rather than creating a political process aimed at encouraging community members 'to initiate conflict in order to advance demands based on rights' (Sites 1998:58). Kavanagh (2007), in her analysis of the Irish government's White Paper on Adult Education (Department of Education and Science 2000), notes that community education is defined in two ways. In the first, community education is simply 'an extension of the service provided by second- and third-level education institutions into the wider community' (Department of Education and Science 2000:110). The second viewpoint is more expansive, incorporating a greater ideological commitment to 'empowerment, both at an individual and a collective level' (Department of Education and Science 2000:110).

Bríd Connolly contends that 'community education is a flexible, emancipating process, which enables people to become more agentic in their own lives and to bring about change in their worlds' (Connolly 2003:9). This statement clearly positions the role and purpose of community education as an activity that is more than simply education that takes place in the community; rather, community education is as much about being a developmental and instrumental process as it is about facilitating educational outcomes. Indeed, from this position one could argue that the process is the outcome.

However, this emphasis on process rather than product is not without its opponents and detractors. Although we normally associate education as being located *in* a school or a college or a university, it does not have to be construed in that way. We would argue that there exists a tension around what would be seen as legitimacy and differential status of these diverse modes of, for want of a better term, provision. In other words, some are seen to be better than others, or greater social value is ascribed to them. Our attendance, progression and successful completion of a prescribed course of study in a formal setting (and arguably to a certain extent some non-formal settings) bestows upon us what Bourdieu and Passeron (1977) would call 'academic capital' or what Sennett and Cobb (1977) refer to as 'badges of success'. The diplomas, certificates and degrees we earn become tradeable commodities, which we can use to secure entry into different parts of the labour market and exchange for 'better' (we will leave you to define that) conditions of employment. But accreditation also plays a powerful symbolic and affective role. The badges of success become markers to the outside world (friends, family, work colleagues, strangers, etc.) of academic achievements and prowess, and enhance our self-esteem and self-confidence as a consequence of being able to navigate and manage productively a course of study.

In other words, for education to occur or to have occurred, and, more important, for our learning to be accepted as being legitimate and valid, it has to happen in a space and place that is given official credence, such as a school, college or university, or at the very least placed somewhere on the National Qualifications Framework. Adult and community education can thus be placed at odds with a society, an education system and economy that increasingly define educational worth, value and contribution in terms of 'hard measureable outcomes' such as progression, accreditation and qualifications. The 'soft outcomes', such as personal and community development, can be more difficult to measure and hence there is the danger (particularly as funding comes under intense scrutiny and pressure) that funding may be more directed towards provision that seems to offer 'better value'.

This shifting away from seeing learning as being equivalent to that which is officially sanctioned raises awkward questions of what we mean by education and to be educated, both as a noun and as a verb. In this view, education is seen not so much in terms of set spaces and places, though this is important, but in terms of relationships and, more important, the meanings attached to them. We also need to be aware that there is also a political dimension at work, as these informal and non-formal 'providers' may be seen as a challenge to the more orthodox conduits of teaching and learning. This notion of challenging orthodoxy by one particular group is captured very well in the next section, where we take a brief look at women's community education (WCE).

Women and Community Education

In writing this chapter we were mindful of the dangers of focusing on one sector of society at the expense of another. However, it would be impossible not to acknowledge and highlight the central and mutually beneficial role that individual women and women's groups have had on adult and (particularly) community education and in turn on society. Emerging in the 1970s,[19] WCE can be viewed in many ways as an organic response by small, often informal, women's groups that came together:

> . . . in order to provide opportunities for women whose communities had been ravaged by poverty, unemployment and emigration . . . These groups were spaces not just for women to engage in personal and educational development, but also opportunities for women to learn together how to act to change their communities. (AONTAS 2009:21)

Although clearly underpinned by a range of theoretical positions that incorporate feminism and Freirean pedagogy, WCE can be also be viewed as a practical response to the frequently unequal societal position that women occupy in Irish society. Recognising that the manifestation of educational disadvantage, although 'usually born out of poverty [is a far more complex issue than simply a lack of money], frequently strips women of a positive self-image, leaving in its wake low self-esteem and little confidence' (NWCI 2001:15). In acknowledging and understanding this complexity and hence the need for an integrated response, Valerie Albertini (2009:24) advises that 'educators in literacy programs and other professionals in social service delivery systems realize the complexity of women's limitations in their social networks and community support systems'.

The AONTAS *Guide to Best Practice of Women's Community Education* (2009) provides a very useful resource in the form of a quality assurance framework (QAF) that encapsulates and guides best practice, values, aspirations, principles and the dimensions of WCE. This document captures very succinctly the extent to which education and community development overlap and while it refers to women's experiences, it could be argued that the point is well made and relevant to any community education experience.

> In the context of WCE, education is not just about providing structured formal learning programmes. Any group that is offering a chance to come together in groups, discuss their experiences, listen to and learn from each other and then act together in some way to address women's inequality is involved in education . . . Likewise, a group that brings women from a community together to engage in community development is also engaged in education. (AONTAS 2009:23)

In keeping with a holistic and student-centred approach to education, Bríd Connolly (2001:4) identified five discernable features of WCE:

1   The participants own the programme.
2   A strong notion of agency and self-reliance; the founders and organisers are agentic.
3   'The curriculum and process of the education are women-centred . . . a distinct shift from the principle that knowledge is located through logical objectivity.'
4   'The facilitation of the groups remains in the hands of the groups.'
5   The development of a common identity between groups; an 'identification of common interests [and a] development of collectivity'.

Again, as with our previous comment with regard to an applicability that goes beyond women's community education experiences, we would contend that the practitioners and providers working with a range of other groups should (if they are not already doing so) incorporate these features into their provision.

IMPLICATIONS FOR PRACTICE

Practitioners who adopt a critical theorist approach to learning need to be aware that it shifts the role and the function of learning, from being a process concerned with just the transfer of skills and knowledge to one of personal and community development and empowerment. Although the latter (i.e. transformation) may be an unintended consequence of the former, it is not part of its 'mission'. As argued by Fleming and Murphy (2006), the utilisation of critical theories should provoke those charged with designing, commissioning or delivering adult and community education to rediscover a critical pedagogy, a pedagogy that goes beyond the transference education model that has characterised much of education delivery in past decades. What this implies is a radical reconstruction and reorientation of the teaching and learning relationship. In quite fundamental terms this is a mode of pedagogy which should encourage greater levels of social analysis, critical reflection and a re-working of the learner–teacher relationship. Crucially, though, this shift in the balance of power also needs to extend beyond the classroom and become 'lifewide'.[20] From this perspective the education process becomes as much an exercise in empowerment as it is about learning skills and/or knowledge. This notion of consciousness-raising demands that practitioners be acutely aware of two things: their own value position; and that of their students. That is, in our rush to save the world, we need to be mindful that we do not become, as Collins (1991) notes, wrapped up in a rhetoric and practice of 'vanguardism and elitism'. As bell hooks (1994:422) presciently remarks, 'teachers must be actively committed to a process of self-actualisation that promotes their own well-being if they teach in a manner that empowers students'. This in part brings into the world of adult education the importance of reflexivity; the act of interrogating and defining one's own values to provide a personal and theoretical point of reference.

In taking a reflexive position it helps to avoid the naive and wholesale absorption of the ideas of others through deference to their status and authority as practitioners and/or theoreticians. That is, we do not accept Fleming's (or Habermas's, Mzeirow's, etc.) work because he is Fleming; we do so because we have subjected it to the same degree of critique as any other writer or commentator. In short, the critical dialogue we have with those ideas and practices that we view as disempowering or repressive (e.g. racism, sexism, etc.) is extended to that which we are largely in agreement with. In turn this criticality is exercised inwardly upon ourselves, as a way of not only setting out the principles (ethical, political, pedagogical, etc.) upon which we base our practice, but to question our very understandings and the meanings we attach to them. It is simply (but uncomfortably) a process of asking: Why do we believe what we do and on what grounds do we hold such beliefs? In other words, nothing is taken for granted.

However, to avoid this becoming merely an exercise in either self-flagellation or self-aggrandisement, it needs to be set within the context of practice. As Whitehead (1989) has argued, as practitioners we need to try and reconcile the differences between what we believe and what we practise in order to construct what he refers to as a 'living educational theory'. For Whitehead, this is about generating one's own theory that is both informed by the work (both conceptual and practical) of others and grounded in our own efforts at reflexivity. This theory (which is always a 'work in progress') is seen as not only being capable of explaining the world (i.e. it is like this because . . .), but also acts to guide our practice; this conjoining of theory and practice is more commonly referred to as *praxis*. But, in turn, this needs to be further contextualised in relation to those students who form, along with ourselves as practitioners, an intricate and delicate web of teaching and learning practices.

What we are implying is that critical self-awareness has to be enmeshed with an understanding of what constitutes an educative experience. The opening up of a dialogue between student and teacher is not just a cognitive activity (a 'meeting of minds' to put it in clichéd terms), but an embodied process. This process is well captured in Table 11.3, which provides an important reminder that educative activities are as much embedded in space and place as they are in the kind of academic relationships we have with each other. Indeed, it goes beyond the traditional roles associated with the student–teacher relationship, and is concerned with the wholeness of the encounter of which the academic is but one, albeit crucial, dimension.

As we know, adult educators usually work with a diverse body of students who bring with them a mix of motivations and personal narratives in terms of their own educational pasts and futures. For some students, the decision to simply attend an adult education class is the culmination of a long process of deliberation and quite possibly framed within a personal history of negative educational experiences (NALA 2009). For some, it may be due to lack of opportunity rather than any other reason. And for others, it is seen as a natural extension of an otherwise unproblematic educational background.

This suggests that, in particular, the crucial early stages of building a relationship with students (individually and collectively) and exploring with them their personal narratives requires great sensitivity and tact. This is underpinned by the need to be ethically attuned to the way in which power permeates and shapes the relationship. In many respects a large proportion of the work of an adult educator is about reconstructing and offering other possibilities of the student–teacher relationship. Again, we return to the notion of reflexivity, in that practitioners are not a dispassionately engaged 'other', but an integral part of this process. Indeed, as Collins (1991:378) also notes, the 'subjectivity of the adult educator is central to any critical practice of adult education'.

In operationalising this discussion we need some mechanism that provides a grounded and practical framework that can help guide and inform practice. Kavanagh (2007) argues that there is a strong connection between the goals and principles of community education and community development:

> Community education attempts to provide learners with the tools to develop their own power and resources needed to address the problems in their communities. The principles of community development and community education are ones of inclusion, participation and diversity.

In this manner, community education is an excellent vehicle for the promotion of the social equality agenda. Table 11.3 provides a useful and practical set of questions that should help guide and inform practitioners.

Table 11.3. Sample template for combining the equality framework with
community education

Framework	Respect recognition	Love, care, solidarity	Resources	Power	Working and learning
Learning Centre	What do you know about the learner's experiences, values?	Do you understand how difficult it is to return to learning?	How can you make room friendly? What can you spend?	Who controls resources? Can you influence them?	Does centre look inviting? Is it warm? Is it accessible?
Learning Environment	How is room set out? Is it like a schoolroom?	Is learner made welcome? Is learner encouraged to participate?	Look at lighting, furniture, materials. Is tea/coffee available?	Who decides how room is set up?	Would you like to learn here?
Curriculum	Are the experiences of the learner taken into account? Is difference looked at?	Are the learners' need understood? Is emotional learning valued?	Are the materials user-friendly? Are they relevant to learner? Is there one for every learner? Do they cost anything?	Who decides the content? Do the learners have a say? Who decides what type of course?	Does the course enable questioning? What type of learning is most valued?
Educator/ Tutor	Do they understand community education processes? Have they empathy with different groups?	Do they understand difference and value it?	What skills/knowl-edge beyond the subject skill do they have?	Do they understand power in the learning setting? Do they facilitate learning?	Are they inclusive of experience as a learning tool? Is learning related to the experiences in the group?
Supports	How is the learner targeted? Advertise-ment or outreach?	Are the barriers that learners face understood?	What is in place as support – childcare, learning etc.?	How is the decision on support made?	Do the supports work? Is evaluation used?

Source: Kavanagh 2007.

GUARDING AGAINST . . .

In Tom Lovett's analysis of the relationship between community education and community development (1997:39), he has argued that:

> . . . the main concern of *community education* is with disadvantaged groups and *communities*. It is part of a long tradition of adult *education* which has sought to compensate for the failures of the formal *education* system and to support a variety of social movements attempting to redress social, economic, cultural and political disadvantage [italics in original].

Lovett's (1997) point about 'rebalancing failures' for disadvantaged communities and groups raises an interesting and relevant point that potentially has implications for practice and hence must be considered. If community education is seen as the concern of 'disadvantaged communities', does it follow that there is the potential for stigmatisation and negative labels being attached to individuals and/or communities that access such provision? This should certainly not deter individuals, communities and organisations from engaging in and promoting educational opportunities. This point is simply a reminder to be aware that as a practitioner your work should be aimed at improving the situation of groups and communities, not contributing to their marginalisation.

CONCLUSION

Adopting a critical theorist approach to learning potentially has huge implications; it shifts the role and the function of learning from being a process simply concerned with the transference of skills and knowledge to one of personal and community development and empowerment. Utilisation of critical theories should provoke those charged with designing, commissioning or delivering adult and community education to rediscover a critical pedagogy, a pedagogy that goes beyond the transferance education model that has characterised much of education delivery in past decades (Fleming and Murphy 2006). This pedagogy should encourage greater levels of social analysis, critical reflection and a re-working of the learner–teacher relationship. Nonetheless, while it is important to be an informed, reflective and critical practitioner, it is also important to engage in practice. It is too easy to get caught up in theoretical debates around the role and purpose of education without using these positions to inform delivery. Theoretical positions should be about informing and guiding practice and not simply to facilitate some dry academic debate for its own sake.

Approaches to community development exist along a continuum which ranges from the conservative to the radical; the role and purpose of education as a vehicle for community development exists alongside this continuum. The generation of social capital for communities and individuals need not necessarily involve huge changes; always be guided by what the community want, not what you as a practitioner think that they want or need. Therefore, in the context of community development we need to be careful not to automatically ascribe radical intentions to education providers (in whatever form) where none may exist. For some groups and learning communities, intentions may be of a smaller and incremental nature, but no less transformative for that. The role and work of the ICA is a good example of 'quietly' changing the lives of rural women (Ferriter 1996).

In assessing the potential benefits to community development processes and outcomes, one needs to be mindful of attributing too much weight to any one factor. Nonetheless, while it may be difficult to attribute a causal link between positive social outcomes and education (Grossman and Kaestner 1997), one can certainly attribute a positive relationship between education and the creation of conditions that in turn enhance and contribute to community development (McClenaghan 2000; CORI 2008).

Notes

1   The mechanics' institutes or, as Inkster (1985) calls them, 'steam intellect societies', first appeared in London and Glasgow in 1823, and then in Dublin in 1824. Their numbers eventually totalled twenty-eight in Ireland, and by the end of the nineteenth century they had either disappeared or had been taken over by the technical schools (Cooke 1999, 2009).

2   Like the mechanics' institutes, the ICA is a voluntary organisation which began its existence in 1910 as the Society of United Irishwomen, which was affiliated to the Irish Agricultural Society.

3   Founded by Tipperary priest Fr (later Canon) Hayes, Muintir na Tíre means the People of the Land or the People of the Countryside. Based on a structure of parish guilds, the community's initiatives were and are based on the principles of self-help and self-reliance.

4   This could be seen as a historical 'bridge' with the national tapestries of, but organisationally disconnected, mechanics' institutes of the nineteenth century. The Agriculture and Technical Instruction (Ireland) Act 1899, which also brought into being the Department of Agriculture and other Industries and Technical Instruction in Ireland, the Agricultural Board and the Board of Technical Instruction, was preceded by the Local Government Act (1898), which could, among other activities, organise and provide technical education in a specified area. It should also be noted that the 1899 Act superseded the 1889 Technical Instruction Act which pertained to the whole of Great Britain and Ireland, whereas the former only related to Ireland. In part this 'Ireland only' Act was due to the agitation of the Technical Educational Association of Ireland, an interest group which fought for better commercial and technical instruction, and which was succeeded by the Irish Technical Instruction Association in 1902.

5   A useful and informative book on the subject is John Coolahan's (1981) *Irish Education: Its History and Structure*.

6   Beginning in 1962, the Department of Education, in co-operation with the Organisation of Economic Co-operation and Development (OECD), undertook a review of second-level education provision, which culminated in the publication of the *Investment in Education* report in 1966. Arguably the major achievement of the report was that it paved the way for the introduction of the free secondary education scheme in 1967.

7   The Commission's rather scathing findings highlighted a litany of inadequacies such as poor research capabilities, inadequate staffing, lack of technological education and failure to take account of population growth predictions. The subsequent development of a network of regional technical colleges (later to become institutes of technology)

and the two national institutes of higher education (NIHE) in Limerick and Dublin (later to become the University of Limerick and Dublin City University respectively) had their origins in the findings of this important report.

8   The Commission reported that some 11 per cent of adults in their survey sample had participated in some form of adult education. This, they noted, was not out of line with countries such as the USA (13 per cent) and England and Wales (16 per cent).

9   'Level 1: People who score this level can perform only at the most rudimentary literacy tasks, that is; those that require the reader to locate a single piece of information in a text, where there is no distracting information and where material is laid out in a manner which facilitates selection of specific information' (Corridan 2002:60).

10   This was established under the terms of the Irish government's Programme for Prosperity and Fairness.

11   Given the rapidly changing economic situation, this state of affairs is extremely fluid. For example, all the senior Traveller training centres are expected to be closed by June 2012.

12   Department of Education and Skills statistics 2009/2010 (Department of Education and Skills 2011:3).

13   Provides part-time further education programmes for young people and adults. Free to those who left school early and who have not completed their Leaving Certificate. Payments are made only to those students who are eligible for: (a) full-time Youthreach; or (b) full-time Traveller Training Programme.

14   The ICA's An Grianan Adult Education College in County Louth was, according to Heverin (2009), Ireland's first residential adult education centre, and was funded by the Kellogg Foundation of America. As noted by Ferriter (1996), the college offered courses not only in the arts and crafts but also on community development and leadership, and was 'seen as the fulfilment of the Association's constitutional requirement that they educate rural women'. (p37).

15   The Community Education Network (CEN) is an umbrella network for over a hundred independent community education groups within the AONTAS membership (http://www.aontas.com/commed/networkcen.html).

16   One could also make the case that many government departments, such as Jobs, Enterprise and Innovation; Justice and Equality; Transport, Tourism and Sport; and Environment, Community and Local Government, have some involvement in funding adult and/or community education initiatives. In fact, dealing with the sheer range of government departments and agencies involved with funding is certainly an issue.

17   The framework provides a way of categorising and comparing awards on a ten-point scale that incorporates everything from a Level 1 certificate (e.g. basic literacy, numeracy) to doctorates at Level 10. For further information see the National Qualifications Authority of Ireland (www.nqai.ie).

18   There is at least one committee for each county, but some counties (e.g. Cork and Waterford) have a county and a city VEC. The present number of thirty-three (July 2011) is subject to review, with a view to reducing the number of VECs through amalgamation.

19   Politicised and more publicly vocal women's groups, such as the Irish Women's Liberation Movement (which began in 1971), Irish Women United (1975), Irish Women's Aid (1975), Adapt (1974), the Rape Crisis Centre (1978) and the Contraceptive Action Programme, began to exert an influence over the direction and content of women's issues.

20   The 1998 Green Paper argued that in addition to learning being 'lifelong' it should also be 'lifewide', i.e. learning opportunities should occur in a wide range of places in addition to conventional educational sites; these should include the home, the community and the workplace.

'From the Inside Out': Using Peer Education in Community Development Practice

A case study of the Tullamore Traveller Primary Healthcare Project (1999 to date)

Lily Kavanagh, Sarah McDonagh, Briggie McInerney, Mary McInerney and Pinkie McInerney (Traveller Community Health Workers), and Ashling Jackson

I Am a Traveller

I am a Traveller
God made me a Traveller
And a Traveller am I.
I could have a castle
That would reach the sky,
Or sail on oceans
Near and wide.
And when the time comes
With dignity I'll die
Because God made me a Traveller
And a Traveller am I.

Mary Hutchinson (on display in Tullamore
Traveller Movement offices, 2010)

CHAPTER SUMMARY

This chapter will show how peer education can be used as an effective way of promoting self-help and mutual aid in community settings. Using the Tullamore Traveller Primary Healthcare Project as a case study, the chapter will discuss how peer education projects can bring about real, tangible differences in people's lives in community settings. The typical steps involved in designing and implementing a peer education model of community development will also be outlined.

INTRODUCTION

In this chapter, the experience of being involved in a peer-led community development project is documented. Five Traveller women reflect on what training for the role of Traveller community health worker involved, and what their work as community health workers, in their own Traveller communities, means on a day-to-day basis. These five women do their work 'from the inside out'. They live in, and are part of, the communities in which they work, and thereby share a common cultural and ethnic identity with the group they work with.

To provide a context for the women's reflections, this chapter initially describes the Irish Traveller community, characteristics of the Traveller community in Ireland, primary healthcare, the Traveller Primary Healthcare Training Programme, and peer education as a method of improving the health status of a traditionally marginalised community. Using the storytelling tradition of the Traveller community, the Tullamore Traveller community health workers share their reflections on their involvement to date in the Tullamore Traveller Primary Healthcare Project. The effectiveness of this project is also reviewed. Finally, the chapter outlines the typical steps involved in designing and implementing a peer education model of community development.

IRISH TRAVELLERS

The Equal Status Act (2000) defines Travellers as:

> . . . the community of people who are commonly called Travellers and who are identified (both by themselves and others) as people with a shared history, culture and traditions including, historically, a nomadic way of life on the island of Ireland. (Government of Ireland 2000:7)

According to Jackson (2009), Travellers are often incorrectly considered part of the nomadic Romani, an ethnic group that originated in a region of India, now widespread throughout Europe. However, while both groups are nomadic, Irish Travellers are native to Ireland. They have their own culture, customs and traditions, as well as being noted for their musical and storytelling abilities. Irish Travellers are Roman Catholic and speak their own language, Cant or Gammon. Pavee Point (2006), an Irish national Traveller representative organisation, identifies language, nomadism, music, storytelling and the Traveller economy as among the important features of Traveller culture and heritage. It is here that there is a contrast with the settled population in Ireland. Being a Traveller is an ascribed status (Kavanagh 2010). This means that for an individual to be called a Traveller, they must have at least one Traveller parent. One cannot just become a Traveller.

Characteristics of the Traveller Community in Ireland

Number of Travellers in Ireland

The All Ireland Traveller Health Study (2010) is the first study of Traveller health status and health needs to involve all Travellers living on the island of Ireland, North and South (DHSSPS and DoHC 2010). The All-Ireland Traveller Health Study arose from a recommendation in the Department of Health and Children's National Traveller Health Strategy 2002–2005 (DoHC 2002): 'A Traveller Needs Assessment and Health Status Study to be carried out to develop and extend the indicators collected in the last survey of Travellers' Health Status and to inform appropriate actions in the area of Travellers' Health'. Traveller health was last examined in the Republic of Ireland by the Health Research Board in 1988 and 1989 (Barry and Daly 1988; Barry et al. 1989). In the All-Ireland Traveller Health Study (2010), Travellers themselves acted as 'peer researchers', which means that they collected the data for the study.

Although the study is primarily focused on the lifestyle and health needs of the Traveller population in both the North and South of Ireland, an enumeration of Travellers living on the island of Ireland was also an important part of the study.

According to the Central Statistics Office (CSO), close to 22,435 Irish Travellers were recorded in the 2006 census. This represented 0.5 per cent of the Irish population at the time of the census (CSO 2007b). However, the All-Ireland Traveller Health Study estimated this figure to be higher – 40,139 Travellers living in the South of Ireland – in 2008, when the fieldwork for this national study was carried out (DHSSPS and DoHC 2010).

Age Breakdown of the Traveller Community

The Traveller community in Ireland has an age structure very different from that of the settled population. According to the 2006 census, two out of every five Travellers were aged under 15 years, compared with one in five for the population as a whole (CSO 2007b). Older Travellers – those aged 65 years and over – accounted for just 2.6 per cent of the total Traveller population, compared with 11 per cent for the general population (CSO 2007b). The distinctive age structure of the Traveller community resulted in a median age of 18 compared with a national figure of 33 (CSO 2007b).

Living Conditions

Of the representative sample interviewed for the All-Ireland Traveller Health Survey, respondents most frequently lived in a house (73.3 per cent Republic of Ireland; 55.4 per cent Northern Ireland), followed by trailer/mobile home or caravan (18.2 per cent Republic of Ireland, 23.8 per cent Northern Ireland). More

Northern Ireland respondents were parked on a transient site (24.3 per cent, compared to 6.8 per cent in the Republic of Ireland), and more Republic of Ireland respondents were parked on an unofficial site (23.8 per cent, compared to 16.7 per cent Northern Ireland) (DHSSPS and DoHC 2010:76).

Health

'Travellers are particularly disadvantaged in terms of health status and access to health services. Generally speaking, they suffer poor health on a level which compares so unfavourably with the settled community that it would probably be unacceptable to any section thereof' (DoHC 2002: section 1.8). On a number of key indicators Traveller health status is poorer than that of the settled population. Life expectancy at birth in Ireland was 76.7 years for males and 81.5 years for females in 2004–2006 (CSO 2009:54). The life expectancy of Traveller men is ten years shorter than for settled men (CPA 2004:3). Traveller women have a life expectancy of twelve years less than settled women (CPA 2004:3). Infant mortality among the settled population in Ireland was 3.7 births per 1,000 population in 2006 (Institut National d'Études Démographique 2008). Infant mortality among Travellers is two and a half times higher than in the settled population (CPA 2004:3).

PRIMARY HEALTHCARE

While the focus on citizen participation emerged from disillusionment with the war on poverty (Hardina 2003), it has been most fully developed and articulated in the fields of health promotion and international community development. In terms of the former, participation in decision-making is not only recognised as a valuable source of knowledge, it is constructed as a fundamental human right: 'People have the right and duty to participate individually and collectively in the planning and implementation of their healthcare' (Declaration of Alma-Ata 1978). The concept of primary healthcare was established at the joint WHO/UNICEF conference in Alma-Ata in 1978, which acknowledged the need to reform the conventional health systems. Health was seen as the concern of society as a whole.

> Primary Health Care (PHC) is essential health care based on practical, scientifically sound and socially acceptable methods and technology made universally accessible to individuals and families in the community, through their full participation and at a cost that the community and the country can afford to maintain at every stage of their development in the spirit of self-reliance and self-determination. It is the first level of contact of individuals, the family and community with the national system, bringing health care as close as possible to where people live and work, and constitutes the first element of a continuing health care process. (Declaration of Alma-Ata 1978)

According to the All-Ireland Traveller Health Study (DHSSPS and DoHC 2010:23), primary healthcare 'is a flexible system that can be adapted to the health problems, culture, way of life and the stage of development reached by the community'. It means enabling individuals and organisations within communities to improve health through informed healthcare, self-help and mutual aid. Of course, these are also characteristics of effective community development practice.

THE TRAVELLER PRIMARY HEALTHCARE TRAINING PROGRAMME

The Traveller Primary Health Care Training Programme was initiated in 1994, as a pilot initiative in the Finglas/Dunsink areas of Community Care Area 6, with funding from the Eastern Health Board. The Traveller Primary Health Care Training Programme is a process through which Travellers gain greater control over the social, political, economic and environmental factors that determine their health (DHSSPS and DoHC 2010). It combines a community development approach on one side, and resources, health skills, health services and health knowledge on the other. This combination is essential for the effective imple-mentation of a primary healthcare approach in the provision of health services to a local Traveller community (DHSSPS and DoHC 2010).

Through using community development principles, such as empowerment, partnership and advocacy, primary healthcare training projects can facilitate the Traveller community to identify and address health issues. Each of these principles can be defined as follows:

1 *Empowerment* – 'Empowerment is achieved through learning and collective organising. It has been defined as "enhancing" people's capacity to influence the decisions that affect their lives and is a central principle of community development' (Gilchrist 2009:66).
2 *Partnership* – In community development practice, partnership means working with all stakeholders in a project. The challenge is to ensure that the working relationship is a fair one, making sure that *all* stakeholders are equally included and consulted. For marginalised groups, there may have to be capacity training, prior to engagement with other stakeholders, so that they are enabled to express opinions, as well as advocate for their broader community in what are traditionally unequal relationships.
3 *Advocacy* – Advocacy work in community development occurs when represen-tatives of communities, on behalf of those communities, promote and seek resolution on community issues and concerns.

Importantly, in the Traveller Primary Health Care Training Programme, the Traveller community participates in every stage of the project, including the initial assessment of the situation, defining the main health problems and issues, setting priorities for the project, implementing the activities, and monitoring and evaluating the results.

The pilot programme in the Finglas/Dunsink area was so successful that it was replicated and adapted nationwide. The *Report of the Task Force on the Traveller Community* (DoE 1995) and the National Travellers' Health Strategy (DoHC 2002) strongly endorsed the work of this first Traveller Primary Health Care Training Programme and recommended its replication. The latter set many targets which are dependent on the development of an effective and inclusive local Traveller health infrastructure, but specifically identified the Traveller Primary Health Care Training Programme as the 'cornerstone' of the strategy and recommended that it should be developed as an effective mechanism to facilitate the implementation of its actions. 'Since 2002, 40 Primary Health Care Training Programmes have been established around the country and they have trained more than 300 Traveller women as Traveller Community Health Workers' (DoHC 2010: 21). Box 12.1 (adapted from Jackson 2009:364–5) describes the Tullamore Traveller Primary Healthcare Project, the case study in this chapter, in more detail.

Box 12.1. The Tullamore Traveller Primary Healthcare Project

Mission Statement of the Primary Healthcare Project
'To support Community Health Workers, to deal with specific Traveller health related issues, in a culturally appropriate way, for both caregiver and care receiver' (Midland Health Board 2004:3).

Summary of the Aims of the Tullamore Traveller Primary Healthcare Project
1 To develop, in consultation with Travellers, FÁS, the Midland Health Board and Tullamore Traveller Movement a primary healthcare project for Travellers.
2 To train Traveller women to work as community health workers among Travellers in their locality.

Background to the Tullamore Traveller Primary Healthcare Project (Midland Health Board)
A health needs assessment study was carried out to determine the health needs of Travellers, according to Travellers, in the Midland region (Duggan-Jackson 2000). A partnership was also set up between Tullamore Traveller Movement, Midland Health Board and FÁS to run the Tullamore Traveller Primary Healthcare Project.

Training to Become a Traveller Community Health Worker
The training of Traveller community health workers involved a number of stages as follows:
Stage One: Capacity building (increasing the capacity (ability) of a community or organisation). Workshops were conducted in Tullamore and surrounding areas to build the capacities of local Traveller women and identify trainees for the project.
Stage Two: Pre-training phase 1999–2001. The focus of this stage was to facilitate Traveller participants to develop an understanding of health in conjunction with community development and personal development.

Some areas in which trainees received training were as follows:

- Numeracy/literacy.
- Confidence/assertiveness skills.
- Communication.
- What primary healthcare is and how Traveller community health workers can provide a primary healthcare service to the local Traveller community.
- How to disseminate health and healthcare information, and respond to health needs in an area, and in so doing, developing a sense of community.

Stage Three: Health intervention phase 2001–3. Trainees were given training in specific aspects of health, identified as being important for Traveller health, e.g. immunisation/dental health/children's health.

Consultation Process in the Project

Consultation was considered essential to the effective development, running and sustainability of the Tullamore Traveller Primary Healthcare Project. This was done as follows:

- Local Travellers were consulted about their own health needs.
- Trainees (Traveller women) were consulted on the design of the project and cultural appropriateness (mainly achieved through evaluation of the project and inclusion of Travellers in that evaluation).
- Inclusion of trainees at steering group meetings (management meetings to organise the running of the project).

Result

Five Traveller women are currently employed as community health workers in Tullamore with the Health Service Executive (HSE) (Mid Leinster).

PEER EDUCATION

The Tullamore Traveller Primary Healthcare Project is a peer education programme. Peer education programmes are usually initiated by health or community professionals, who recruit members of the 'target' community to serve as peer educators. Peer educators are trained in relevant health information and communication skills and they, in turn, seek to promote health-enhancing knowledge and skills among their community (peers). Since the Traveller community health workers live and work in their local communities, this health education model is most likely to promote health-enhancing behaviour change. 'Only a Traveller knows a Traveller' (McInerney 2010), so Travellers are more likely to be able to share health information in a culturally appropriate way than an 'outside' health professional from the settled community, no matter how highly trained they are, trying to impart that same information. Later in this chapter, the effects of this model of health education will be outlined, proving how effective the Tullamore Traveller Primary Healthcare Project has been to date.

Although located broadly in the field of social psychology, peer education does not appear to have its roots in a particular school of thought. This is further complicated by the fact that many peer education programmes do not outline the theoretical basis for their work (Johns 2007). Most programmes draw on more than one theory base, which often overlap, making examples difficult to identify (Johns 2007). 'It can be concluded that rather than the practical application of theory, peer education rests on lay principles and assumptions. It would seem to be a method in search of a theory rather than the application of theory to practice' (Turner and Shepherd 1999:235). This may be because there is no one overarching theory explaining peer education projects. However, there are theories in social psychology, sociology and education that can be applied to it. These theories explain why peer education is beneficial. For that reason, some of them are reviewed here. From the perspective of trying to achieve best practice in community development, these theoretical perspectives can help guide community development workers in the planning and design of peer education interventions.

Theory of Reasoned Action

Derived from social psychology, the theory of reasoned action was proposed by Ajzen and Fishbein (1980; Fishbein and Ajzen 1975). This theory states that a person's voluntary behaviour is determined by his/her attitude towards that behaviour and how he/she thinks other people would view them if they performed the behaviour. Therefore, within an ethnic group, such as Travellers, it is very likely that Traveller health attitudes and beliefs will be shaped by their cultural socialisation, as well as an expectation to follow custom and practice. Health advice from a fellow Traveller will be given more importance than advice given by someone outside the Traveller community.

Social Learning Theory

This theory is largely based on the work of psychologist Albert Bandura. According to Bandura:

> Learning would be exceedingly laborious, not to mention hazardous, if people had to rely solely on the effects of their own actions to inform them what to do. Fortunately, most human behaviour is learned observationally through modelling: from observing others, one forms an idea of how new behaviours are performed, and on later occasions, this coded information serves as a guide for action. (Bandura 1977:22)

The key predictors of successful behaviour change are confidence (self-efficacy) in the ability to carry out an action and expectation that a particular goal will be achieved (outcome expectancy) (Foster *et al.* 2007). Traveller community health workers act as health role models and exemplars within their own communities. This brings about a change in health behaviours and attitudes because the Traveller community health workers are 'in' the Traveller community, so health behaviour change is initiated from within.

Diffusion of Innovations Theory

According to this theory, new information is more likely to be adopted and learned from those who are well integrated and practising the new behaviours (Johns 2007). For this reason, the Traveller Primary Healthcare Projects are successful because the Traveller community health workers are themselves Travellers. Therefore, health advice is more easily accepted by the broader Traveller community. The role of opinion leaders in a community, acting as agents for behaviour change, is a key element of this theory. Their influence on group norms or customs is predominantly seen as a result of person-to-person exchanges and discussions. Person-to-person exchanges and discussions are methods of working used by Traveller community health workers.

Theory of Participatory Education

The theory of participatory education has been important in the development of peer education (Freire 1970). Participatory or empowerment models of education are based on an understanding that powerlessness at the community or group level, and the economic and social conditions inherent in the lack of power, are major risk factors for poor health (Amaro 1995). This theory states that empowerment and full participation of the people affected by a given problem are key to behaviour change. In the context of peer education, this means that the inclusion of interactive experimental learning activities are extremely important, and peer educators can be influential teachers and role models. Peer educators should be trustworthy and credible opinion leaders within the target group. All the community health workers in the Tullamore Traveller Primary Healthcare Project are respected in their own communities, both as community health workers and also, importantly, as individuals. This is especially important in the Traveller community where the target audience is not reached through formally planned activities, but through everyday social contacts. The process of peers talking among themselves and determining a course of action is central to the success of a peer education project.

OUR STORY SO FAR: TULLAMORE TRAVELLER COMMUNITY HEALTH WORKERS

Storytelling is an important characteristic of Traveller culture. It has been used for generations to pass on norms and values, and as a way of maintaining Traveller identity. The following is the collective account of our experiences and reflections on being involved in a peer education project.

'We decided to become trainees in the Traveller Primary Healthcare Project in 1999. All of us have always had an interest in Travellers, especially in improving health and education in the local Traveller communities. Some of us were worried about what people would think of us, like who do we think we are, doing this work, and how we would be viewed. The funny thing is we didn't realise how good it would be, in fact, we had no idea what an effect a project like this could have on the lives of those in our communities and on our own lives.

'We are like liaisons between the Traveller community and the health services. There are real signs that that this project works so well. Immunisations have gone up and the number of Traveller women going for health checks has gone up. In Tullamore, more Travellers got the swine flu injection than the settled people because of the work we do. In other ways, the effects are very clear too; for example, we have apprentices coming up behind us. By apprentices we mean that the younger ones are interested and want to get involved in this type of work and these types of projects. Personally, it has given us great confidence.

'Other projects have come out of this project. Men have come on board. That's a really big thing. There will be another Primary Healthcare Project starting up soon and four men will be among the trainees. There's a Men's Horse Project running now, where male workers work with older men to try to get them involved with health services. [Funding for this project was cut in Budget 2011.] Travellers Drugs Outreach Projects have also started up. This is a taboo subject among Travellers because people are ashamed, but there is more and more of it. Suicide is also a really big thing too and that is related to conflict that is going on.

'We have done other things as well. We worked on the All-Ireland Traveller Health Status Study (2010) as peer researchers. We have given presentations to social care and nursing students about Traveller health, discrimination, and of course, the Primary Healthcare Project. We are all involved on committees for different things, such as accommodation, domestic violence, health, education, etc. We represent Travellers to get things done. Sometimes it works and sometimes it doesn't. Accommodation is still a big issue. Some Travellers are still living in terrible accommodation and on unserviced halting sites. Some of us are living in houses, some on the serviced halting site in Tullamore, and some of us on an unserviced halting site outside Tullamore. RTÉ came to the unserviced halting site a while back with a local politician, but nothing was ever done about the site. The unserviced halting sites are just not working. Things have not changed over the years. While we know we are doing really good work and making a difference, as a Traveller in this society you are really up against it.

'We do find that people react differently to what we are trying to do. For example, when we started the dental programme, which was a major success [discussed below], one family ran us, with our dental floss and toothbrushes [everyone starts laughing as they remember this]. When we went back to that family, a year later, they ran us again [again, everyone laughs]. Sometimes people, especially older people, feel insulted, even if we let them know that other families are getting toothbrushes. They think it's like charity and are too proud to take the help. Some people then are very happy – it really depends.

'One thing that is so obvious from the work we do is that everything affects health, both physical and mental. Although we are working with the local Traveller community, as community health workers, we are also living it ourselves, and have to face it ourselves. It's a 24/7 job; there's no doubt about that. We have our phones on all the time because there are ongoing problems. We cope with that by being able to bring it back here [to the Primary Healthcare Project office], and that really helps us not to burn out with this work. We have been great friends for the last twenty years, which means we can always talk with each other. While the training and work are very good, and our confidence has developed enormously as a group and individually, it is also very challenging work. It works so well because it is a peer-led project. However, that means for us, we are sometimes put in difficult circumstances. Confidentiality is a very big issue; if you let information out, it's very serious, and they [the local Traveller community] won't trust you. Sometimes it's very difficult to know how to act, especially in very sensitive circumstances, like in child protection issues, because we also live in the community. We can talk to each other, and to the primary healthcare project co-ordinators, especially about very sensitive issues. That helps!

'The work is hard in another way too because when you are visiting one family, it is not just one issue, there could be ten issues. Sometimes we go into a family and there's no work to do, just listen – the person may just need a shoulder to cry on. Because we have now been going in for years, we are trusted. People know we won't go mouthing off.

'It is very frustrating work at times, though, especially when you cannot get services quickly for families, if they need them, especially families you know are in trouble, and you just can't get a social worker to visit, or get them things they need. It could be an emergency and they won't get to see a social worker for a week.

'The job is not just about health, either. To be honest, we have to know about a lot of different things, even outside of health, because people look to us for advice. That is why it is a 24/7 job. We have had to tell families to go to MABS [Money Advice and Budgeting Service] and St Vincent de Paul. Traveller families are really badly hit by the recession. For example, they are afraid of losing their fuel allowance, uniform grants, and their Christmas bonus is also gone. We have to be able to give advice on all these issues and tell people where to go.'

Interestingly, the increasing complexity of the role of community health workers in the local Traveller community may well be a reflection of how integrated the women have become as community health workers in their own communities.

EFFECTIVENESS OF TULLAMORE TRAVELLER PRIMARY HEALTHCARE PROJECT

As a model of promoting health, the Primary Healthcare Training Programmes have received international recognition for their work:

> For achievement worthy of international recognition, this WHO 50th anniversary commemorative certificate for a national community-based health project that promotes health for all, values of equity, solidarity, participation, intersectoral approaches and partnership is awarded to the Primary Health Care for Travellers Project, Dublin, Ireland. (Jo Asvall MD, Regional Director, WHO Regional Office for Europe, September 1998 (cited in DHSSPS and DoHC 2010:25))

An example of the success of the Tullamore Traveller community health workers' work was evident in an evaluation of the oral health promotion programme for Traveller families in County Offaly. This evaluation showed a 31 per cent increase in the number of mothers adding fruit to children's lunch boxes, as a result of oral health education delivered by the Traveller community health workers (HSE – Mid Leinster 2009:1). The main foods reportedly included in children's lunch boxes post intervention were sandwiches, fruit, fruit juices and dairy products (HSE – Mid Leinster 2009:1).

Figure 12.1. Oral hygiene pre- and post-intervention

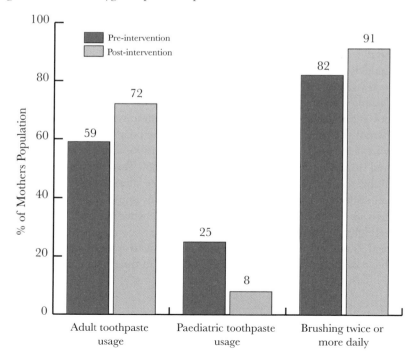

Figure 12.1 shows that 91 per cent of adults and children brush their teeth twice or more daily after intervention by the Traveller community health workers. Also, as a result of the oral health intervention, there was a 10 per cent reduction in the use of abrasive toothpastes, a 12 per cent reduction in the number of adult smokers and a 15 per cent reduction in the number of adults who take sugar in their tea (HSE – Mid Leinster 2009:2).

Another example of the success of the Tullamore Traveller community health workers is:

> We feel that cervical screening is now much higher than it would tradition-ally have been. This is a big thing because it used to be the case that people would be afraid to say the word [cancer], in case they would catch it, but now as a result of health interventions through a peer-led education project, this is no longer the case. In fact, local Traveller women are more active in trying to prevent health problems. (Traveller community health workers)

DESIGNING AND IMPLEMENTING A PEER-LED EDUCATION MODEL OF COMMUNITY DEVELOPMENT

Peer-led models of primary healthcare work because they work from the 'inside out', rather than having a more top-down approach. Table 12.1 outlines the typical steps involved in designing and implementing a peer-led education model of community development. Although this chapter focused exclusively on Traveller Primary Healthcare Projects, as an example of peer education programmes, the steps outlined in the table can be applied to any peer education programme with any community group.

CONCLUSION

The most important feature of peer education projects is that they give value to the lived experience of the peer educators and see them as experts on their own lives and, importantly, experts on what their target community is probably experiencing. Peer education projects provide those in the target community with the skills and knowledge to effectively implement a given intervention/project in that community. Not only is the intervention effective, but both the peer educators and the broader target community become empowered as a result. This augurs very well for the sustainability of the peer education programme, and possible follow-on programmes, as a result of the original initiative.

Table 12.1. Typical steps involved in designing and implementing a peer education model of community development

Step 1	Acquire domain knowledge	'Domain knowledge' is defined here as knowledge about a community or group that a community development worker hopes to work with. This knowledge means acquiring information on the target group's: • mores • norms • values and beliefs • characteristics
Step 2	Needs analysis	Conduct a needs analysis in collaboration with the target community to identify priority project areas. This can be done using quantitative or qualitative research techniques. This should be carried out in consultation with the target community through, for example, identifying and involving opinion leaders.
Step 3	Agree on a project area with the target community	Consultation including the target group, to identify what the priority area(s) should be.
Step 4	Identify peer educators	Identify peer educators within the target community, with the assistance of opinion leaders. Indeed, the opinion leaders may become the peer educators.
Step 5	Capacity building	The capacity-building stage empowers the peer educators to participate fully and as expected in their role.
Step 6	Training as peer educators	Training as peer educators to fulfil the requirements of the project as follows: 1 capacity building 2 specialised skills to meet the needs of the target community.
Step 7	Implementation	Running the peer education project.
Step 8	Evaluation	Evaluation to monitor the process of the peer-led education project should be built into the day-to-day workings of the project. The evaluation should also measure the outcomes of the project, to ensure that the project achieves its aims and objectives.

13

Community-Based Youth and Family Interventions: Moving from Evidence-Informed to Evidence-Based Practice

Cormac Forkan

CHAPTER SUMMARY
This chapter will draw a distinction between an evidence-based versus an evidence-informed way of working in youth and family interventions. It will illustrate, with the use of a case study from a community-based family support project, how such projects can introduce and utilise an evidence-based approach to their work, by engaging in a system of tracking the perceived social support levels among adolescents attending their project. Finally, the implications of this research for the practice, policy and research communities will be discussed.

INTRODUCTION

Considerable public expenditure is invested annually in a plethora of community-based youth and family interventions in Ireland. One of the primary arguments underpinning this endeavour is that early intervention with young people and families is a successful way of enabling the positive development of participants in these projects. Therefore, building a reservoir of knowledge on what works in applied practice settings is of core importance to policy makers, practitioners, young people and families themselves.

AN EVIDENCE-BASED METHODOLOGY

For many centuries, the Church's moral dynasties provided a body of secure knowledge, on the basis of which important decisions were made. However, with the development of complex political systems, particularly since the Industrial Revolution, there has been an increasing move towards adopting an evidence-based policy methodology in decision making (Pawson 2006). The coming together of 'social knowing and political doing' has been a long process (Pawson 2006). In the USA in 1969, Donald T. Campbell pointed to an ever-growing 'experimenting society', encapsulating an experimental approach to social reform.

This meant that new programmes designed to deal with specific problems were implemented and monitored to see what outcomes were achieved. Due to the continued development of this approach in contemporary society, it is normal to find that agencies and governments are less inclined to take professional views on trust, but instead demand supporting evidence. This evidential approach will hopefully avoid situations such as those from the past, when, for example, everyone in society knew for certain that the world was flat! However, alongside the literature supporting an evidence-based approach to policy, there are some who argue that evidence can be cynically exploited and used in the interests of those in power (Pawson 2006). For example, the Iraq War that began in 2003 was supported on the grounds of evidence pointing to the existence of weapons of mass destruction – evidence that was later disproved by impartial experts.

EVIDENCE-BASED VERSUS EVIDENCE-INFORMED PRACTICE

There is a growing demand for community-based youth and family interventions to be evidence-based, which underlines a shift towards more results-based accountability in all facets of life (Coleman *et al.* 2003). Using an evidence-based approach provides the potential for more practitioners to use evidence in their daily work. An evidence-based approach is appealing since it is grounded in rationality, and is focused on quality of care and cost-effectiveness (Usher and Wildfire 2003). In the clinical setting, an evidence-based approach brings services more in line with the best available clinical science evidence, using practices that are shown to be safe and effective (Chaffin and Friedrich 2004). The roots of evidence-based practice can be found primarily in evidence-based healthcare, but more recently in social work and child welfare. As suggested by Rosen (2003), a growing evidence base emanating from the implementation of evidence-based practice can guide the development, implementation and evaluation of new programmes and practices.

When discussing evidence-based practice, the core question is, of course, what constitutes evidence? Kazdin and Weisz (2003) define 'evidence' as replicable procedures that have outcomes that can be reproduced by others. In the world of the sciences, whether social or natural, the most reliable form of evidence is generated using a randomised control trial (RCT). For Chaffin and Friedrich (2004:1098), evidence-based practice is 'the competent and high-fidelity implementation of practices that have been demonstrated safe and effective, usually in randomised control trials'. Evidence-*informed* practices differ from evidence-based practices in that they are more subjective, driven by personal values and subject to the social contexts of the time. In general, youth care practice in the contemporary world is largely evidence-informed (Veerman and van Yperen 2007).

There are obvious dangers with evidence-informed practice. One example is from the Scared Straight Boot Camps run for juvenile delinquents in the USA.

Table 13.1. Contrasting evidence-based practice with traditional evidence-informed practice

	Traditional evidence-informed practice	Evidence-based practice
1 Source of knowledge	• Accumulated subjective experience with individual cases • Opinion about practice outcomes emphasised – 'In my experience . . .'	• Well-designed, randomised trials and other controlled clinical research • Facts about practice outcomes emphasised – 'The data show that . . .'
2 Knowledge location and access	• Hierarchical • Knowledge is possessed by opinion leaders and gurus • Charismatic expert driven	• Democratic • Knowledge is available to anyone willing to read the published scientific research or research reviews • IT-driven
3 Method of achieving progress	• Haphazard, fortuitous • Based on changing values, fads, fashions and leaders	• Systematic, predictable • Based on incremental and cumulative programmes of outcome research
4 Practitioner expertise	• Quasi-mystical personal qualities and intuition	• Specific, teachable, learnable skills and behaviour
5 View of practice	• Art • Creative artistic process with fluid boundaries	• Craftsmanship • Creativity within the boundaries of the supported models and protocols
6 Research–practice link	• Indirect • Inferential	• Direct • Integral and fundamental to practice
7 How research is summarised and applied to practice	• Individual subjective practitioner synthesis of whatever literature is consumed	• Best practices work group or collaborative summary based on exhaustive reviews of the outcome research and meta-analysis
8 Programme evaluation	• Inputs (credentials of practitioners) • Outputs (number of clients served, number of service units delivered)	• Outcomes (measurable 'bottom-line' client benefits)
9 Location of research	• Mostly in laboratory settings and divorced from practice	• Field clients routinely enrolled in trials in order to test benefits and refine services
10 Quality control	• Focuses on how well service rationales are conceptualised and the credentials of who provides them	• Focuses on how well services are behaviourally delivered vis-à-vis a prescriptive protocol
11 Practice visibility	• Actual practice is seldom observed by anyone other than the practitioner and the client	• Direct peer or consultant observation of actual practice and specific feedback is common
12 Assumptions about outcomes	• Faith • Service programmes in general are seen as good and are assumed to be beneficial	• Scepticism • Knowledge that interventions may be inert or even harmful • Benefit must be empirically demonstrated, not assumed

Source: adapted from Chaffin and Friedrich 2004:1101.

After undergoing controlled outcomes research, it was confirmed that the boot camps did not produce any better outcomes, and often produced worse ones (Petrosino et al. 2000). Therefore, there is no way of knowing what works with evidence-informed practice and, more important, no way to separate out the things that work from those that do not. Considering this, Chaffin and Friedrich (2004:1100) suggest that, 'in the traditional evidence-informed practice culture, we can expect only that tomorrow's interventions will look different from today's – we cannot confidently expect that they will work any better'.

Table 13.1 is taken from Chaffin and Friedrich (2004); it contrasts an evidence-based approach with traditional evidence-informed practice. With the traditional approach, knowledge is generated from subjective experience with individual cases, as distinct from an RCT used in evidence-based practice. In evidence-informed practice, progress can be haphazard, while in evidence-based practice it is systematic and predictable. Therefore, in a traditional approach, assumptions about the outcomes are based on faith rather than on the empirically demonstrated outcomes generated by an evidence-based approach.

Despite the obvious benefits of using evidence-based practice, Chaffin and Friedrich (2004) argue that the full implementation of this approach into everyday practice faces a number of barriers. For example, funding is a key issue: many funders of child-based programmes do not allow for costs of adapting new technologies, initial training, supervision and quality monitoring. In addition, limited leadership in specific organisations may lead to no change occurring, further compounded by a lack of incentives that link rewards, such as funding, to client outcomes. The absence of turnkey training packages in evidence-based practice models impedes institutional change, as does the resistant practitioner who may feel that the implementation of this approach would involve them surrendering their creativity and flexibility.

When mining the existing literature to find the level of evidential support for interventions for children and adolescents, Kazdin (2000) found that there were 1,500 controlled investigations of interventions. After a meta-analysis of these studies, the effect size was shown to range from 0.40 to 0.80, with a mean of 0.70. These results show a moderate to large effect size. However, only 40–50 of those interventions underwent RCT-type evaluations. Therefore, a considerable number of the interventions used with young people on an everyday basis have no RCT-based empirically sound information (Veerman and van Yperen 2007). In addition, Weisz et al. (1992) suggest that the positive picture of the effects of youth care may be inflated due to the over-inclusion of well-controlled studies conducted in specialised settings carefully created for the studies in question. For example, the chosen interventions may involve ten sessions or fewer; often only address one problem; have a clearly defined manual to direct the work; and may involve therapists who are well trained and supervised. This is all in contrast to the multiple-problem scenarios facing real on-the-ground youth care workers. Similarly, the results of a review of ten quasi-experimental studies performed in practice between 1942 and 1993 found the effect sizes to be no more than 0.01, with a range of –0.40 to 0.29 (Weisz *et al.* 1992). Therefore, there is very little empirical support for interventions used in practice. These results were supported by another study with four additional interventions (Weisz and Jensen 2001).

It is clear, therefore, that in reality only a few interventions in the area of youth and family support have been, or will ever be, evaluated using an RCT. Therefore, the majority of evidence created by projects relating to the effectiveness of their interventions will at best be evidence-informed and not evidence-based. To bridge the gap between these two forms of evidence, Veerman and van Yperen (2007) present a model in which evidence generated from youth and family-based projects could be categorised on a four-point scale, ranging from minimum-level evidence to the higher-end RCT 'gold standard' level of evidence. They argue that it is not as simple as providing a 'Yes/No' approach to all interventions with regard to their effectiveness. Instead, four different levels of evidence can be gathered and utilised. These are discussed briefly below (see also Table 13.2).

Level 1 – Descriptive Evidence

This type of evidence would involve a clear description of the core elements of an intervention, such as goals, activities and target groups. The types of research that can generate this level of evidence range from analysis of documents to descriptive studies. When this descriptive evidence is generated, it can be very relevant to practitioners: it can provide an overview of the interventions, as well as an inventory of the core elements that can more easily be communicated to clients, students, colleagues and managers. Descriptive evidence can also provide information on the 'potential' effectiveness of interventions.

Level 2 – Theoretical Evidence

Theoretical evidence provides a more sophisticated and higher level of evidence for practitioners than descriptive evidence. Theoretical evidence identifies both a sound theory that underpins the intervention, and how and why this particular intervention will lead to specific outcomes. A well-articulated theory underpinning an intervention will help to explain why a particular course of action may be expected to be beneficial to a client. Reviews, meta-analyses and expert knowledge studies are the main types of research used in generating this level of evidence. Theoretical evidence provides a plausible explanation for the potential effectiveness of interventions.

Level 3 – Indicative Evidence

Indicative evidence refers to a situation where a systematic evaluation shows that desired changes have occurred with the clients engaged with the intervention. In most cases, a treatment may be considered successful when 95 per cent of the clients are satisfied, when the treatment goals are achieved in 90 per cent of cases and when 80 per cent of cases show behaviour within a range according to a standardised assessment instrument (Veerman and van Yperen 2007). However, at this level of evidence, it is still unclear which elements of the intervention 'cause' the outcome(s). Nevertheless, research at this level can provide good preliminary evidence, when the data have been collected across multiple sites and have been replicated on a number of occasions. Therefore, indicative evidence illustrates the functionality of a particular approach. The types of research that can generate this level of evidence range from client-based satisfaction studies and monitoring studies, to more macro benchmark studies and quasi-experimental studies. In Table 13.2, those methods mentioned above the dotted line have more potential to generate higher levels of indicative knowledge than those methods below the line.

Level 4 – Causal Evidence

With causal evidence, it is possible to judge whether or not a particular intervention is efficacious. The core question that this level of evidence can answer is whether the intervention itself has caused the outcome. An RCT or repeated case studies research approach can reveal the elements of the intervention that are responsible for certain outcomes being achieved.

DEVELOPING AN EVIDENCE-BASED APPROACH: A CASE STUDY

The author's interest in evidence-based practice was sparked during his time working as a frontline youth worker for Foróige, the national youth development organisation in Ireland, during the 1990s. During this work, the author was acutely aware that he was practice rich but evidence poor. This experience, coupled with his experience in academia since then, has fostered an interest in the need to develop systems to understand outcomes for children in a more evidence-based way.

Curious to investigate an evidence-based approach in Ireland, the author located a community-based family support project that was willing to participate in the study. The first task undertaken was to examine the nature of data collected on the outcomes of those attending the project. The author found that, apart from the collation of throughput data, which was complemented by qualitative commentary on programme delivery, no outcomes data were routinely collected by the project staff. Therefore, the project and its various programmes were being run along evidence-informed lines.

It was agreed with the staff that, given this situation, the study would *explore how the project could introduce and utilise an evidence-based approach to their work, by engaging in a system of tracking the perceived social support levels among adolescents*

Table 13.2. Levels of evidence, parameters of evidence, types of research and effectiveness of interventions

Levels of evidence	Parameters of evidence	Types of research	Effectiveness of interventions
4 Causal	As in 1, 2 and 3, but there is now sound and substantial evidence that the outcome is caused by the intervention and/or clear evidence showing which ingredients of the intervention are responsible for the outcome.	• RCT • Repeated case studies (N = 1 designs)	Efficacious
3 Indicative	As in 1 and 2, but it has now been demonstrated that the intervention clearly leads to the desired outcomes (e.g. goals are attained, target problems decrease, competencies increase, clients are satisfied).	• Quasi-experimental studies • Theory of change studies • Norm-referenced approaches .... • Benchmark studies • Client satisfaction studies • Goal attainment studies • Monitoring studies • Quality assurance studies	Functional
2 Theoretical	As in 1, but the intervention now has a plausible rationale (i.e. a programme theory) to explain why it should work with whom.	• Reviews • Meta-analyses • Expert knowledge studies	Plausible
1 Descriptive	The essential elements of the intervention (e.g. goals, target groups, methods and activities, requirements) have been made explicit.	• Descriptive studies • Observational studies • Analysis of documents • Conduct of interviews	Potential

Source: Veerman and van Yperen 2007.

attending the project over a one-year period. While the data generated would not be at Level 4 in Veerman's and van Yperen's (2007) model, the methodology chosen would generate *indicative evidence* (at Level 3) for the project, which would help them to become evidence-based in their work.

Social Support

Groundbreaking social research conducted in 1967 (Holmes and Rahe 1967) on the effect of life stress on health proved that those with the higher levels of social support would suffer fewer negative health outcomes following stressful events than those with lower levels of social support. With the publication of two pivotal articles, one by Sidney Cobb (1976) and one by John Cassel (1976), the concept of social support was for the first time introduced to a global audience. Both authors pointed out the centrality of social relationships and support in the maintenance of health and as a buffer to stress (House *et al.* 1988). In addition, Cassel (1976) argued that social support is a protective factor, provided by important network members, that helps modify a person's biological resistance to disease.

For Cobb (1976), social support is information held by the subject whereby they believe that they are cared for, which he refers to as emotional support. It is also information held by the subject that they are esteemed and valued, referred to as 'esteem support', as well as information held by the subject that they belong to a network of communication and mutual obligation. For Cobb, social support can be found at work during the major periods of transition in a person's life. The definition of social support in contemporary theory defines it as 'both the structures of an individual's social life (for example, group membership or existence of familial ties) and the more explicit functions they may serve (for example, provision of useful advice or emotional support)' (Uchino 2004; Pinkerton and Dolan 2007). As suggested by Cutrona (1996), most research on social support shows that those who have received it have better mental health, fewer physical health problems and lower rates of mortality.

Given the importance of understanding the levels and types of social support in the lives of the adolescents with whom it works, the project agreed that *tracking the perceived social support levels among adolescents attending the project over a one-year period* would be useful. To enable this, the social provisions scale or SPS (Cutrona and Russell 1987) was used (see Appendix 1, below). A major factor leading to the decision to use the SPS in this study was that in 2002, Cutrona and Dolan adapted the original SPS and produced the SPS child version for use with children and adolescents in Ireland.

The SPS measures both the sources (perceived level of support from friends, parents, siblings and other adults) and the types (concrete, emotional, esteem and advice) of perceived support (Dolan 2003). In an attempt to simplify and operationalise the concept of social support, Cutrona and Russell (1990), Cutrona (2000) and Barrera (2000) identified four main types of support:

1   *Concrete support* – physical and practical assistance given to others, e.g. childminding for a family member to free them to do a particular task.
2   *Emotional support* – typified by being there for someone, providing a listening ear, empathising with the person in relation to a specific event. This type of

support provides the recipient with a sense of acceptance, which may help strengthen their self-esteem during a challenge (Uchino 2004).

3   *Advice support* – dual-sided support, since the advice given is more than information that may be required by the person; the information may also provide them with emotional reassurance.

4   *Esteem support* – typified by support that helps the recipient see that they are valued and have worth.

After reviewing the categories of young people involved in the project, it was decided to invite all young people attending the project to participate in the study. A list of the twenty-two potential participants was drawn up and a letter sent to each child's parents, seeking consent for their child to be involved in the study. The mean age of this group was 13 years of age. Following the receipt of written parental consent allowing the adolescents (n = 22) to participate in the study, the author administered the SPS on a one-to-one basis with each young person. By Time 2 (T2), one year later, eighteen of the twenty-two had participated in the data collection. This resulted in a retention rate of 82 per cent being achieved between T1 and T2.

Presentation of Results

Using the data corresponding to the 'Yes' rating from the SPS, it was possible to investigate the difference in the perceived social support scores by sources and types for the respondents between T1 and T2 (see Table 13.3). Parents were the greatest source of support, both at T1 (93 per cent) and T2 (87 per cent), and had dropped by 6 per cent between these two periods. Friends were the second best source of support, achieving an average support score of 85 per cent at T1, while this had declined to 83 per cent at T2. Other adults were the second last supporter, accounting for 93 per cent of support at T1, falling to 74 per cent at T2. Siblings were by far the least supportive of the respondents, scoring 76 per cent at T1 and falling to 64 per cent at T2.

Using the data in Table 13.3, it was also possible to determine the rate of change of the type of support between T1 and T2 by source of support. The horizontal line marked '0' in Figure 13.1 represents no change at T2 in the extent of support. Therefore, any point above the line indicates a trend towards an increase in support, while below the line indicates a trend towards a drop in support. The key findings are:

- *Concrete support* had worsened at T2 for all sources of support, with the largest decrease being from siblings (–20 per cent).
- *Emotional support* had worsened at T2 for all sources of support, with the largest decrease being from other adults (–8 per cent).
- *Esteem support* increased for parents (1 per cent) and increased by 14 per cent for friends, while falling by 30 per cent for other adults and by 7 per cent for siblings.

- *Advice support* from all sources fell sharply at T2, with friends falling by 14 per cent, siblings by 16 per cent, parents by 17 per cent and other adults by 23 per cent.

Table 13.3. Changes in the mean perceived social support score at T1 and T2, by sources and types of support for respondents

Support type	Parents (%)	Friends (%)	Other adults (%)	Siblings (%)
Concrete support at T1	91	95	100	81
Emotional support at T1	100	91	91	81
Esteem support at T1	82	64	86	68
Advice support at T1	100	91	95	72
Total score	373	341	372	302
Mean score	93	85	93	76
Concrete support T2	89	89	83	61
T2–T1 range	–2	–6	–17	–20
Emotional support T2	94	89	83	77
T2–T1 range	–6	–2	–8	–4
Esteem support T2	83	78	56	61
T2–T1 range	+1	+14	–30	–7
Advice support T2	83	77	72	56
T2–T1 range	–17	–14	–23	–16
Total score	349	333	294	255
Mean score	87	83	74	64

Discussion of Findings

Prior to the study, the project did not have a mechanism in place for monitoring outcomes for the adolescents with whom it worked and was, therefore, evidence-informed rather than being evidence-based. However, after tracking the perceived social support of these adolescents over a one-year period, a number of key findings emerged.

1 Perceived Availability of High Levels of Social Support Over Time

The majority of participants perceived the availability of high levels of social support. More importantly, the perception of high levels of social support was

Figure 13.1. Changes in the mean perceived social support score between T1 and T2, by sources and types of support for respondents

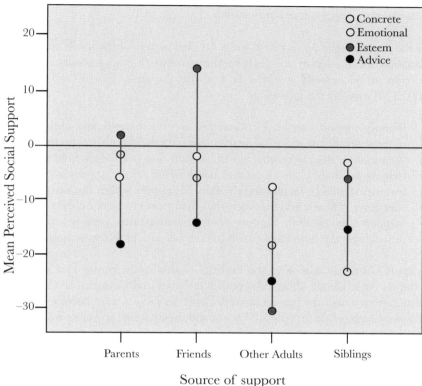

Source of support

consistent over the period of the study (one year). This finding is important because it shows that the project was associated with maintaining high levels of perceived social support for the adolescents over the duration of the study.

2 Parents Perceived as the Strongest Source of Social Support

The data collected using the SPS child version clearly shows the pivotal role of parents in the adolescents' lives. The results reveal that adolescents perceived their parents to be the greatest source of social support for them, both at T1 and T2. This is an important finding because it negates the traditional 'storm and stress' perception of adolescents' relationships with their parents.

3 Patterns in Perceived Social Support from Other Sources

(a) *Friends:* the data showed that adolescents perceived their friends to be their second best source of support (after parents).

(b) *Other adults and siblings:* the results showed that adolescents perceived other adults as their third source of perceived support (after parents and friends). Siblings were perceived to be the worst source of social support across all four types of support explored in this study.

For the first time the project now had a detailed picture of the levels and types of perceived social support for each of the participating adolescents. The next question raised by staff was how best to use the data. To this end, Cutrona (2000:120) suggests the following:

> Family support can be a critical resource for parents and children who are striving to overcome adverse circumstances. However, supportive interventions are not always effective . . . support is most effective from those with whom we share close emotional bonds. Thus, the . . . professional's first priority should be facilitating the **flow of support** within the existing social networks of family and friends, rather than trying to 'graft on' new sources of support. In general, support that communicates genuine caring, yet encourages the individual to solve his or her own problems is most effective.

To apply Cutrona's advice to the findings of this study, Figure 13.2 offers two scenarios. An evidence-informed approach is shown in the diagram on the left, the position from which the project started. Here, the project was unable to facilitate the *flow of support* between the adolescent and their parents and close supporters as they did not have outcomes-based data. The project could only offer generic, gut-based support, rather than needs-led, evidence-based support, based on the individual needs of the adolescent participants. Therefore, due to the lack of data, the project's approach could be described as more hit-and-miss, represented in the diagram on the left by the solid arrowed lines. However, occasionally, as is the case in projects that are evidence-informed, the intervention provided does exactly meet the need of the adolescent, characterised in the diagram by a dotted arrowed line.

The evidence-based approach being explored by this study is shown in the diagram on the right of Figure 13.2. Due to the longitudinal measurement of the adolescent's perceived social support, the project can use the data to create interventions that are optimally matched to the needs of the adolescents. The end result is that the project can accurately facilitate the flow of support within the existing social networks of the young person and enable a sustainable ecological support network for the person into the future.

Implications for Practice, Policy and Research

It is the opinion of the author that community-based youth and family interventions in Ireland have a number of choices for the future (Davis and Smith 2009). First,

Figure 13.2. Difference between using an evidence-based approach and an evidence-informed approach

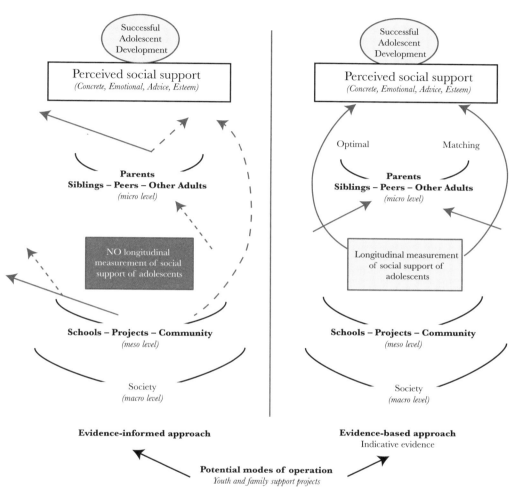

they can opt to do nothing, maintain the status quo and decide not to engage in an evidence-based approach to their work. Second, they can tinker at the edges of their work and perhaps partly introduce an evidence-based approach. Alternatively, they can opt for an evidence-based approach and radically overhaul their way of doing business. If this last direction is chosen, the ensuing evidence-based approach will initiate a discussion, particularly needed in Ireland, on how best to create an agreed framework of evidence for the sector (Canavan 2009). This is very much in line with the *Agenda for Children's Services* (Office of the Minister for Children 2007), which re-emphasises the government's commitment to the delivery of evidence-based services to children, families and their communities.

Since the findings of this research have implications for the practice, policy and research communities, the author has created a number of messages for each sector to consider. It is hoped that these will encourage all concerned with community-based youth and family projects to consider how they can introduce and utilise an evidence-based approach in their work, particularly by engaging in a system of tracking the social support levels among service users for service design and provision.

Messages for Practice

Use an evidence-based approach. This study highlights the usefulness of community-based youth and family projects engaging in the measurement of perceived social support for adolescents as a tool in evidence-based practice. An evidence-based approach can help practitioners identify outcomes, plan interventions and monitor results in a coherent and systematic way. Practitioners who engage in this way of working are also allowing themselves to critically reflect on their practice. This shows a commitment to ensuring that their practice does make a difference (Sanders and Munford 2006). In addition, an evidence-based approach can help them with their reporting to their funders. Social support measurement will also help practitioners identify gaps in perceived social support for adolescents with whom they work. Practitioners can then more effectively increase the flow of support from informal sources and thus encourage natural sources of support. Working in this manner will mobilise support for adolescents from within the space where they live their lives (Davis and Smith 2009).

- *Training needs:* To develop an evidence-based approach, practitioners will need to identify their training needs and engage in the necessary training.
- *An ecological approach:* This study has shown the overwhelming importance of informal supporters in the lives of the adolescent participants. Parents hold the central position in this regard. Therefore, all projects that engage with adolescents need to work with members of the adolescents' social ecology, namely their parents, friends, siblings and other adults. As Dolan (2003:239) suggests, the motto for practice needs to be 'working with parents as a way of working with adolescents'.
- *Supporting parents:* To be 'good enough' parents and continue being central supporters of adolescents, practitioners can help increase the flow of informal support for parents themselves, as well as providing formal support when needed.
- *Bonds with friends:* Friends were identified as a strong source of perceived support for the adolescent participants in this study. Therefore, while working with adolescents, practitioners can consciously enable adolescents to develop closer bonds with their friends.
- *Relationship with siblings and other adults:* Siblings were identified as the weakest perceived source of support among the adolescents in the study. Awareness of

this fact will lead practitioners to investigate whether this is the case in their own settings and, if so, why. If it is the case, they could introduce ways to enable an increased flow of support from this source of support. Conflict resolution-type interventions could be used to help overcome difficulties between siblings. Strengthening the relationship between adolescents and other adults in their social ecology is also a core task for practitioners.

Messages for Policy Makers

- *Requiring an evidence-based approach:* In light of the drive towards early intervention and prevention, policy makers and funders need to require all community-based youth and family projects that work with adolescents to approach service design and provision in an evidence-based way. This model of working dovetails with the seven National Service Outcomes for Children in Ireland and the way of working as outlined in the *Agenda for Children's Services* (Office of the Minister for Children 2007).
- *Sustainability:* To create a culture of evidence-based practice in community-based youth and family projects, it will be necessary to upskill and train practitioners. Policy makers will need to ensure that opportunities for this are created so that the work of evidence-based practice can be sustained.
- *An ecological approach:* As noted above, informal supporters have an overwhelming importance in the lives of adolescents. Therefore, policy needs to investigate ways of ensuring that all projects that engage with adolescents work with members of their social ecology, namely their parents, friends, siblings and other adults.

Messages for Research

- *Tentative practice design framework:* This study has introduced a tentative model for developing and using an evidence-based approach in youth and family projects. In collaboration with the practice world, the research community can now test this framework through additional studies, preferably designed to be longitudinal in nature.
- *Dissemination of and access to research findings:* In any given year, multiple studies relevant to practitioners who work with adolescents are conducted both in Ireland and internationally. However, due to the often guarded nature of the academic publishing system and distribution, practitioners never get access to this cutting-edge knowledge. The research community and practitioners need to investigate ways of overcoming this issue.
- *Adolescent-friendly methodologies:* A core duty of the research world is to continually investigate how to improve research methodologies suitable for research with adolescents. This will involve focusing on both qualitative and quantitative approaches and tools.

CONCLUSION

This chapter set out to address three areas. The first of these was to draw a distinction between an evidence-based versus an evidence-informed way of working in youth and family interventions. Second, with the use of a case study from a community-based family support project, the chapter illustrated how such projects can introduce and utilise an evidence-based approach to their work, by engaging in a system of tracking the perceived social support levels among adolescents attending their project. Third, the chapter discussed the implications of this research for the practice, policy and research communities.

APPENDIX 1. SOCIAL PROVISIONS SCALE (SPS CHILD VERSION)

The tool shown here is not the full child-friendly version as developed by Cutrona and Dolan. Please contact the author of this chapter at cormac.forkan@nuigalway.ie for more information on how to access the full tool.

Official Use Only

Respondent Number: _____   Age: _____ Years

Sex of Respondent :   M   F   Date: / /

Total: _____

In answering the next 4 questions, please think about your current relationships with your *friends*. If you feel a question accurately describes your relationships with your friends, you would say 'yes'. If the question does not describe your relationships, you would say 'no'. If you cannot decide whether the question describes your relationships with your friends, you may say 'sometimes'.

1 Are there friends you can depend on to help you, if you really need it?
   NO   SOMETIMES   YES

2 Do your relationships with your friends provide you with a sense of acceptance and happiness?
   NO   SOMETIMES   YES

3 Do you feel your talents and abilities are recognised by your friends?
   NO   SOMETIMES   YES

4 Is there a friend you could trust to turn to for advice, if you were having problems?
   NO   SOMETIMES   YES

In answering the next set of questions, please think about your current relationships with your parent(s)/carer.

5   Can you depend on your parent(s)/carer to help you, if you really need it?
NO   SOMETIMES   YES

6   Do your relationships with your parent(s)/carer provide you with a sense of acceptance and happiness?
NO   SOMETIMES   YES

7   Do you feel your talents and abilities are recognised by your parent(s)/carer?
NO   SOMETIMES   YES

8   Could you turn to your parent(s)/carer for advice, if you were having problems?
NO   SOMETIMES   YES

In answering the next set of questions, please think about your current relationships with your brother(s) and/or sisters(s).

9   Can you depend on your brother(s)/sister(s) to help you, if you really need it?
NO   SOMETIMES   YES

10 Do your relationships with your brother(s)/sister(s) provide you with a sense of acceptance and happiness?
NO   SOMETIMES   YES

11 Do you feel your talents and abilities are recognised by your brother(s)/sister(s)?
NO   SOMETIMES   YES

12 Could you turn to your brother(s)/sister(s) for advice, if you were having problems?
NO   SOMETIMES   YES

In answering the next set of questions, please think about your current relationships with any other adult person in your community, for example a teacher, sports coach or other adult who you know and who supports you.

13 Can you depend on other adult(s) you know to help you, if you really need it?
NO   SOMETIMES   YES

14 Do your relationships with this adult(s) provide you with a sense of acceptance and happiness?
NO   SOMETIMES   YES

15 Do you feel your talents and abilities are recognised by this adult?
NO   SOMETIMES   YES

16 Could you turn to another adult for advice, if you were having problems?
NO   SOMETIMES   YES

Evaluation as a Mechanism for Empowerment in Community Development Practice

Ashling Jackson

> All truths are easy to understand once they are discovered; the point is to
> discover them.
>
> (Galileo [1632] 1967)

CHAPTER OBJECTIVES

This chapter will discuss the merits of empowerment evaluations for community
development practice. The stages involved in designing and implementing an
empowerment evaluation will be documented. Barriers to conducting empowerment
evaluations and possible solutions to overcome these will be outlined. Finally, how
to assess whether empowerment evaluation works will also be described.

INTRODUCTION

Well-conducted evaluations are very important in community development
practice to gauge how successful a project is, identify areas that require
improvement, and often to ensure continued funding of a project. Evaluation can
be defined as the systematic analysis and interpretation of how a community
development project/intervention operates and the effects of it. There are many
types of evaluations which can be used in community development practice. First,
traditional evaluation is conducted by someone external to a community
development project who manages the evaluation study to assess the merits of a
project and makes recommendations for improvement, if necessary. In this type of
evaluation, stakeholders are the object of study in the evaluation. Second,
collaborative evaluation is 'any evaluation in which there is a significant degree of
collaboration or cooperation between evaluators and stakeholders in planning
and/or conducting the evaluation' (Cousins *et al.* 1996:210). Here, stakeholders are
the object of study but also participate in the evaluation process. Third is
participatory evaluation, whose roots are in the citizen participation programmes
that emerged in the United States in the 1960s, and in a growing awareness of the

importance of representing multiple perspectives in political decision-making (Plottu and Plottu 2009). 'Process use' is an important characteristic here. Process use means that there is a focus on the impact of participating in the evaluation process in addition to generating findings and evaluation reports (Díaz-Puente *et al.* 2007). Last, an *empowerment* evaluation, which is a type of participatory evaluation, occurs when the target community takes an active role in the evaluation. The community is not passive in the evaluation process, nor is it merely collaborating, but instead is actively taking part and engaged in a constant process of consultation with the evaluators. In this type of evaluation, the evaluator may plan, manage and provide training to the target community, so that they are enabled to participate in the evaluation, but the target community also takes a lead in the evaluation process. When used like this, evaluation becomes a mechanism for empowerment. If we believe that community development is a 'process whereby those who are marginalised and excluded are enabled to gain in self confidence, to join with others and to participate in actions to change their situation and to tackle the problems that face their community' (Motherway 2006:2), then for an evaluation to be 'community development' in nature, the evaluation should be empowering, i.e. designed and conducted in consultation and partnership *with and by* the target community.

In this chapter, I will take a closer look at empowerment evaluation, stages of an empowerment evaluation, barriers to empowerment evaluation and how they can be overcome, as well as outlining criteria against which empowerment evaluations can be measured to see how effective they are. Finally, and in conclusion, I will argue that empowerment evaluations may well be a cost-effective approach to evaluation in community development practice.

A CLOSER LOOK AT EMPOWERMENT EVALUATION

Fetterman and Wandersman (2005:28) define empowerment evaluation as an:

> . . . evaluation approach that increases the probability of achieving programme success by:
> 1   Providing programme stakeholders with tools for assessing the planning, implementation and self-evaluation of their programme and
> 2   Mainstreaming evaluation as part of the planning and management of the programme/organisation.

'Although there are many participatory evaluation approaches, empowerment evaluation places an explicit emphasis on building the evaluation capacity of individuals and organisations, so that the evaluation is built into the day to day management practices of organisations' (Cox *et al.* 2010:11). Empowerment evaluation gives the stakeholders the primary role in the evaluation activities (Patton 2008), focusing on building their capacities and training them to conduct their own evaluations. So from a community development perspective, evaluation can in itself be a tool to 'enable [the target community] to gain in self confidence, to join with others and to participate in actions to change their situation and to tackle the problems that face their community' (Motherway 2006:2). If evaluation is used in this way, there can be no doubt that it will supplement other capacity-building initiatives in a community development project.

Empowerment evaluation shares some values and methods with other approaches to evaluation, including traditional evaluation and collaborative and participatory evaluation. However, according to Wandersman *et al.* (2005), it is the set of empowerment evaluation principles considered in their entirety that distinguishes it from other evaluation approaches. These principles of empowerment evaluation make empowerment evaluations very suitable for community development projects, and are summarised under the headings 'Direct outcomes for participants', 'Direct outcomes for the community' and 'Direct outcomes for society' in Table 14.1.

Table 14.1. Direct outcomes for participants, direct outcomes for the community and direct outcomes for society as a result of empowerment evaluations

Direct outcomes for participants	Direct outcomes for the community	Direct outcomes for society
Dialogue The empowerment evaluation should encourage extensive exchange and dialogue between and within interest groups. The aim is to enhance understanding of interests, values and views amongst the various participants (House 2005).	**Inclusion** This means working with under-represented and powerless groups, not just sponsors and well-organised groups, as key stakeholders in the evaluation process. This does not mean that every interest, value or view concerned will be given equal weight, merely that all relevant ones should be considered in designing and conducting the evaluation (House 2005). Because the community owns the process of evaluation and the completed evaluation study, the inclusion of the community is guaranteed. This is very important for groups who are marginalised, or typically have no voice in society.	**Democratic participation** 'As with the principles of community ownership and inclusion, democratic participation is a principle that is seen as critical for establishing stakeholder buy-in. Democratic buy-in also: 1 underscores the importance of deliberation and authentic collaboration as a critical process for maximizing use of the skills and knowledge that exist in the community and 2 emphasizes that fairness and due process are fundamental parts of the empowerment evaluation process' (Wandersman *et al.* 2005:33).
Deliberation The aim of an empowerment evaluation is to achieve, through rational discussion, a set of outcomes, values and conclusions involving all those concerned. It may be only through participation in the empowerment evaluation process that stakeholders are able to formulate and construct their interest in interaction with others (House 2005).	**Community knowledge** Community members have a distinct advantage over those not living, or not involved, in their communities. They have real community knowledge from their community experience. Therefore, their involvement in empowerment evaluations can bring an added value dimension to the final evaluation report.	**Social justice** Empowerment evaluation gives marginalised communities the tools to evaluate their own programmes and a sense of control that they may not traditionally have. 'The aim of empowerment evaluation is to make a difference with an eye towards the larger social good' (Wandersman *et al.* 2005:34).

Direct outcomes for participants	Direct outcomes for the community	Direct outcomes for society
Capacity building As an empowerment evaluation gives the stakeholders the primary role in the evaluation activities (Patton 2008), the evaluation process itself can be used as a capacity-building initiative. Increasing stakeholder ability to plan, implement and monitor evaluations means that evaluation expertise can build up in a community development project. This expertise, while benefiting the current empowerment evaluation project, can also be used to carry out subsequent evaluations.	**Community ownership** Empowerment evaluation is inclusive and does not view stakeholders, especially the target community, as passive objects to be researched. Instead, the community shapes the evaluation process, owning the process of evaluation and the completed evaluation study.	
	Evidence-based strategies 'Empowerment evaluators believe that part of their role is to assist stakeholders in combining evidence-based knowledge – regarding what works – and the communities' knowledge of context and participation when planning and implementing interventions' (Wandersman *et al.* 2005:35). If this occurs, which is inevitable in an empowerment evaluation, recommendations from an empowerment evaluation are likely to be practical, realistic and feasible.	
	Organisational learning For an empowerment evaluation to work, organisations must to willing to engage in and, importantly, trust the empowerment evaluation process	
	Accountability Not only does an empowerment evaluation build evaluation capacity among stakeholders, especially the target community, but it must also be accountable, i.e. demonstrate clearly the outcomes of a programme/ intervention, what needs to be improved, can the programme be replicated/expanded and how can this be done?	

Source: Wandersman *et al.* 2005.

According to Plottu and Plottu (2009), the aim of empowerment evaluations is to produce an evaluation process which is value-free. This means that empowerment evaluations should try to be independent of the value systems and objectives of any particular stakeholder. Plottu and Plottu (2009) also raise the question, though, as to whether empowerment evaluations can ever actually achieve value-free judgements on the process and outcome of the evaluation study. The evaluator as a stakeholder will contribute to the evolution of the decision process and the construction of the final choice (Plottu and Plottu 2009). 'It is not possible for evaluators to assume a position on the sidelines . . . in the hope that our practice will not perturb the situation, or influence it via some form of unwanted bias' (Greene 2002:2–3). It can be argued that empowerment evaluations not only empower those who are marginalised and excluded, i.e. the target community, through the actual process of conducting the evaluation, but are also more likely to reflect the views of *all* stakeholders. So while there is no guarantee that they will be completely value-free, they are far more likely to reflect the views of the stakeholders/community than other types of evaluation. It is also more likely that stakeholders will adhere to the recommendations of the evaluation if they themselves have agreed on, and participated in, its formulation and implementation.

In empowerment evaluations, active participation, capacity building and learning by all relevant actors become a fundamental, rather than an instrumental condition, and the approach focuses on facilitating collective rather than individual learning. For this very reason, empowerment evaluations are ideal for community development settings, as the ethos of a community development process is to empower individuals and communities through engagement and participation.

CARRYING OUT AN EMPOWERMENT EVALUATION

Baur *et al.* (2010) highlight the importance of fostering mutual understanding and learning processes in addressing the challenges of working with stakeholders in unequal relationships. The inclusion and full participation of marginalised groups in evaluation is thus a challenge for evaluators. It raises questions about how to include all stakeholders in the evaluation process in a way that empowers marginalised stakeholder groups and at the same time is acceptable for the dominant stakeholder groups.

In 2007, the American Evaluation Association outlined that evaluation studies should be conducted in the following way:

1   An evaluation study should be based on systematic inquiry. This means that it should be conducted properly and with 'technical adequacy' (Cronbach 1982). It should measure how effective an intervention is, using the most appropriate research design. This will vary depending on the type of project/intervention being evaluated.
2   The evaluation team need to have the skills and competencies to conduct the evaluation. This is particularly important in an empowerment evaluation. Using an empowerment evaluation approach can be a helpful way to learn about, as well as conduct effective evaluations with, culturally diverse groups.

The evaluation must reflect the highest level of performance in evaluation (American Evaluation Association 2007).

3   Integrity/honesty is essential in evaluation studies. Round table discussions and use of an evaluation framework (as discussed in Table 14.2) ensure that principles of integrity and honesty are adhered to. Realistic timescales have to be set within budget constraints. The scope of results and how the evaluation will be used must also be specified at the start of an evaluation. The process of the evaluation should be very transparent. This will be helped by providing regular updates to all stakeholders, as well as ensuring that there is ongoing consultation with all stakeholders.

4   Respect for people can be assured by abiding by current professional ethics, standards and regulations regarding confidentiality, informed consent and potential risks or harms to participants. The aim of any evaluation is to 'seek to maximise the benefits and reduce any unnecessary harm that might occur from an evaluation' (American Evaluation Association 2007:129). An evaluator has 'to carefully judge when the benefits from the evaluation or procedure should be foregone because of potential risks' (American Evaluation Association 2007:129). Importantly, in community development evaluations, an evaluator must understand, respect and take into account differences among stakeholders, such as culture, religion, gender, disability, age, sexual orientation and ethnicity (American Evaluation Association 2007).

5   The responsibilities for general and public welfare are also important. General and public welfare are taken into consideration by focusing not only on the immediate operations and outcomes of the evaluation, but also on the broad assumptions, implications and potential side effects of the evaluation report, and, of course, the implementation of recommendations.

Table 14.2 outlines in more detail the stages involved in carrying out an empowerment evaluation, as well as recommendations for actions at each stage.

The role of the empowerment evaluator is one of facilitator, organiser, trainer, manager and planner. The role of the stakeholders, including marginalised communities, is one of learner/evaluation trainee and, importantly, expert on the issues of living in a marginalised community.

As can be seen from Table 14.2, ensuring participation in evaluation is a very rigorous process.

> It presupposes a certain number of stages and activities: informing, motivating, training stakeholders; allowing participants to construct a shared vision; guaranteeing conditions for balanced confrontation of points of view and providing financial means, which in terms of timing are not necessarily compatible with available resources, nor the timeframe of public decision-making. (Plottu and Plottu 2009)

Table 14.2. Stages in carrying out an empowerment evaluation and recommendations for actions at each stage

Stage 1: Preliminary capacity building for the target community
Capacity-building exercises may need to be conducted in the following areas:
* confidence building
* assertiveness skills
* numeracy and literacy skills
* voicing an opinion
* dealing with conflicting opinions in discussion groups
* being able to listen to and understand the opinion of others, even if they are contrary to personally held opinions.

Stage 2: Engaging *all* stakeholders – round table discussion
The following can be discussed:
1   What empowerment evaluation is.
2   Purpose of empowerment evaluation.
3   Value of it for the current project.
4   Capacity building.
5   Potential for transferability of skills acquired to future projects.
6   Agreeing an evaluation agreement (see Stage 2(a)).
7   Designing an evaluation framework (see Stage 2(b)).
8   Possible research methodologies that could be used. The purpose of discussing how the evaluation could be conducted is to demystify the process and identify any possible barriers/problems that there may be in using particular research methodologies. Training will be given at a later stage.
9   Responsibility of the evaluators.
10 Role of the stakeholders.
11 Training required.
12 Timescales for completion.
This discussion might not be completed at one meeting: it could take a number of meetings.
Ongoing consultation with stakeholders at all stages of the evaluation process reduces suspicion, increases the likelihood of co-operation and motivation, broadens the knowledge base for all involved, as well as allowing different perspectives to be considered. Most important, it increases the likelihood that recommendations will be implemented.

Stage 2(a): Agreeing an evaluation agreement for an empowerment evaluation	Stage 2(b): Designing an evaluation framework for an empowerment evaluation
An evaluation agreement summarises procedures and clarifies roles/responsibilities in the evaluation. This agreement should reflect a 'doing with' rather than a 'doing for' philosophy. It provides a basis for modifying/renegotiating, if required. An empowerment evaluation agreement may contain the following:	An empowerment evaluation framework, or strategy, is an outline of how an evaluation study is to be carried out. The following issues should be considered:
1 Description of the purpose of the evaluation.	1 What is the best way to conduct the evaluation?
2 Identification of the stakeholders, especially the users of a project.	• Quantitative methodology.
	• Qualitative methodology.
3 How the evaluation will be carried out, i.e. method of evaluation.	• A combination?
	• Ethics.
4 How stakeholders, especially the target community, will be empowered in the evaluation process.	2 How can the integrity of data gathered be verified?
	• Validity.
5 The timescale for the evaluation.	• Reliability.
6 The budget necessary to conduct the evaluation.	• Rigour.
7 Who is responsible for implementing recommendations arising out of the evaluation.	3 What are the constraints on the evaluation, e.g. time and resources?
	4 What are the timescales?
8 Signing off on the evaluation agreement by all stakeholders. This is helpful to confirm the commitment of all stakeholders to the empowerment evaluation process.	5 Who is responsible for implementing the recommendations? There should be discussion at this point about what will happen if the evaluation results are negative, i.e. what that will mean for the continuity of the project; what will it mean for those employed in the project?
	6 What are the agreed deadlines for interim reports and final evaluation reports?

Stage 3: Conducting the empowerment evaluation

Training the target community to conduct the evaluation can be done in the following ways:
1   Formal training (literacy/numeracy/research methods).
2   Role play exercises (interviews and focus groups).
3   Simulation exercises (interviews and focus groups).
4   Peer-assisted training: members of the target community helping each other/demonstrating.
Carrying out the fieldwork can be done by:
1   Assisting an evaluator.
2   Shadowing an evaluator.
3   Target community members working in pairs/small teams to conduct the research.
Stage 3 should be characterised by ongoing consultation with the target community.

Stage 4: Compiling the final report

An empowerment evaluation report should include the following:
1   Aims/objectives of the project being evaluated.
2   Purpose of an empowerment evaluation for this project.
3   How was it ensured that this was an empowerment evaluation and not a collaborative/traditional evaluation?
4   How exactly was the evaluation carried out?
5   Why was the evaluation carried out in this way?
6   How were the results analysed?
7   Did the research method fairly and ethically record the views of all involved in all stages of the project? According to whom?
8   Stages of the evaluation:
    • planning
    • implementation
    • how these were carried out.
9   Results of the evaluation
10 Were the aims(s)/objectives of the project achieved?
11 Recommendations
12 Value of using an empowerment evaluation strategy – future use and transferability of skills.

Stage 5: Implementing the recommendations

BARRIERS TO EMPOWERMENT EVALUATION

This section discusses some common barriers to empowerment evaluation and proposes solutions to overcome them.

Table 14.3. Barriers to empowerment evaluation and possible solutions

Barrier	Possible solution
Training marginalised groups to take part in evaluation	1 Capacity building, to ensure that people are confident to express their views and participate, is essential. 2 Training in research methods, so as to be able to conduct the evaluation, is also necessary. 3 Training sessions are often necessary in order to introduce the limits and expectations of an evaluation, its timeframe, the stakes and what is to be expected from participants. 4 Training marginalised groups to take part should be included in the timeframe and budget when designing the evaluation framework.
Enabling marginalised groups to build a common view	1 Allowing time, such as in the round table discussions referred to in Table 14.2, to allow community members, or representatives of the community as 'bearers of a shared vision of a locality or region to debate with confidence and defend their "project" before other stakeholders such as public decision-makers or funding agencies' (Floc'hlay and Plottu 1998:266) 2 Prior training in areas such as assertiveness and voicing an opinion may be necessary.
Getting 'buy-in' from the broader target community	1 Clear information about what the empowerment evaluation is and what it will do should be disseminated. This can be done in the following ways. • Arrange a meeting in a local hall. • Arrange meetings with representatives of local groups/organisations. • Ask local opinion leaders to spread the word and/or become involved in the empowerment evaluation. • Advertise though local community groups/newsletters. • Use 'word of mouth'. 2 Emphasise the advantages of involvement: • All views will be heard. Depending on available funding: • Continued service provision. • Improved service provision. • New service provision. 'The aim is to create a dynamic and friendly atmosphere so as to give the project a sense of social engagement and to ensure lasting mobilization' (Plottu and Plottu 2009:353).
The empowerment evaluation process must be supervised	To ensure 'technical adequacy' (Cronbach 1982) an empowerment evaluation must be supervised by someone skilled in evaluation. However, there is no reason to assume that this will be required for every project. Cox et al. (2010: 11) emphasise that once the evaluation capacity of individuals and organisations develops, as happens in empowerment evaluations, the evaluation is 'built into the day-to-day management practices of organisations'. Therefore, the skills acquired initially can be transferred to other projects and can build up in an organisation/project.
Quality of data	1 High-quality data is ensured if the evaluation process is supervised by an expert evaluator. This level of expert supervision may not be necessary in subsequent empowerment evaluations. 2 Empowerment evaluation provides a team of peer researchers, who have already built up trust in a community and also know how 'true' is the information that they are receiving. Ensuring that they are adequately trained in research methods means that very high-quality data can emerge from an empowerment evaluation. 3 Carrying out a pilot study, prior to the main evaluation study, can provide sufficient experience to carry out an evaluation study.

Barrier	Possible solution
Fear of job loss, if an evaluation produces negative results	1 This should be discussed at the design of an evaluation framework stage. 2 Regular updates and interim findings to be made available to all stakeholders, including those managing/working on a project. 3 Ongoing consultation with all stakeholders 4 Flexibility in the operation of the project. If an evaluation update or interim report highlights that something is not working in a project, there should be flexibility built into the operation of the project to adapt it accordingly.
Disruption to activities of the project/ organisation during the data collection phase	An empowerment evaluation naturally includes staff and management in the planning process. The time needed to conduct the evaluation should be built into the evaluation framework, as well as who will need to be involved. If the activities of a project will be disrupted during the data collection phase, this should be discussed and agreed in advance with the project co-ordinators/community development workers. Of course, this should be kept to a minimum.
Resistance to carrying out an evaluation in this way	1 Outline in initial meetings and round table discussion (Table 14.2) the advantages of an empowerment evaluation. 2 Emphasise that the integrity of data collected will not be compromised but may, in fact, be enhanced. 3 Ensure regular updates are provided to all stakeholders to minimise suspicion and mistrust.

HOW TO ENSURE THAT EMPOWERMENT EVALUATION WORKS

For an empowerment evaluation to work, it must fulfil the claims it makes (Cousins 2005; Patton 2005). I argue that an empowerment evaluation itself needs to be evaluated against the following criteria:

1   Did the evaluation effectively analyse and interpret how an intervention operated and its effects?
2   Were all stakeholders satisfied with the evaluation process?
3   Were all stakeholders satisfied that the evaluation report reflected how the intervention/project *really* worked?
4   Was the empowerment conducted ethically? (American Evaluation Association 2007)
5   Was the evaluation inquiry systematic?
6   What was the learning derived from the process of conducting and participating in an empowerment evaluation?
7   How can acquired evaluation skills be transferred to other projects?

CONCLUSION

Plottu and Plottu (2009) argue that in the case of sustainable development, approaches to participation in evaluation, through its emancipatory function for the weakest participants, constitutes an action in favour of sustainable development. Its most important characteristic is that people from marginalised communities become trained in evaluation methods and these skills are easily transferable to other projects. Contrary to what some commentators suggest (Plottu and Plottu 2009), it can be a cost-effective way of completing evaluation in community development and voluntary projects. As we live in recessionary times, the cost of running and evaluating community development projects is becoming an ever more critical issue in Ireland. In Budget 2011 (Ireland), the government announced budget cuts to community development programmes and projects in Ireland. Budget 2011 saw gross funding for the Department of Community, Equality and Gaeltacht Affairs (whose responsibilities are now divided between several newly formed departments), which provided funding for the community and voluntary sector in Ireland, reduced by 13 per cent (Carey 2010).

In the challenging economic times in which we live, I argue that this evaluation approach may well be the way forward for the community and voluntary sector, both to ensure that evaluations are carried out to best practice standards, and because they can be carried out with restricted funding and resources. Empowerment evaluation, by the fact that it builds capacity in the target community, is a 'very good value' evaluation method from a community development perspective. In the true spirit of best practice in community development, it acts as a mechanism for empowerment. However, if the transferability of evaluation skills is included as a purpose of evaluation, as happens with empowerment evaluations, that learning can be transferred to subsequent projects, or even later stages of the original project. Therefore, reliance on an 'expert' empowerment evaluator diminishes. In this way, follow-on evaluation studies can become very cost-effective.

Conclusion: Community Development – Making Society Better

Colm O'Doherty and Ashling Jackson

> Community is not to do with desire, as some have suggested, but with a sense of who **we** are, a shared recognition of what we have in common. So the kind of attachment that is characteristic of community is not to do with being 'tied down' in some way but, on the contrary, is the condition for our liberation, through others. (Somerville 2011:239)

This book has gathered together some of the key policy and theory influences shaping community development practice in Ireland today. Collectively the chapters included here provide us with rich examples of how community development creates common bonds through common experiences, in spite of continuing funding constraints. While each chapter in the book has a different story to tell, all of them assert the social value of community development, and provide the reader with an understanding of how it can assist people to acquire the skills, as well as the confidence, to improve the quality of their lives. The pivotal position held by community development in Irish civil society and its central importance in pursuing individual and collective well-being in the face of an uncertain future, triggered by unpredictable drivers of change, is a central thread in all the chapters. Community development builds a culture of shared interest which provides a social platform for consciousness-raising and the challenging of values at an individual and societal level.

Community development has become synonymous with civil society activity. As we have a strong tradition of community development activity in Ireland, this gives a very uplifting insight into the type of society we actually live in. Civil societies are venerated for contributing to democratisation and good governance, to active citizenship and community development, to social relations and societal integration (Purdue 2007). Drawing upon Walzer (1995), Deakin (2001) posits that civil society encompasses a range of diverse forms of association or social organisation which, regardless of their goals, are formed on a voluntary and independent basis.

The Carnegie Trust, in its *Inquiry into the Future of Civil Society in the UK and Ireland* (Mulgan 2010), described civil society as having three interlinked dimensions.

Table 15.1. Carnegie Trust definition of civil society

Civil society as associational life	Civil society as a 'good society'	Civil society as the arenas for public deliberation
Civil society is where people come together voluntarily for the benefit of themselves, others (or sometimes both together), for actions that lie beyond either the government or for private-profit business. It includes formal organisations such as voluntary and community organisations, faith-based organisations, trade unions, mutuals and co-operatives. It also includes informal groups, from the very local to global social movements.	The term civil society is sometimes used as a shorthand term for the type of society we want to live in. The values of civil society associations that have strongly influenced the Commission's view of a 'good society' include a commitment to social justice (fairness, equality of treatment, opportunities and outcomes); mutuality, and a belief in the interdependence of lives ('I thrive if you thrive') and the golden rule that can be found in all traditions (behave towards others as you would have them behave towards you); the related sense of solidarity that comes from people acting together; a strong commitment to freedom, particularly freedom from oppressive power in all forms; and, in recent years, a growing engagement with the ecological values of harmony and balance with nature.	A third sense of the term civil society refers to the places where people and organisations discuss common interests, develop solutions to society's most pressing problems and try to reconcile differences peacefully. These arenas sit alongside, and influence, those in the media and politics. They may be physical – a community centre, or meetings and events hosted by civil society groups, or public bodies, or they may be virtual – on the web.

Source: Mulgan 2010:16.

It is clear from the different chapters in this book that community development in contemporary Ireland has fully embraced the concept of civil society and represents an activity embedded in the middle ground of Irish society. In fact, the presence of a strong and constantly evolving community development sector encapsulates the nature of civil society in Ireland. However, community development activity, like most aspects of life in modern Ireland, is vulnerable to macro social and economic forces. Although community development can be a mechanism for social change in a rapidly changing society, we are all currently living in an economic reality in which civil society and the 'middle ground' of community development activity have been squeezed by the economic crash and face serious challenges in the future. While community development cannot take responsibility for dealing with the social consequences of wider economic restructuring or crisis – neither should it be expected to (Craig 1998) – it does affect the social reality in which community development workers work.

Historically, community development has been centrally concerned with democracy: in many contexts, its professional legitimacy has been justified by its strategic position as mediator in the relationship between the state and its citizens, through various forms of participation and community engagement. (Shaw 2011:ii128)

Whilst community development offers opportunities for participation and community engagement, it is always framed and regulated by the changing imperatives of policy. Adequate and appropriate social policy can facilitate and support community development activities, but can also restrict it in recessionary times, such as we are experiencing at the moment. For Shaw (2011), this has inevitably produced contradictions and tensions which, in turn, have framed the possibilities and constraints for practice. Negotiating these has always been a core challenge for practitioners. While it can be argued that the strongest position for community development is in the spaces and boundaries between local people and policy makers (Miller and Ahmed 1997), 'there is a danger that this leaves community workers stuck in the middle, as distinct from strategically positioned, between marketised state policy and democratic politics' (Shaw 2011:ii128). As we have seen in the various chapters in this book, exercising personal and collective agency in these spaces is central to the dynamic of critical community development participation (Martin 1999). Therefore, community development workers and the nature of community development practice will have to continue to be resourceful and pioneer creative solutions to overcome continuing challenges in community settings. On a positive note, these challenges are also opportunities for community development to represent a site of resistance, in civil society, to the dominant or hegemonic ideas which foster a belief that people are essentially selfish, acquisitive and materialistic.

It is a virtual axiom of orthodox economics that **more** is always **better**. At national level, all considerations pale beside the need to keep GDP figures ticking upwards. At the individual level, the pursuit of individual wealth has risen beyond mere social acceptability to become synonymous with 'aspiration' and even, in some quarters, touted as a moral good. (New Economics Foundation 2011:14)

It could be said that the above quote characterised life in Celtic Tiger Ireland, and may, to some degree, still do so. However, the need for community development projects/organisations and competent community development workers, before the Celtic Tiger period, during it and, importantly, at the moment, means that there is an ongoing need to address inequality and marginalisation in Irish society. Drawing on the wise words of Lao Tzu in a well-known Chinese proverb, 'Give a man a fish; you have fed him for today. Teach a man to fish; and you have fed him for a lifetime', it would seem that community development should remain as a logical and practical way to empower disadvantaged communities and reduce marginalisation in Irish society in the long term.

Contributors' Profiles

We would like to sincerely thank each of our chapter authors for their contribution to this book. We really appreciate the time and effort you have given in helping us to make this project possible. It has been a pleasure to work with you.

Ashling and Colm

Delores Crerar MA co-ordinates the interagency partnership of the Gateway Project, Athlone. She previously worked as a co-ordinator on Strand 1 of the Equality for Women Measure and has spent many years working directly with young people and communities.

Dr Tom Farrelly is a social science lecturer on the Nursing and Social Care degree programmes in the Institute of Technology, Tralee. He has a long association with literacy provision, having acted as a tutor with KLEAR in Dublin and as a tutor and workplace literacy co-ordinator for the Kerry Education Service/Kerry County Council joint project.

Dr Cormac Forkan is a lecturer in the School of Political Science and Sociology at NUI Galway and the programme co-ordinator for the BA in Youth and Family Studies. He is also a staff member of the Child and Family Research Centre at the university.

Dr Ashling Jackson is a senior lecturer in Child and Social Care Studies at Athlone Institute of Technology. She lectures in the areas of sociology, community development and research methods, and has worked extensively with disadvantaged groups in community settings, most notably the Traveller community.

Lily Kavanagh has worked as a community health worker with the Primary Healthcare Project for Travellers in Tullamore for the last nine years. She works directly with Traveller families in Tullamore town.

Dr Andrew Loxley is a sociologist and a PhD graduate from the University of Bath. He has worked in Trinity College Dublin since 2002, both as Director of Postgraduate Teaching and Learning, and Director of Research. He has recently been involved in a number of projects looking at the changing nature of Irish higher education.

Sarah McDonagh has worked as a community health worker with the Primary Healthcare Project for Travellers in Tullamore for the last nine years. She works directly with Traveller families in Tullamore town.

Briggie McInerney has worked as a community health worker with the Primary Healthcare Project for Travellers in Tullamore for the last nine years. She works directly with Traveller families in Birr town.

Mary McInerney has worked as a community health worker with the Primary Healthcare Project for Travellers in Tullamore for the last nine years. She works directly with Traveller families in Tullamore, Edenderry, Ferbane and Clara. She has an interest in Traveller accommodation issues, as well as in preventing violence against women.

Pinkie McInerney has worked as a community health worker with the Primary Healthcare Project for Travellers in Tullamore for the last nine years. She works directly with Traveller families in Clara and Birr.

Steve McNamara DipHE MA has worked in the community and voluntary sector, voluntarily and professionally, since the early 1980s. He currently works in the RAPID Programme based in Limerick City Council and teaches diploma courses in Youth and Community Work and Community Development, as well as an MA programme in Social Care Management at Limerick IT.

Bernadette Naughton MSocSc (Social Work) is a lecturer in Applied Social Studies at Athlone Institute of Technology. She lectures in the areas of psychology, community development and applied social care. Bernadette's experience includes the assessment and treatment of child sexual abuse, residential child care, community child protection and working with marginalised sectors of the community.

Dr Patricia Neville is a sociologist and has taught sociology and social studies at a variety of FE and HE institutions in Ireland. She is currently a visiting scholar with the Department of Gender Studies, Queen's University, Ontario.

Dr Féilim Ó hAdhmaill has been a lecturer in the School of Applied Social Studies at University College Cork since June 2006, where he teaches Social Policy and Community Development and is Programme Director for the Master's in Third Sector Management. He has an extensive background in community activism and in the community and voluntary sector in the North. He is a founder member of the UCC Science Shop.

Déirdre O'Byrne BA, MSocSc has worked for twenty years as a practitioner, trainer and adviser on community development and project management in the community and voluntary sector. She teaches on diploma courses on Non-formal Guidance and Youth and Community at University College Cork. She also works in the areas of professional evaluation and research for third-sector organisations.

Colm O'Doherty is head of the Department of Humanities and Social Studies at the Institute of Technology Tralee. After eighteen years of front-line practice in social work, family support and community development, he took on a pivotal role in community and social work education at University College Cork. He has published and researched widely.

Gerard Phillips is project leader with the HSE Springboard Project in Cork City, where his work involved setting up the project and developing the initiative in two RAPID areas. He has previously worked in both practice and academic settings and is an accredited member of the Irish Association for Counselling and Psychotherapy. He has published a longitudinal study about working with persistent and serious offenders.

References

CHAPTER 1. SETTING THE SCENE

Checkoway, B. (1995) 'Six strategies of community change', *Community Development Journal* 30: 2–20.

— (1997) 'Core concepts for community change', *Journal of Community Practice* 4: 11–29.

— (2011) 'Community development, social diversity, and the new metropolis', *Community Development Journal* 46, April: ii5–ii14.

DeFilippis, J. and Saegert, S. (eds) (2008) *The Community Development Reader*. Routledge: New York.

Fahey, T. and Layte, R. (2007) 'Family and Sexuality' in T. Fahey, H. Russell and C.T. Whelan, *Best of Times? The Social Impact of the Celtic Tiger*. Dublin: Institute of Public Administration.

O'Connell, M. (2001) *Changed Utterly*. Dublin: Liffey Press.

O'Connor, P. (2006) 'Private troubles, public issues: the Irish sociological imagination', *Irish Journal of Sociology* 15(2): 5–22.

Wellstone, P. (2002) *Heroes for a Better World* [online], <http://www.betterworld heroes.com/ pages-w/wellstone-quotes.htm> accessed 15 August 2011.

Zukin, C., Keeter, S., Andolina, M. *et al.* (2006) *A New Engagement? Political Participation, Civic Life, and the Changing American Citizen*. New York: Oxford University Press.

CHAPTER 2. THE VALUE OF COMMUNITY DEVELOPMENT

Barry, S. (2008) *The Secret Scripture*. London: Faber & Faber.

Bauman, Z. (2001) *Community – Seeking Safety in an Insecure World*. Cambridge: Polity Press.

— (2008) *The Art of Life*. Cambridge: Polity Press.

CWC (Community Workers' Co-operative) (2008) *Towards Standards for Quality Community Work*. Galway: CWC.

Delaney, L. (2009) 'Well-being Under Conditions of Abundance: Ireland from 1990 to 2007'. Paper given at the Statistical and Social Inquiry Society Barrington Lecture, 13 May.

Field, J. (2003) *Social Capital*. London: Routledge.

Jordan, B. (2008) *Welfare and Well-being – Social Value in Public Policy*. Bristol: Policy Press.

Layard, R. (2005) *Happiness – Lessons from a New Science*. London: Penguin.

Layard, R. and Dunn, J. (2009) *A Good Childhood – Searching for Values in a Competitive Age*. London: Penguin.

O'Doherty, C. (2007) *A New Agenda for Family Support – Providing Services that Create Social Capital*. Dublin: Blackhall.

Packham, C. (2008) *Active Citizenship and Community Learning*. Exeter: Learning Matters.

Putnam, R.D. (2000) *Bowling Alone: The Collapse and Revival of American Community*. New York: Simon & Schuster.

Searle, B.A. (2008) *Well-being: In Search of a Good Life?* Bristol: Policy Press.

Twelvetrees, A. (2008) *Community Work I*. Basingstoke: Palgrave Macmillan.

Wilkinson, R. and Pickett, K. (2009) *The Spirit Level – Why More Equal Societies Almost Always do Better*. London: Allen Lane.

CHAPTER 3. INVESTIGATING THE DE-POLITICISATION OF COMMUNITY DEVELOPMENT

Alinsky, S.D. (1969) *Reveille for Radicals*. New York: Random House.

— (1972) *Rules for Radicals: A Pragmatic Primer for Realistic Radicals*. New York: Vintage.

Allen, K. (2000) *The Celtic Tiger: The Myth of Social Partnership in Ireland*. Manchester and New York: Manchester University Press.

— (2009) *Ireland's Economic Crash: A Radical Agenda for Change*. Dublin: Liffey Press.

Begg, D. (2009) 'Social Partnership and the Failure of Social Development'. Paper given at Cork Institute of Technology, 15 January.

Billis, D. (1993) *Organising Public and Voluntary Agencies*. London: Routledge.

Bon, V. (2007) *The Community Development and Family and Community Services Resource Centre Programmes: Who We Are and Where We Come From*. Limerick: SMWCDSA.

Butcher, H. (2007) *Critical Community Practice*. Bristol: Policy Press.

Byrne, F. (2009) Speech at launch of Community Asset Management Agency (CAMA), Dublin (unpublished).

Chubb, B. (1970) *The Government and Politics of Ireland* (with a historical introduction by David Thornley). Stanford, CA: Stanford University Press.

Clarke, J. and Newman, J. (1997) *The Managerial State: Power, Politics and Ideology in the Remaking of the Welfare State*. London: Sage.

Collins, M., Healy, S. and Reynolds, B. (eds) (2010) *Agenda for a New Ireland: Policies to Ensure Economic Development, Social Equity and Sustainability*. Dublin: Social Justice Ireland.

Craig, G., Derricourt, N. and Loney, M. (eds) (1982) *Community Work and the State: Towards a Radical Practice*. Community Work 8. London: Routledge.

Craig, G. and Mayo, M. (1995) *Community Empowerment: A Reader in Participation and Development*. London: Zed Books.

Craig, G., Mayo, M., Popple, K., Shaw, M. and Taylor, M. (2011) *The Community Development Reader: History, Themes and Issues*. Bristol: Policy Press.

Crosland, C.A.R. (1956) *The Future of Socialism*. London: Jonathan Cape.

Curno, P. (ed.) (1978) *Political Issues and Community Work*. London: Routledge.

CWC (Community Workers' Co-operative) (2000) *Strategies for Social Partnership*. Galway: CWC.

— (2003) *Wealth, Power, Inequality: Challenges for Community Work in a New Era*. Galway: CWC.

— (2008) *Towards Standards for Quality Community Work*. Galway: CWC.

— (2010) 'Defending Ireland's communities' (press release), February 2010.

DSCFA (Department of Social, Community and Family Affairs) (1999) *The National Community Development Programme: United Against Poverty*. Dublin: Government Publications.

— (2000) *White Paper on a Framework for Supporting Voluntary Activity and for Developing the Relationship between the State and the Community and Voluntary Sector*. Dublin: Government Publications.

Duggan, C. and Ronayne, T. (1991) *Working Partners? The State and Community Sector*. Dublin: Work Research Centre.

Family Support Agency (2010) *FRC Programme SPEAK Report 2009* [online], <http://www.fsa.ie/funding-grants-/family-resource-centre-programme>.

Faughnan, P. and Kelleher, P. (1992) 'The Voluntary Sector and the State: A Study of Organisations in One Region'. Ireland: Conference of Major Religious Superiors (Ireland).

Forde, C., Kiely, E. and Meade, R. (eds) (2009) *Youth and Community Work in Ireland: Critical Perspectives*. Dublin: Blackhall.

Fukuyama, F. (1993) *The End of History and the Last Man*. Harmondsworth: Penguin.

Galbraith, J.K. (1992) *The Culture of Contentment*. London: Sinclair-Stevenson.

Gaynor, N. (2005) *In-Active Citizenship and the De-politicalisation of Community Development in Ireland*. Dublin: Dublin City University.

Geoghegan, M. (2008) 'The Contested Meaning of Civil Society: Community Development in Ireland, 1980–2007', PhD thesis <http://library.ucc.ie/record=1839290>, accessed 28 September 2010.

Harvey, B. (2004) 'Poverty, social exclusion and the new member states', *Action on Poverty Today* 5(2).

— (2010) *Analysis of Implications of 2010 Budget for the Voluntary and Community Sector*. Dublin: Impact.

Harvey, H. and MacDonald, M. (1993) *Doing Sociology: A Practical Introduction*. London: Macmillan.

Hazelkorn, E. (1986) 'Class, Clientelism and the Political Process in the Republic of Ireland' in P. Clancy, S. Drudy, K. Lynch and L. O'Dowd (eds), *Ireland: A Sociological Profile*. Dublin: Institute of Public Administration, pp. 326–43.

Higgins, M.D. (1982) *The Limits of Clientelism: Towards an Assessment of Irish Politics* in C. Clapham (ed.), *Private Patronage and Public Power: Political Clientelism in the Modern State*. London: Frances Pinter, pp. 114–41.

Hurley, L. (1992) *The Historical Development of Irish Youth Work*. Wexford: Irish Youth Work Centre.

Inclusion Ireland [website] <http://www.inclusionireland.ie> accessed 24 September 2010.

Jacobson, D., Kirby, P. and Ó Broin, D. (eds) (2006) *Taming the Tiger: Social Exclusion in a Globalised Ireland*. Dublin: TASC/New Island Press.

Kane, E. and O'Reilly-de Brún, M. (2001) *Doing Your Own Research*. London: Marion Boyars.

Kelleher, P. and Whelan, M. (1992) *Dublin Communities in Action*. Dublin: Community Action Network and Combat Poverty Agency.

Kirby, P. (2002) *The Celtic Tiger in Distress: Growth with Inequality in Ireland*. Basingstoke: Palgrave.

— (2004) 'Globalisation, the Celtic Tiger and social outcomes: is Ireland a model or a mirage?', *Globalisations* 1(2).

— (2005) 'The Irish State and the Celtic Tiger: A "Flexible Developmental State" or a Competition State?', in G. Harrison (ed.) *Global Encounter: International Political Economy, Development and Globalisation*. Basingstoke: Palgrave Macmillan.

— (2007) *Economic Success, Social Failure: Ireland of the Celtic Tiger*. Paper given at Community Development: A Tool for Anti-Poverty Work in Ireland Conference, Brandon, Tralee, Co. Kerry.

Kirby, P. and Murphy, M. (2008) *A Better Ireland is Possible: Towards an Alternative Vision for Ireland*. Galway: Community Platform.

Kitchener, M., Kirkpatrick, I. and Whipp, R. (2002) *Supervising Professional Work under New Public Management: Evidence from an 'Invisible Trade'*, <http://www.onlinelibrary.wiley.com> accessed 29 September 2010.

Klein, N. (2007) *The Shock Doctrine: The Rise of Disaster Capitalism*. London: Penguin.

Ledwith, M. (2005) *Community Development: A Critical Approach*. Bristol: Policy Press.

Lewis, H. (2006) *New Trends in Community Development*. Derry: International Conflict Research Institute (INCORE), University of Ulster.

Lynch, K. (1999) *Equality in Education*. Dublin: Gill & Macmillan.

Marshall, T.H. and Bottomore, T. (1991) *Citizenship and Social Class*. London: Pluto Press.

May, T. (2001) *Social Research: Issues, Methods and Process*. Milton Keynes: Open University Press.

Mayo, M. (1975) 'Community Development: A Radical Alternative?', in R. Bailey and M. Brake (eds), *Radical Social Work*. London: Edward Arnold.

McCarthy, C. (2009) *Report of the Special Group on Public Service Numbers and Expenditure Programmes*. Government Publications, Dublin.

McDyer, J. (1982) *Fr McDyer of Glencolmcille: An Autobiography*. Brandon, Dingle.

Meade, R. (2005) 'We hate it here, please let us stay! Irish social partnership and the community/voluntary sector's conflicted experiences of recognition',

Critical Social Policy 15(3), <http://www.ucc.ie/library> accessed 11 January 2010.

Meade, R. and O'Donovan, O. (2002) 'Editorial introduction: corporatism and the ongoing debate about the relationship between the state and community development', *Community Development Journal* 37(1), <http://www.ucc.ie/library> accessed 27 April 2010.

Millar, M. (2008) 'Social Inclusion and the Welfare State: Who Cares?', in M. Adshead, P. Kirby and M. Millar, *Contesting the State: Lessons from the Irish Case*. Manchester: Manchester University Press.

Motherway, B. (2006) *The Role of Community Development in Tackling Poverty in Ireland*. Dublin: Combat Poverty Agency.

Muintir na Tíre [website] <http://www.muintir.ie> accessed 24 September 2010.

Murphy, M. (2000) 'Is Social Partnership the Only Route to Social Inclusion and, if so, Where is the Voice of the Excluded?', in Community Workers' Co-operative, *Strategies for Social Partnership*.

O'Brien, M. and Penna, S. (1998) *Theorising Welfare: Enlightenment and Modern Society*. London: Sage.

O'Carroll, J.P. (1987) 'Strokes, cute hoors and sneaking regarders: the influence of local culture on Irish political style', *Irish Political Studies* 2(1).

O'Connor, T. (2009) 'The structural failure of Irish economic development and employment policy', *Irish Journal of Public Policy* 2(1).

— (2010) *A Cost Benefit Analysis of CDPs in the Cork and Kerry Area*. Report prepared for the CDP Community Forum, Cork, 16 January 2010.

OECD (Organisation for Economic Co-operation and Development) (2008) *Education at a Glance*, <http://www.ucc.ie/library/electronicresources> accessed 19 April 2010.

O'Neill, K. (2010) Untitled presentation, SIPTU Conference, 25 September.

O'Reilly, E. (2004) 'Imagine the Future – An Irish Perspective'. Paper presented to 7th Annual Céifin Conference, 3 November, <http://www.ceifin.com> accessed 26 April 2010.

O'Sullivan, P. (2007) The *Wealth of the Nation. How Ireland's Wealthy will Invest in the Next Decade*. Dublin: Bank of Ireland Private Banking Ltd.

O'Toole, F. (2003) *After the Ball*. Dublin: New Island.

Plunkett, H. (1914) *Agricultural Co-Operation and the Present War: An Appeal to the Department and the Societies*. Dublin: Irish Agricultural Organisation Society.

Pobal [website] <http://www.pobal.ie> accessed 24 September 2010.

— (1999) 'Community development strategies and actions within the integrated local development programme', *Insights* 11. Dublin: Pobal.

Popple, K. (1995) *Analysing Community Work*. Bristol: Open University Press.

Programme for National Recovery (1989). Dublin: Government Publications.

Sarantakos, S. (1998) *Working with Social Research*. Sydney: Macmillan.

Seers, D. and Jay, L. (1971) *Development in a Divided World*. Harmondsworth: Penguin.

Tallon, F. (1993) *Getting Down to Work*. Dublin: Gill & Macmillan.

Titmuss, R. (1968) *Commitment to Welfare*. New York: Pantheon.

Tucker, V. (1989) 'Community Work and Social Change', in Combat Poverty Agency, *Community Work in Ireland: Trends in the 80s, Options for the 90s*. Dublin: CPA.

Twelvetrees, A. (1985) *Democracy and the Neighbourhood*. London: National Federation of Community Organisations.

Walsh, J., Craig, S. and McCafferty, D. (1998) *Local Partnerships for Social Inclusion?* Dublin: Oak Tree Press.

Whelan, M. (1989) 'Training and Professionalisation in Community Work', in Combat Poverty Agency, *Community Work in Ireland: Trends in the 80s, Options for the 90s*. Dublin: CPA.

White, M. (2010) Seanad Éireann Debates, Vol.203, No.13 (on Community Development), 1 July 2010.

Younghusband, E. (1968) *Community Work and Social Change: The Report of a Study Group on Training set up by the Calouste Gulbenkian Foundation*. London: Calouste Gulbenkian Foundation.

CHAPTER 4. CHANGING THE RULES OF THE GAME: SUPPORTING COMMUNITY DEVELOPMENT

CDX/National Empowerment Partnership (2008) *Empowering Evaluation: Evaluating Empowerment*. Sheffield: CDX.

CWC (Community Workers' Co-operative) (2008) *Towards Standards for Quality Community Work*. Galway: Community Workers' Co-operative.

Dean, H. (2010) *Understanding Human Needs*. Bristol: Policy Press.

Eurostat (2010) *Combating Poverty and Social Exclusion: A Statistical Portrait of the European Union 2010*. Brussels: Eurostat.

Jordan, B. (2007) *Social Work and Well-being*. Dorset: Russell House.

Ledwith, M. (2005) *Community Development: A Critical Approach*. Bristol: Policy Press/BASW.

NESC (National Economic and Social Council) (2009) *Well-being Matters: A Social Report for Ireland*, Vol. 1. Dublin: NESC.

Oppenheim, C., Cox, E. and Platt, R. (2010) *Regeneration through Co-operation: Creating a Framework for Communities to Act Together*. Manchester: Co-operatives UK.

Saarnio, T., Nissinen, P., Salminen, M., Potzsch, T., Sheikh, L. and Fuller, P. (2006) *Yari Manual: Working Model for Working with Young People at Risk*. Italy: EU Leonardo Programme.

South and Mid West Community Development Support Agency (2010) *History of the Support Agency*. Limerick: South and Mid West Community Development Support Agency.

Updike, J. (1992) *Matters of State*. Keynote speech at the 111th Chicago Humanities Festival, From Freedom to Equality.

CHAPTER 5. ACHIEVING CULTURALLY COMPETENT PRACTICE IN COMMUNITY DEVELOPMENT SETTINGS

Allen-Meares, P. (2007) 'Cultural competence: an ethical requirement' *Journal of Ethnic and Cultural Diversity in Social Work* 16(3): 1531–3212.

Amnesty International (2002) *Opinion Poll for Amnesty International*. Dublin: Lansdowne Marketing Research.

Barrett, A. and McCarthy, Y. (2006) *Immigrants in a Booming Economy: Analysing their Earnings and Welfare Dependence*. IZA Discussion Papers 2457, Institute for the Study of Labour (IZA) Labour 21(4).

Chu, Y.K. and Goode, T. (2009) *Cultural and Linguistic Competencies*. New York: Old Post.

CSO (Central Statistics Office) (2006) *EU Survey on Income and Living Conditions (EUSILC)*. Dublin: Stationery Office.

— (2008) *Census 2006. Non-Irish Nationals Living in Ireland*. Dublin: Stationery Office.

Devore, W. and Schlesinger, E.G. (1999) *Ethnic-Sensitive Social Work Practice* (5th edn). Boston, MA: Allyn & Bacon.

Dewees, M. (2001) 'Building cultural competence for work with diverse families: strategies from the privileged side', *Journal of Ethnic and Cultural Diversity in Social Work* 9(3/4).

Gannon, M.J. and Pillai, R. (2010) *Understanding Global Cultures: Metaphorical Journeys through 29 Nations, Clusters of Nations, Continents, and Diversity* (4th edn). USA: Sage.

Gelman, C. (2004) 'Empirically based principles for culturally competent practice with Latinos', *Journal of Ethnic and Cultural Diversity* 13(1): 83–108.

Glicken, M.D. (2004) *Using the Strengths Perspective in Social Work Practice*. USA: Pearson Education.

Green, J.W. (1995) *Cultural Awareness in the Human Services: A Multi-ethnic Approach*. Boston: Allyn & Bacon.

Hanley, J. (1999) 'Beyond the tip of the iceberg: five stages toward cultural competence', *Reaching Today's Youth* 3(2): 9–12.

Haraway, D. (1992) *Primate Visions: Gender, Race and Nature in the World of Modern Science*. London: Verso Editions.

Hegarty, F. (2007) *Black African Women in the Irish Labour Market*. Dublin: Dublin Inner City Partnership.

Jandt, F.E (2010) *An Introduction to Intercultural Communication: Identities in a Global Community* (6th edn). USA: Sage.

McGinnity, F., O'Connell, P., Quinn, E. and Williams J. (2006) *Migrants' Experience of Racism and Discrimination in Ireland: Results of a Survey Conducted by the Economic and Social Research Institute for the European Union Monitoring Centre on Racism and Xenophobia*. Dublin: Economic and Social Research Institute.

McGoldrick, M. and Giordano, J. (1996) Preface, in M. McGoldrick, J.K. Pearce and J. Giordano (eds) *Ethnicity and Family Therapy* (2nd edn). New York: Guilford Press, pp. ix–xiii.

Mederos, F. and Woldeguiorguis, I. (2003) 'Beyond cultural competence: what child protection managers need to know and do'. *Journal of Child Welfare* 82(2): 125–42.

MRCI (Migrant Rights Centre Ireland) (2008) *Tools for Social Change: A Resource Guide for Community Work with Migrant Workers and their Families in Ireland.* Dublin: MRCI.

— (2010) *Racism and Migrant Workers in Ireland*: policy paper. Dublin: MRCI.

NASW (National Association of Social Workers) (2001) *Standards for Cultural Competence in Social Work Practice.* Washington, DC: NASW.

NCCRI (National Consultative Committee on Racism and Interculturalism) (2003) *Submission to the Department of Community, Rural and Gaeltacht Affairs on the Inclusion of Ethnic Minorities in Community and Local Development Strategies.* Ireland: NCCRI.

Office of the Refugee Applications Commissioner (2010) *Monthly Statistical Report: September.* Dublin: Stationery Office.

Purnell, L. (2008) *Transcultural Health Care: A Culturally Competent Approach.* Philadelphia: F.A. Davis.

Rack, P. (1982) *Race, Culture and Mental Disorder.* London: Tavistock.

Robert Smyth Academy (2011) *Abnormality: Deviation from Statistical Norms* [website], <http://psychology4a.com/Abnormal%202.htm> accessed 1 November 2011.

Roberts, R. *et al.* (1990) *Developing Culturally Competent Programs for Families of Children with Special Needs.* Washington, DC.

Schlesinger, E.G and Devore, W. (2007) *Reflections on Practice and Research with Multicultural Populations: Past, Present, and Beyond Ethnic Sensitive Social Work Practice: Back to the Future.* New York: Haworth Press.

Walker, B.A. (1994) *Valuing Difference: the Concept and a Model* in C. Mabey and P. Iles (eds) *Managing Learning.* London: Routledge and Open University.

Weaver, H. (1999) 'Indigenous people and the social work profession: defining culturally competent services', *Journal of Social Work* 44(3).

Woodroffe, A. (2007) 'Societal cultural competence and cultural community well-being', *Forum on Public Policy* 1 (Winter).

CHAPTER 6. COMMUNITY DEVELOPMENT, CONFLICT AND POWER IN THE NORTH OF IRELAND

Acheson, N., Harvey, B. and Williamson, A. (2005) 'State welfare and the development of voluntary action: the case of Ireland, North and South', *Voluntas* 16(2), June 2005.

Acheson, N. and Milofsky, C. (2008) 'Peace building and participation in Northern Ireland: local social movements and the policy process since the "Good Friday" Agreement', *Ethnopolitics* 7(1): 63–80.

Akenson, D.H. (1973) *Education and Enmity: The Control of Schooling in Northern Ireland 1920–50*. Newton Abbot: David and Charles.

Alinsky, S. (1969) *Reveille for Radicals*. New York: Random House.

— (1971) *Rules for Radicals*. New York: Vintage Books.

Anderson, T., Finn, A., Hamilton, A. and McCartney, C. (1988) *Violence and Communities: The Impact of Political Violence in Northern Ireland on Intra-Community, Inter-Community and Community-State Relationships*. Coleraine: Centre for the Study of Conflict, University of Ulster.

Aunger, E.A. (1976) 'Religion and occupational class in Northern Ireland', *Economic and Social Review* 7(1).

Baird Report (1980) *You and Your Baby: Report of the Advisory Committee on Infant Mortality and Handicap in Northern Ireland*. Belfast: HMSO.

Ball, D. (1971) 'Council and community', *New Society* 7 January, 18–19.

Barritt, D.P. and Carter, C.F. (1962) *The Northern Ireland Problem: A Study in Group Relations*. Oxford: Oxford University Press.

Beckett, J.C. and Glasscock, R.E. (1967) *Belfast: The Origin and Growth of an Industrial City*. London: BBC.

Bell, J.B. (1979) *The Secret Army: The IRA 1966–1979*. Dublin: Academy Press.

BIP (Belfast Interface Project) (1998) *Interface Communities and the Peace Process*. Belfast: BIP.

Birrell, D. and Williamson, A. (1983) 'Northern Ireland's Integrated Health and Personal Social Services Structure' in A. Williamson and G. Room (eds), *Health and Welfare States of Britain: An Inter-Country Comparison*. London: Heinemann.

— (2001) 'The voluntary–community sector and political development in Northern Ireland since 1972', *Voluntas* 12(3): 205–20.

Boal, F.W. and Douglas, J.N.H. (eds) (1982) *Integration and Division: Geographical Perspectives on the Northern Ireland Problem*. London: Academic Press.

Bocock, R. (1986) *Hegemony*. London: Tavistock Press.

Boyd, A. (1969) *Holy War in Belfast*. Tralee: Anvil Books.

— (1995) 'The Orange Order, 1795–1995 – outlook and influence of a key element in the culture of Protestant Ulster', *History Today* 45(9): 16–23.

Brody, J. (1974) 'Planning for People' in D. Jones and M. Mayo (eds), *Community Work: One*. London: Routledge & Kegan Paul, pp. 44–5.

Buckland, P. (1979) *The Factory of Grievances: Devolved Government in Northern Ireland, 1921–39*. Dublin: Gill & Macmillan.

Budge, I. and O'Leary, C. (1973) *Belfast: Approach to Crisis: A Study of Belfast Politics, 1613–1970*. London: Macmillan.

Burton, F. (1978) *The Politics of Legitimacy: Struggles in a Belfast Community*. London: Routledge & Kegan Paul.

Cairns, E., Van Til, J. and Williamson, A. (2004) *Social Capital, Collectivism-Individualism and Community Background in Northern Ireland; A Report to the Office of the First Minister and the Deputy First Minister and the Head of the*

Voluntary and Community Unit of the Department for Social Development [online], <http://www.ofmdfmni.gov.uk/socialcapital.pdf> accessed 2 May 2011.

CAJ (Committee on the Administration of Justice) (2010) CAJ's response to the Office of First Minister and Deputy First Minister's consultation on Cohesion, Sharing and Integration, November 2010, CAJ, Belfast.

Calouste Gulbenkian Foundation (1968) *Community Work and Social Change.* London: Longman.

Cameron Commission (1969) *Disturbances in Northern Ireland: Report of the Commission appointed by the Governor of Northern Ireland.* Belfast: HMSO.

Cochrane, F. and Dunn, S. (2002) *People Power? The Role of the Voluntary and Community Sector in the Northern Ireland Conflict.* Cork: Cork University Press.

Collins, J. (1990) 'Political attitudes and integrated education in Northern Ireland', *Studies* 79(316): 409–19.

Corish, P.T. (1981) *The Catholic Community in the Seventeenth and Eighteenth Centuries.* Dublin: Helicon.

Cormack, R.J. and Osborne, R.D. (1991) *Discrimination and Public Policy in Northern Ireland.* Oxford: Clarendon Press.

CRC (Community Relations Council) (1991) *Community Development in Protestant Areas.* Belfast: CRC.

— (2003) *A Shared Future: Response by the Community Relations Council.* Belfast: CRC.

— (2005) *A Shared Future: From Consultation to Action.* Belfast: CRC.

CRU (Community Relations Unit) (2005) *A Shared Future – Improving Relations in Northern Ireland: The Policy and Strategic Framework for Good Relations in Northern Ireland.* Belfast: CRU and Office of the First Minister and Deputy First Minister (OFMDFM).

CSO (Central Statistical Office) (1987) *Regional Trends 22.* London: HMSO.

CWC (Community Workers' Co-operative) (2007) *Building Peace and Democracy in Ireland North and South: The Role of the Community and Voluntary Sector.* CWC.

Darby, J. (ed.) (1983) *Northern Ireland: The Background to the Conflict.* Belfast: Appletree.

— (1986) *Intimidation and the Control of the Conflict in Northern Ireland.* Dublin: Gill & Macmillan.

Darby, J. and Morris, G. (1974) *Intimidation in Housing.* Belfast: Northern Ireland Community Relations Commission.

Darby, J. and Williamson, A. (1978) *Violence and the Social Services in Northern Ireland: Lessons of Devolution.* Dublin: Gill & Macmillan.

Deane, E. (1981) 'Community Work in the 70s' in H. Fraser *et al.*, *Community Work in a Divided Society, Community Action in Northern Ireland*, Vol. 1, No. 1. Belfast: Farset Press.

Deloitte MCS Ltd (2004) *Research to Develop a Methodology for Identifying Areas of Weak Community Infrastructure*, Final Report. Belfast: Department for Social Development.

Devlin, P. (1981) *Yes, We Have no Bananas: Outdoor Relief in Belfast, 1920–39.* Belfast: Blackstaff Press.

DFPNI (Department of Finance and Personnel Northern Ireland) (2010) *2010–11 Northern Ireland Public Sector Pay and Workforce Technical Annex,* April [online], <http://www.dfpni.gov.uk/2010-11-pay-and-workforce-technical-annex.pdf> accessed 21 August 2011.

— (2011) *Northern Ireland Net Fiscal Balance Report, 2008–09* [online], <http://www.dfpni.gov.uk/northern-ireland-net-fiscal-balance-report-08-09.pdf> accessed 20 August 2011.

Dunn, S. (1986) 'The role of education in the Northern Ireland conflict', *Oxford Review of Education* 12(3): 233–42.

Dunn, S., Morgan, V. and Wilson, D. (1989) 'Perceptions of school integration in Northern Ireland', *CORE* 13(2).

Farrell, M. (1976) *Northern Ireland: The Orange State.* London: Pluto Press.

Frazer, H. and Fitzduff, M. (1994) *Improving Community Relations,* CRC Pamphlet No.3. Belfast: CRC.

Freire, P. (1973) *Pedagogy of the Oppressed.* Harmondsworth: Penguin.

Gaffkin, F. (1976) 'Self-Help in a Catholic Working-Class Community'. Unpublished MSc thesis, Queen's University Belfast.

Gilligan, C., and Tonge, J. (eds) (1997) *Peace or War? Understanding the Peace Process in Northern Ireland.* Aldershot: Ashgate.

Graham, B. (2008) 'Containment and the Politics of Loyalist-Based Conflict Transformation', in M. Busteed, F. Neal and J. Tonge (eds) *Irish Protestant Identities.* Manchester: Manchester University Press.

Griffiths, H. (1974a) *The NICRC: A Case Study in Agency Conflict.* Coleraine: New University of Ulster.

— (1974b) 'Carrying on in the Middle of Violent Conflict: Some Observations of Experience in Northern Ireland' in D. Jones and M. Mayo (eds) *Community Work One.* London: Routledge & Kegan Paul.

— (1975) 'Paramilitary groups and other community action groups in Northern Ireland today', *International Review of Community Development* 33(4).

— (1978) 'Community Reaction and Voluntary Involvement' in J. Darby and A. Williamson (eds) *Violence and the Social Services in Northern Ireland.* London: Heineman, pp. 165–94.

Hall, M. (ed.) (1993) *Life on the Interface: Belfast 'Peaceline' Community Groups Confront Common Issues,* Island Pamphlets No.1. Newtownabbey: Island Publications.

Harris, R. (1972) *Prejudice and Tolerance in Ulster: A Study of Neighbours and Strangers in a Border Community.* Manchester: Manchester University Press.

Hayes, M. (1972) 'Community relations and the role of the community relations commission in Northern Ireland', *Administration* 20(4).

Heatley, C. (2004) *Interface: Flashpoints in Northern Ireland.* Belfast: Lagan Books.

Heenan, D. and McLaughlin, R. (2002) 'Re-assessing the role of credit unions in community development: a case study of Derry Credit Union, Northern Ireland', *Community Development Journal* 37(3): 249–59.

Hughes, J., Donnelly, C., Robinson, G. and Dowds, L. (2003) *Community Relations in Northern Ireland: The Long View*, ARK Northern Ireland Social and Political Archive [online], <http://www.ark.ac.uk/publications/occasional/occpaper2.PDF> accessed 20 August 2011.

Jones, E. (1956) 'The segregation of Roman Catholics and Protestants in Belfast', *Sociological Review* 4(2).

— (1960) *A Social Geography of Belfast*. London: Oxford University Press.

Kelly, G. (1998) *Mediation in Practice: A Report of the Art of Mediation Project*. Derry: INCORE [online], <http://cain.ulst.ac.uk/issues/parade/kelly.htm> accessed 20 August 2011.

Kennedy, L. (1986) *Two Ulsters: The Case for Repartition*. Belfast: Queen's University Belfast.

Kilmurray, A. (2009) 'Governmentality and community action: the application of an analytical approach', *Irish Journal of Community Work*, Issue 1, July, 98–113.

Lewis, H. (2006) *New Trends in Community Development*. Derry: INCORE [online], <http://www.incore.ulst.ac.uk/policy/lilp/New_Trends_Com_Dev.pdf> accessed 20 August 2011.

Lovett, T. (1997) 'Community education and community development: the Northern Ireland experience', *Studies in the Education of Adults* 29(1): 39–50.

Lundy, P. and McGovern, M. (2006) 'Participation, truth and partiality: participatory action research, community-based truth-telling and post-conflict transition in Northern Ireland', *Sociology* 40(1): 71–88.

Mallie, E. and McKittrick, D. (1996) *The Fight for Peace: The Secret Story Behind the Irish Peace Process*. London: Heinemann.

Marris, P. (1974) 'Experimenting in Social Reforms' in D. Jones and M. Mayo (eds) *Community Work One*. London: Routledge & Kegan Paul, pp. 256–8.

Maud Report (1967) *Report of the Royal Commission on Local Government in England*, Chairman Sir John Maud. London: HMSO.

McCann, E. (1973) *War and an Irish Town*. London: Pluto Books.

McCorry, J. and Morrisey, M. (1989) 'Community, crime and punishment in West Belfast', *Howard Journal* 28(4): 282–90.

McCready, S. (2001) *Empowering People: Community Development and Conflict 1969–1999*. Belfast: HMSO.

McEvoy, K. and Shirlow, P. (2009) 'Re-imagining DDR ex-combatants, leadership and moral agency in conflict transformation', *Theoretical Criminology* 13(1): 31–59.

McKittrick, D., Kelters, S., Feeney, B. and Thornton, C. (2004) *Lost Lives: The Stories of the Men, Women and Children Who Died Through the Northern Ireland Troubles* (3rd edn). Edinburgh: Mainstream.

Mitchell, C., Gribben, V. and Kelly, R. (2005) *Loyalist Conflict Transformation Initiatives*. Belfast: OFMDFM.

Moody, T.W. and Beckett, J.C. (eds) (1955) *Ulster Since 1800: A Political and Economic Survey*. London: Oxford University Press.

Moriarty, G. and Nihill, C. (2011) 'Nationalist violence continues in Ardoyne', *Irish Times* 13 July 2011.

Morrow, D. (2000) *Community Relations and Peace Building: What Have We Learned? Reflections by Recipients of Grant Aid from the European Programme of the Northern Ireland Community Relations Council, Belfast, Northern Ireland.* Belfast: CRC.

Munck, R., Rolston, B. and Moore, G. (1987) *Belfast in the Thirties: An Oral History.* Belfast: Blackstaff Press.

NICRC (Northern Ireland Community Relations Commission) (1971) *Flight: A Report on Population Movement in Belfast During August 1971.* Belfast: NICRC.

NUU (New University of Ulster) Social Administration Department Research Team (1975) *Community Action and Community Perceptions of the Social Services in Northern Ireland.* Coleraine: NUU.

Ó hAdhmaill, F. (1983) 'Alternatives to the Northern Ireland Dual Education System', unpublished BSc thesis, University of Ulster.

— (1990) 'The Function and Dynamics of the Ghetto; A Study of Nationalist West Belfast', unpublished PhD thesis, University of Ulster.

O'Brien, T. (ed.) *Social and Economic Self-Help in Ireland.* Derry: Institute of Continuing Education, Magee College.

O'Dowd, L., Rolston, B. and Tomlinson, M. (1980) *Northern Ireland: Between Civil Rights and Civil War.* Belfast: CSE Books.

O'Prey, M. and Magowan, J. (2001) *Weak Community Infrastructure: A Support Priority.* Belfast: Northern Ireland Voluntary Trust.

Osborne, R.D. and Cormack, R.J. (1987) 'Religion, occupations and employment 1971–1981', Fair Employment Agency Research Paper no. II. Belfast: FEA.

Political Vetting of Community Work Working Group (1990) *The Political Vetting of Community Work in Northern Ireland.* Belfast: Northern Ireland Council for Voluntary Action.

Putnam, R. (2000) *Bowling Alone.* New York: Simon & Schuster.

Robson, T. (2000) *The State and Community Action.* London: Pluto Press.

Rolston, B. (1984) 'Whatever happened to community politics?' *Fortnight*, July/August, 5–6.

Rose, R. (1971) *Governing Without Consensus: An Irish Perspective.* London: Faber & Faber.

Ruane, J. and Todd, J. (1996) *The Dynamics of Conflict in Northern Ireland.* Cambridge: Cambridge University Press.

Rural Community Network (2003) *Border Protestants and Community Development.* Cookstown: Rural Community Network.

Seebohm Report (1968) *Committee on Local Authority and Allied Personal Social Services Report*, Cmnd 3703. London: HMSO.

Shirlow, P., Graham, B., McEvoy, K., Ó hAdhmaill, F. and Purvis, D. (2005) *Politically Motivated Former Prisoner Groups: Community Activism and Conflict Transformation, A Research Report submitted to the Northern Ireland Community Relations Council.* Belfast: CRC.

Singleton, D. (1985) 'Housing and planning policy in Northern Ireland: problems of implementation in a divided community', *Policy and Politics* 13(3): 305–26.

Skeffington Report (1960) *Committee on Public Participation in Planning, People and Planning*. London: HMSO.

Smith, C.S. and Anderson B. (1972) 'Political Participation through Community Action' in G. Parry (ed.) *Participation in Politics*. Manchester: Manchester University Press, pp. 303–18.

Smith, D.J. and Chambers, G. (1991) *Equality and Inequality in Northern Ireland, Part 4: Public Housing*. London: Policy Studies Institute.

— (1991) *Inequality in Northern Ireland*. Oxford: Clarendon Press.

Sutton, M. (2001) *Sutton Index of Deaths, 1969–2001*, available online at Conflict Archive on the Internet (CAIN) <http://cain.ulst.ac.uk/sutton/index.html>.

Thomason, G. (1961) *Community Development in Ireland*. Tipperary: Muintir na Tíre Publications.

Voluntary Activity Unit (1999) *The Story of Community Infrastructure in Northern Ireland*. Belfast: Department of Health and Social Services.

Weiner, R. (1976) 'The Shankill: power in participation', *The Planner* 62(4): 102–3.

— (1978) *The Rape and Plunder of the Shankill*. Belfast: Farset Co-operative Press.

Whyte, J. (1983) 'How Much Discrimination Was There Under the Unionist Regime 1921–1968?' in T. Gallagher and J. O'Connell (eds) *Contemporary Irish Studies*. Manchester: Manchester University Press.

Williamson, A. (ed.) (1995) *Beyond Violence: The Role of Voluntary and Community Action in Building a Sustainable Peace in Northern Ireland*. Belfast: CRC.

Williamson, A.P., Beattie, R.S. and Osborne, S.P. (2004) 'Addressing fragmentation and social exclusion through community involvement in rural regeneration partnerships: evidence from the Northern Ireland experience', *Policy and Politics* 32: 350–69.

Wolfenden, J.B. (1978) *The Future of Voluntary Organizations: The Report of the Wolfenden Committee*. London: Croom Helm.

CHAPTER 7. WHAT IS FAMILY SUPPORT ANYWAY?

Audit Commission (UK) (1994) *Seen but not Heard*. London: Stationery Office.

Browne, V. (2010) 'And so it's agreed – we will change nothing', *Irish Times* 13 October, p. 14.

Buchanan, A. (2002) 'Family Support' in D. Mc Neish, T. Newman and H. Roberts (eds), *What Works For Children?* Buckingham: Open University Press.

Canavan, J., Dolan, P. and Pinkerton, J. (2000) *Family Support: Direction from Diversity*. London: Jessica Kingsley.

Canavan, J. and O Brien, M. (2005) *Ballinasloe Family Support Service: Evaluation Report*. Galway: Child and Family Research and Policy Unit, WHB/NUI Galway.

Cannan, C. and Warren, C. (1997) *Social Action with Children and Families: A Community Development Approach to Child and Family Welfare*. London: Routledge.

Daly, M. (ed.) (2007) *Parenting in Contemporary Europe: A Positive Approach.* Strasbourg: Council of Europe Publications.

Daly, M. and Clavero, S. (2002) *Contemporary Family Policy: A Comparative Review of Ireland, France, Germany, Sweeden and the UK.* Dublin: Institute of Public Administration.

Daly, M. and Leonard, M. (2002) *Against All Odds: Family Life on a Low Income in Ireland.* Dublin: Institute of Public Administration.

Danziger, S. and Waldfogel, J. (2000) *Investing in Children: What Do We Know? What Should We Do?,* CASE Paper 34. London: Centre for the Analysis of Social Exclusion.

D'Cruz, H. and Stagnitti, K. (2008) 'Reconstructing child welfare through participatory and child-centred practice: a conceptual approach', *Child and Family Social Work* 13(2): 156–65.

Dolan, J., Canavan, J. and Pinkerton, J. (2006) *Family Support as Reflective Practice.* London: Jessica Kingsley.

Fahey, T. and Russell, H. (2001) *Family Formation in Ireland: Trends, Data Needs and Implication,* Policy Research Series No. 43. Dublin: Economic and Social Research Institute.

Garrett, P.M. (2009) *'Transforming' Children's Services? Social Work, Neoliberalism and 'Modern' World.* Maidenhead: Open University Press.

Ghate, D. and Hazel, N. (2002), *Parenting in Poor Environments: Stress, Support and Coping.* London: Jessica Kingsley.

Gill, O. and Jack, G. (2007) *The Child and Family in Context: Developing Ecological Practice in Disadvantaged Communities.* Dorset: Russell House.

Gilligan, R. (2000) 'Family Support: Issues and Prospects' in J. Canavan, P. Dolan and J. Pinkerton (eds), *Family Support: Direction from Diversity.* London: Jessica Kingsley.

Hantrais, L. and Letablier, M.T. (1996) *Families and Family Policies in Europe.* London: Longman.

Home-Start International (2005) *Transitional Report, Learning from Families, Policies and Practices to Combat Social Exclusion amongst Families with Young Children in Europe.* London: Home-Start International.

HSE (Health Service Executive) (2010) *Roscommon Child Care Case: Report of the Inquiry Team to the Health Service Executive* [online], <http://www.hse.ie/eng/services/Publications/services/Children/RoscommonChildCareCase.pdf> accessed 14 January 2011.

Jameson, F. (2000) 'Postmodernism or the Cultural Logic of Late Capitalism' in M. Hardt and K. Weeks (eds) *The Jameson Reader.* Oxford: Blackwell.

Katz, I. and Pinkerton, J. (eds) (2003) *Evaluating Family Support: Thinking Internationally, Thinking Critically.* Chichester: Wiley.

Lederach, J.P. (1995) *Preparing for Peace: Conflict Transformation across Cultures.* New York: Syracuse University Press.

Luepnitz, D.A. (1988) *The Family Interpreted Psychoanalysis, Feminism, and Family Therapy.* USA: Basic Books.

McKeown, K., Haase, T. and Pratschke, J. (2001) *Springboard Promoting Family Well-being: Through Family Support Services, Final Evaluation of Springboard January 2000 to May 2001*. Dublin: Department of Health and Children.

Mullaly, B. (2007) *The New Structural Social Work* (3rd edn). Ontario: Oxford University Press.

NICHE Springboard (2007) *Residents' Experiences of Helping Agencies, Experiences, Reflections and Recommendations*. Cork: NICHE.

O'Doherty, C. (2007) *A New Agenda for Family Support: Providing Services that Create Social Capital*. Dublin: Blackhall.

Oliver, P. (2010) *Foucault: The Key Ideas*. London: Hodder Education.

O Toole, S. (2002), *North Lee Springboard Initiative Report*, internal report compiled for the Child Care Manager's Office and North Lee Community Work Department, October.

Parton, N. (1991) *Governing the Family: Child Care, Child Protection and the State*. London: Macmillan.

Phillips, G. (2008) 'Resilience in practice interventions', *Child Care in Practice* 14(1): 45–54.

Quinton, D. (2004) *Supporting Parents: Messages from Research*. London: Jessica Kingsley.

Rogers, C.R. (1961) *On Becoming a Person: A Therapist's View of Psychotherapy*. London: Constable.

Sandbaek, M. (2007) 'Services to Support Positive Parenting' in M. Daly (ed.), *Parenting in Contemporary Europe: A Positive Approach*. Strasbourg: Council of Europe Publications.

Ungar, M. (ed.) (2005) *Handbook for Working with Children and Youth: Pathways to Resilience across Cultures and Contexts*. Thousand Oaks, CA: Sage.

Warren, C. (1997) 'Family Support and the Journey to Empowerment' in C. Cannan and C. Warren, *Social Action with Children and Families: A Community Development Approach to Child and Family Welfare*. London: Routledge.

Weissberg, R.P., Kumfer, K.L. and Seligman, M.E.E.P. (2003), 'Prevention that works for children and youth: an introduction', *American Psychologist* June/July, 58(6–7), 425–32.

Westoby, P. (2008) 'Developing a community development approach through engaging resettling Southern Sudanese refugees within Australia', *Community Development Journal* 43(4): 483–95.

CHAPTER 8. NURTURING COLLABORATIVE RELATIONSHIPS AND DEVELOPING LOCAL COMMUNITIES

Atkinson, M., Wilkin, A., Stott, A., Doherty, P. and Kinder, K. (2002) *Multi-Agency Working: A Detailed Study*, LGA Research Report 26. Slough: NFER

Bertram, T., Pascal, C., Bokhari, S., Gasper, M., Holterman, S., John, K. and Nelson, C. (2002) *Early Excellence Centre Pilot Programme 3rd Annual Evaluation Report 2001–2002*. Birmingham: Centre for Research in Early Childhood.

Bisno, H. (1988) *Managing Conflict*. London: Sage.

Browne, G. Roberts, J., Gafni, A., Bryne, C., Kertyzia, J. and Loney, P. (2004) 'Conceptualising and validating the human services integration measure', *International Journal of Integrated Care* 4: 1–12.

Butterworth, J., Foley, S. and Metzel, D. (2001) *Developing Interagency Agreements: Four Questions to Consider*. Virgina: Commonwealth University, Community Door Institution Brief No. 14.

Cheminais, R. (2009) *Effective Multi-Agency Partnerships: Putting Every Child Matters into Practice*. London: Sage.

Cornwall, A. (2008) 'Unpacking "participation": models, meanings and practices', *Community Development Journal* 43(3): 269–83.

Costongs, C. and Springett, J. (1997) 'Joint working and the production of a city health plan: the Liverpool experience', *Health Promotion International* 12(1): 9–19.

Cunningham-Smith, V. (2004) 'Interagency collaboration: a mixed bag', *Developing Practice*, Autumn: 15–18, in Human Community Services (2010) *Interagency Collaboration: Making it Work*, Research to Practice Notes. New South Wales Government.

CWC (Community Workers' Co-operative) (2008) *Towards Standards for Quality Community Work. An All-Ireland Statement of Values, Principles and Work Standards*. Galway: CWC.

Darlington, Y. and Feeney, J.A. (2008) 'Collaboration between mental health and child protection services: professionals' perceptions of best practice', *Child and Youth Service Review* 30(2): 187–98.

Darlington, Y., Feeney, J.A. and Rixon, K. (2005) 'Interagency collaboration between child protection and mental health services: practices, attitudes and barriers', *Child Abuse and Neglect* 29(10): 1085–98.

Department for Education (UK) (2006) *Every Child Matters: Change for Children: Benefits of Multi-agency Working* [online], <http://www.everychildmatters.gov.uk/deliveringservices/multiagencyworking> accessed 8 September 2010.

Dolan, P., Pinkerton, J. and Canavan, J. (2006) *Family Support as Reflective Practice*. London: Jessica Kingsley.

Drabble, L. (2007) 'Pathways to collaboration: exploring values and collaborative practices between child welfare and substance abuse treatment fields', *Child Maltreatment* 12(1): 31–42.

Dunlop, J.M. and Holosko, M.J. (2004) 'The story behind the story of collaborative networks – relationships do matter!', *Journal of Health and Social Policy* 19(3): 1–18.

Ervin, N. (2004) 'Assessing interagency collaboration through perceptions of families', *Journal of Community Health Nursing* 21(1): 49–60.

Fine, M., Pancharatnam, K. and Thomson, C. (2005) *Coordinated and Integrated Human Service Delivery Models*, SPRC Report 1/05. Sydney: Social Policy Research Centre, University of New South Wales.

Friedman, S.R., Reynolds, J., Quan, M.A., Call, S., Crusto, C.A. and Kaufman, J.S. (2007). 'Measuring changes in interagency collaboration: an examination of the Bridgeport Safe Start initiative', *Evaluation and Program Planning*, 30(3): 294–306.

Frost, N. (2005) *Professionalism, Partnership and Joined-up Thinking. A Research Review of Front-Line Working with Children and Families*. UK: Research in Practice (www.rip.org.uk).

Gardner, S. (1996) 'Accountability in Community Building' in Civic Practices Network, *Story-Making: United Way and Community Building* [online], <http://www.cpn.org/topics/community/uwaystorymaking.htlm#building> accessed 5 September 2009.

Garrett, P.M. (2004) 'Talking child protection: the police and social workers "working together"', *Journal of Social Work* 4(1): 77–97.

Gray, B. (1989) *Collaborating: Finding Common Ground for Multiparty Problems*. San Francisco: Jossey-Bass.

Green, B.L., Rockhill, A. and Burrus, S. (2008) 'The role of interagency collaboration for substance-abusing families involved with child welfare', *Child Welfare* 87(1): 29–61.

Halsey, K., Gulliver, C., Johnson, A., Martin, K and Kinder, K. (2005) *Evaluation of Behaviour and Education Support Teams*, Research Brief RB706. Nottingham: DfES.

Hardiker, P., Exton, K. and Baker, M. (1991) *Policies and Practices in Preventive Child Care*. Aldershot: Ashgate.

Harlow, E. and Shardlow, S.M. (2006) 'International models of hospital interdisciplinary teams for the identification, assessment, and treatment of child abuse', *Social Work in Health Care* 46(4): 1–16.

Hartman, A. (1995) 'Diagrammatic assessment of family relationships', *Families in Society* 76: 111–22.

Head, B.W. (2008) 'Assessing network-based collaborations: effectiveness for whom?' *Public Management Review* 10(6): 733–49.

Henderson, M. and P. (2004) *Partnerships for Service Delivery: Review of the Research and Practice Literature: Report to the Queensland Department of Communities, Brisbane* (Henderson Report). Brisbane: Department of Communities 2005.

Hopkin, L. (2006) 'Competition and cooperation: coordinating services to establish a lifelong learning hub', *Social City* 1: 1–11.

Hultberg, E.-L., Glendinning, C., Allebeck, P. and Lonnroth, K. (2005) 'Using pooled budgets to integrate health and welfare services: a comparison of experiments in England and Sweden', *Health and Social Care in the Community* 13: 531–41.

Katz, I. and Hetherington, R. (2006) 'Co-operating and communicating: a European perspective on integrating services for children', *Child Abuse Review* 15: 429–39.

Lennie, J. (2006) *Learnings, Case Studies and Guidelines for Establishing Shared and Collaborative Service Delivery in the Non-Government Sector: Evaluation of the*

Multi-Tenant Service Centre (MTSC) Pilot Project. Brisbane: Queensland Department of Communities.

— (2007) *Challenges and Strategies for the Sustainability and Viability of Non-Profit Multi-Tenant Service Centres: A Literature Review*. Brisbane: Queensland Department of Communities.

Lloyd, G., Stead, J. and Kendrick, A. (2001) *Hanging on in there. A Study of Inter-agency Work to Prevent School Exclusion in Three Local Authorities*. London: NCB.

Mackinnon Partnership (2005) *Easton EMAP, Lockleaze and Knowle West & Filwood Youth Inclusion and Support Panels (YISPs): An Evaluation Report to Bristol Youth Offending Team*. Middlesex: Mackinnon Partnerships.

McInnes, K. (2007) *A Practitioner's Guide to Interagency Working in Children's Centres: A Review of Literature*. London: Barnardo's.

McTernan, E. and Godfrey, A. (2006) 'Children's services planning in Northern Ireland: developing a planned model to address rights and needs', *Child Care in Practice* 12(3): 219–40.

Melcher, J. (1999) *Putting the Pieces Together*, Best Practice Briefs no.3 1998–1999. Michigan: Michigan State University Outreach Partnership.

Metcalfe, J., Riedinger, M., McKenzie, M. and Cook, L. (2007) *Cross-sector Collaboration for Child and Youth Services*. West Perth, WA: Australian Research Alliance for Children and Youth.

Norris, A. (2005) *Capacity Building Through Community and Government Collaboration*, Proceedings of the International Conference on Engaging Communities, 14–17 August 2005, Brisbane Convention and Exhibition Centre [online], <http://www.engagingcommunities2005.org/abstract/Norris-Andrew-final.pdf> accessed 5 July 2008.

NSW DCS (New South Wales Department of Community Services) (2005). *Interagency Guidelines for Child Protection Intervention*. New South Wales Government.

Richardson, S. and Asthana, S. (2006) 'Interagency information sharing in health and social care services: the role of the professional culture', *British Journal of Social Work* 36: 657–69.

Simpson, A., Miller, C. and Bowers, L. (2003) 'The history of the care programme approach in England: where did it go wrong?' *Journal of Mental Health* 12: 489–504.

Sloper, P. (2004) 'Facilitators and barriers for co-ordinated multi-agency services', *Child Care, Health and Development* 30: 571–80.

Sylva, K., Sammons, P., Melhuish, E., Siraj-Blatchford, I. and Taggart, B. (1997–2003) *The Effective Provision of Pre-School Education (EPPE) Project*. London: Institute of Education, University of London.

Tomlinson, K. (2003) *Effective Interagency Working: A Review of the Literature and Examples from Practice*, Local Government Association Research Report 40. Slough: NFER.

Townsend, A. and Shelley, K. (2008) 'Validating an instrument for assessing work-force collaboration', *Community College Journal of Research and Practice* 32: 101–12.

Townsley, R., Abbot, D. and Watson, D. (2003) *Making a Difference? Exploring the Impact of Multi-Agency Working on Disabled Children with Complex Health Care Needs, their Families and the Professionals who Support them*. Bristol: Norah Fry Research Centre, University of Bristol, <http://www.bris.ac.uk/Depts/NorahFry> accessed 12 July 2008.

Valentine, K., Fisher, K. and Thomson, C. (2006) 'Making integration happen: the Families First policy experience', *Child Abuse Review* 15(6): 414–28.

Walker, R. (2010) *Forging New Links with the Community Services Sector to Build a Better Health Care System*. Queensland Council of Social Services.

Walsh, P., McGregor-Lowndes, M. and Newton, C.J. (2006). *Shared Services: Lessons from the Public and Private Sectors for the Nonprofit Sector*. Brisbane: Centre of Philanthropy and Nonprofit Studies, University of Queensland.

Whyte, B. (1997) 'Crossing boundaries: an exercise in partnership provision', *British Journal of Social Work* 27: 679–704.

CHAPTER 9. VOLUNTEERS AS MANAGERS OF FAMILY RESOURCE CENTRES

Broaderick, S. (2002) 'Community development in Ireland – a policy review', *Community Development Journal* 37(1): 101–10.

Bussell, H. and Forbes, D. (2002) 'Understanding the volunteer market: the what, where, who and why of volunteering', *International Journal of Nonprofit and Voluntary Sector Marketing*, 7(3): 244–57.

Connolly, P. (2006) 'Management style in the non-profit sector in Ireland', *Irish Journal of Management* 26(2): 129–47.

Cuskelly, G., Taylor, T., Hoye, R. and Darcy, S. (2006) 'Volunteer management practices and volunteer retention: a human resource management approach', *Sport Management Review* 9: 141–63.

Department of Social Protection (2010) 'Minister Ó Cuív announces arrangements for 5,000 new Tús work placement opportunities in the community sector' (press release), 21 December [online], <http://www.welfare.ie/EN/Press/Releases/2010/Pages/pr211210.aspx> accessed 9 February 2011.

Donnelly-Cox, G., Donoghue, F. and Hayes, T. (2001) 'Conceptualizing the third sector in Ireland, North and South', *Voluntas: International Journal of Voluntary and Nonprofit Organizations* 12(3): 195–204.

Forsyth, J. (1999) 'Volunteer management strategies: balancing risk and reward', *Nonprofit World* 17(3): 40–3.

FRC (Family Resource Centre) National Forum (2006) 'Supporting Families, Building Communities 2006–2009 Strategic Plan' [online], <http://www.frcnf.com/documents.Summaryfinalversion.pdf> accessed 19 January 2011.

— (2009a) 'Cuts to Family Resource Centres would cripple local economies and communities' (press release), 3 August.

— (2009b) 'Continuation of Family Resource Centres is welcome but many challenges lie ahead' (press release), 14 December.

FSA (Family Support Agency) (2007a) *Family and Community Services Resources Centre Programme. SPEAK FRC National Database: Trends 2004–2007.* Dublin: Family Support Agency.

— (2007b) *Family and Community Services Resources Centre Programme. Resources, Activities, Partners and Achievements 2007.* Dublin: Family Support Agency.

— (2008) *Family and Community Services Resources Centre Programme. Resources, Activities, Partners and Achievements 2008.* Dublin: Family Support Agency.

— (2009) *Family and Community Services Resources Centre Programme. Resources, Activities, Partners and Achievements 2009.* Dublin: Family Support Agency.

Gaynor, N. (2009) 'In-active citizenship and the depoliticization of community development in Ireland', *Community Development Journal*, July: 1–15.

Hager, M.A. and Brudney, J.L. (2004) *Volunteer Management Practices and Retention of Volunteers.* Chicago, IL: Urban Institute.

Halfpenny, P. and Reid, M. (2002) 'Research on the voluntary sector: an overview', *Policy and Politics*, 30(4): 533–50.

Lee, A. (2003) 'Community development in Ireland', *Community Development Journal* 38(1), January: 48–58.

McCarthy, C. (2009) *Report of the Special Group on Public Service Numbers and Expenditure Programmes.* Dublin: Government Publications.

Milligan, C. and Fyfe, N.R. (2005) 'Preserving space for volunteers: exploring the links between voluntary welfare organisations, volunteering and citizenship', *Urban Studies* 42(3): 417–33.

Varley, T. (1999) 'More Power to the People? The Politics of Community Action in Late Twentieth-Century Ireland' in S. Healy and B. Reynolds (eds), *Social Policy in Ireland: Principles, Practice and Problems.* Dublin: Oak Tree Press, pp. 387–409.

Wheel, The (2005) *Sector Skills. Addressing the Training Needs of the Community and Voluntary Sector.* Dublin: The Wheel.

CHAPTER 10. FAMILY RESOURCE CENTRES, COMMUNITY DEVELOPMENT AND RESTORATIVE JUSTICE: COMPATIBLE ENDEAVOURS?

Anslow, G. (2001) 'Victim/Offender Mediation Service' in P. Keeley (ed.), *Restorative Justice – Challenges and Benefits for Irish Society.* Dublin: Victim/Offender Mediation Service.

Ashworth, A. (2002) 'Responsibilities, rights and restorative justice', *British Journal of Criminology* 43(3): 578–95.

Bon, V. (2007) *Voluntary Management Committees: The Community Development and Family and Community Services Resource Centre Programmes South and Mid West Regions – Who We Are and Where We Come From.* Limerick: SMWCDSA.

Bryman, A. (2004) *Social Research Methods* (2nd edn). Oxford: Oxford University Press.

CDX (Community Development Exchange) 2009 'What is Community Development?' [online], <http://www.cdx.org.uk/what-is-community-development> accessed 10 March 2009.

Changing Ireland (2006), Spring: issue 17. Limerick: Community Development Network Moyross.

Craig, G., Gorman, M. and Vercseg, I. (2004) *The Budapest Declaration – Building European Civil Society through Community Development* [online], <http://www.cdf.org.uk/SITE/UPLOAD/DOCUMENT/The_Budapest_Declaration.pdf> accessed 10 March 2009.

CWC (Community Workers' Co-operative) (2008) *Towards Standards in Quality Community Work*. Galway: Community Workers' Co-op [online] <http://www.cwc.ie/news/StandardsForQualityCommunity_01.12.08/Towards%20Standards%20for%20Quality%20Community%20Work%20-%20complete.pdf> accessed 20 March 2009.

Denscombe, M. (2007) *The Good Research Guide* (3rd edn). Maidenhead: Open University Press.

DJELR (Department of Justice, Equality and Law Reform) (2007) 'National Commission on Restorative Justice established' (press release). Dublin: Department of Justice, Equality and Law Reform [online], <http://www.justice.ie/en/JELR/Pages/PR07000321> accessed 13 March 2009.

FCWTG (Federation of Community Work Training Groups) (2001) *Making Changes – Practice into Policy*. Sheffield: FCWTG [online], <http://www.fcdl.org.uk/publications/documents/cdl/making_changes.doc> accessed 10 February 2009.

FSA (Family Support Agency) (2007) *Family and Community Services Resource Centre Programme 2007: A Guide for Community Groups* [online], <http://www.fsa.ie/familyresource/FRCGuidelinesforInclusion2007.doc> accessed 20 March 2009.

— (2008a) *Family Support Agency* [online], <http://www.fsa.ie/familyresource/index.html> accessed 20 March 2009.

— (2008b) *SPEAK FRC National Database: Trends 2004–2007*. Dublin: FSA.

— (2008c) *Family and Community Services Resource Centre Programme: Resources, Activities, Partners and Achievements 2007*. Dublin: FSA [online], <http://www.fsa.ie/leadmin/user_upload/Files/SPEAK_2007_final_report.pdf> accessed 7 March 2009.

Graef, R. (2001) *Why Restorative Justice?* London: Calouste Gulbenkian Foundation.

Haverty, M. (2009) *Integrating Wholesale Restorative Justice within Irish Society: Issues and Considerations Facing Policy Makers* [online], <http://works.bepress.com/cgi/viewcontent.cgi?article=1000&context=martin_haverty> accessed 18 April 2009.

Henderson, P. and Salmon, H. (2001) *Social Inclusion and Community Development*. London: Community Development Foundation.

Johnstone, G. (2002) *Restorative Justice – Ideas, Values, Debates.* Cullompton: Willan.

— (2003) 'Introduction: restorative approaches to criminal justice' in *A Restorative Justice Reader – Texts, Sources, Context.* Cullompton: Willan.

Johnstone, G. and Van Ness, D.W. (eds) (2007a) *The Handbook of Restorative Justice.* Cullompton: Willan.

— (2007b) 'The Meaning of Restorative Justice' in *The Handbook of Restorative Justice.* Cullompton: Willan.

Keeley, P. (2001a) 'Conference Overview' in *Restorative Justice – Challenges and Benefits for Irish Society*; Dublin: Victim/Offender Mediation Service.

— (2001b) *Restorative Justice – Challenges and Benefits for Irish Society*; Dublin: Victim/Offender Mediation Service.

Kitzinger, J. (1995) 'Qualitative research: introducing focus groups', *British Medical Journal* 311: 299–302.

Kitzinger, J. and Barbour, R.S. (eds) (1999): *Developing Focus Group Research: Politics, Theory and Practice.* London: Sage.

Ledwith, M. (2005) *Community Development – A Critical Approach.* Bristol: Policy Press.

Lee, A. (2006) *Community Development: Current Issues and Challenges.* Dublin: Combat Poverty Agency.

Levant, S., Cullen, F.T., Fulton, B. and Wozniak, J.F. (1999) 'Reconsidering restorative justice: the corruption of benevolence revisited', *Crime and Delinquency* 45(1) 3–27.

Lincoln, Y.S. and Guba, E.G. (1985) *Naturalistic Enquiry.* Newbury Park: Sage.

Marshall, T. (1996) 'The evolution of restorative justice in Britain', *European Journal of Criminal Policy and Research* 4(4): 21–43.

McCold, P. (1998) 'Restorative Justice – Variations on a Theme' in L. Walgrave (ed.), *Restorative Justice for Juveniles: Potentialities, Risks and Problems for Research : A Selection of Papers Presented at the International Conference, Leuven, May 12–14, 1997.* Leuven, Belgium: Leuven University Press.

— (2004) 'What is the Role of Community in Restorative Justice?' in H. Zehr and B. Toews (eds) (2004) *Critical Issues in Restorative Justice.* Monsey, NY: Criminal Justice Press.

McCold, P. and Wachtel, B. (1998) 'Community is not a Place: A New Look at Community Justice Initiatives' in Johnstone, G. (ed.) *A Restorative Justice Reader – Texts, Sources, Context.* Cullompton: Willan.

Meagher, A. (2006) 'Editorial' in *Changing Ireland*, issue 17. Limerick: Community Development Network Moyross.

Motherway, B. (2006) *The Role of Community Development in Tackling Poverty in Ireland – A Literature Review.* Dublin: Combat Poverty Agency.

NCRJ (National Commission on Restorative Justice) (2008) *Interim Report March 2008.* Dublin: NCRJ.

NCRP (Nenagh Community Reparation Project) (2008) *Development of the Nenagh Community Reparation Project* [online], <http://www.nenaghreparation.org/development_printer.htm> accessed 2 May 2008.

Newman, P., Duan, N., Rudy, E.T. and Johnston-Roberts, K. (2004) 'HIV and risk prevention in a post-vaccine context', *Vaccine* 22: 1954–63.

Oireachtas (2007) *Joint Committee on Justice, Equality, Defence and Women's Rights Report on Restorative Justice.* Dublin: Houses of the Oireachtas.

PAULO (2003) *National Occupational Standards in Community Development Work.* Grantham (Lincs): PAULO [online], <http://www.fcdl.org.uk/publications/documents/nos/Standards%20040703.pdf> accessed 12 February 2009.

Powell, F. and Geoghegan, M. (2004) *The Politics of Community Development.* Dublin: A. & A. Farmar.

Raye, B.E. and Roberts, A. (2007) 'Restorative Processes' in G. Johnstone and D.W. Van Ness (eds), *The Handbook of Restorative Justice.* Cullompton: Willan.

Schiff, M. (2007) 'Satisfying the Needs of Stakeholders' in Johnstone, G. and Van D.W. (eds), *The Handbook of Restorative Justice.* Cullompton: Willan.

SMWCDSA (South and Mid-West Community Development Support Agency) (2007, 2008): *Minutes of Anti-Social Behaviour Sub-group Meetings.* Unpublished: facilitated by SMWCDSA staff.

Umbreit, M. (1999) *What is Restorative Justice?* [online], http://cehd.umn.edu/ssw/rjp/Resources/RJ_Dialogue_Resources/RJ_Principles/What_is_RJ.pdf, accessed 12 January 2009.

Van Ness, D. (2002) 'The Shape of Things to Come: A Framework for Thinking About a Restorative Justice System' in E. Weitekamp and H. Kerner (eds), *Restorative Justice: Theoretical Foundations.* Cullompton: Willan, pp.1–20.

— (2003) 'Creating Restorative Systems' in G. Johnstone (ed.), *A Restorative Justice Reader.* Cullompton: Willan.

Wallis, P. and Tudor, B. (2008) *The Pocket Guide to Restorative Justice.* London: Jessica Kingsley.

Weitekamp. E. and Kerner, H. (eds) (2002): *Restorative Justice: Theoretical Foundations.* Cullompton: Willan.

Zehr, H. (2002) *The Little Book of Restorative Justice.* Intercourse, PA: Good Books.

— (2005): *Changing Lenses – A New Focus for Crime and Justice.* Scottdale, PA: Herald Press.

Zehr, H. and Mika, H. (1998) 'Appendix 1: Fundamental Principles of Restorative Justice' in Zehr, H. (2002) *The Little Book of Restorative Justice.* Intercourse, PA: Good Books.

Zehr, H. and Toews, B. (eds) (2004) *Critical Issues in Restorative Justice.* Monsey, NY: Criminal Justice Press.

Zernova, M and Wright, M. (2007) 'Alternative Visions of Restorative Justice' in G. Johnstone and D.W. Van Ness (eds), *Handbook of Restorative Justice.* Cullompton: Willan.

CHAPTER 11. EDUCATION: A TOOL FOR COMMUNITY DEVELOPMENT

Action Group on Access to Third Level Education (2001) *Report of the Action Group on Access to Third Level Education.* Dublin: Stationery Office.

Albertini, V. (2009) 'Social networks and community support: sustaining women in need of community-based adult education programs', *New Directions for Adult and Continuing Education* 122, Summer: 23–32.

AONTAS (2009) *Flower Power: Aontás Guide to Best Practice of Women's Community Education.* Dublin: AONTAS.

— (2011) *Community Education: More than Just a Course – Exploring the Outcomes and Impact of Department of Education and Skills Funded Community Education.* Dublin: AONTAS.

Bailey, N. (2009) *Integrating Development Education into Adult Education using Active Citizenship as a Focus.* Dublin: AONTAS.

Bourdieu, P. and Passeron, J-C. (1977) *Reproduction in Education, Society and Culture.* London: Sage.

Collins, M. (1991) *Adult Education as Vocation.* London: Routledge.

Connolly, B. (2001) *Women's Community Education in Ireland.* Dublin: AONTAS.

— (2003) 'Community education: listening to the voices', *Adult Learner – The Irish Journal of Adult and Community Education* 9–19.

Cooke, J. (1999) 'The Dublin Mechanics' Institute', *Dublin Historical Record* 52(1): 15–31.

— (2009) *A History of the Irish Vocational Education Association, 1902–2002.* Naas: Irish Vocational Education Association.

Coolahan, J. (1981) *Irish Education: Its History and Structure.* Dublin: Institute of Public Administration.

CORI (Conference of Religious in Ireland) (2008) *Planning for Progress and Fairness: Policies to Ensure Economic Development, Social Equity and Sustainability – CORI Justice Socio-Economic Review.* Dublin: CORI Justice.

Corridan, M. (2002) *Moving from the Margins: A Study of Male Participation in Adult Literacy.* Dublin: Dublin Adult Learning Centre.

CWC (Community Workers' Co-operative) (2008) *Towards Standards for Quality Community Work.* Dublin: CWC Publications.

Department of Education (1966) *Investment in Education.* Dublin: Stationery Office

— (1967) *Report of the Commission on Higher Education.* Dublin: Stationery Office.

Department of Education and Science (1998) *Green Paper: Adult Education in an Era of Learning.* Dublin: Stationery Office.

— (2000) *Learning for Life: White Paper on Adult Education.* Dublin: Stationery Office.

Department of Education and Skills (2011) *Education Statistics 2009/2010.* Dublin: Stationery Office.

Department of the Taoiseach (1999a) *Opportunities, Challenges and Capacities for Choice* (NESC Report 104). Dublin: Stationery Office.

— (1999b) *The Programme for Prosperity and Fairness*. Dublin: Stationery Office.

Englund, T. (2006) 'Jürgen Habermas and education', *Journal of Curriculum Studies* 38(5): 499–501.

Faure, E. (1972) *Learning to Be: The World of Education, Today and Tomorrow* (Faure Report). Paris: UNESCO.

Ferriter, D. (1996) *Mothers, Maidens and Myths*. Dublin: FÁS.

Fitzsimons, C. (2010) 'Professionalism in community work and its implications for radical community education', *Adult Learner – The Irish Journal of Adult and Community Education in Ireland*, 53–71.

Fleming, T. (2008) 'We are condemned to learn: towards higher education as a learning society', *Level 3*, issue 6 [online], <http://level3.dit.ie/html/issue6/fleming/fleming.pdf> accessed 11 September 2009.

Fleming, T. and Murphy, M. (2006) 'The Application of the Ideas of Habermas to Adult Learning' in P. Sutherland and J. Crowther (eds), *Lifelong Learning: Concepts and Contexts*. London: Routledge, pp. 48–57.

Freire, P. (1970) *Pedagogy of the Oppressed*. London: Penguin.

— (1973) *Education for Critical Consciousness*. New York: Seabury Press.

Government of Ireland (1984) *Lifelong Learning: Report of the Commission on Adult Education*. Dublin: Stationery Office.

— (1995) *Charting Our Education Future: White Paper on Education*. Dublin: Stationery Office.

— (1999a) Qualifications (Education and Training) Act. Dublin: Stationery Office.

— (1999b) *National Development Plan 2000–2006*. Dublin: Stationery Office.

— (2007a) *Towards 2016*. Dublin: Stationery Office.

— (2007b) *National Development Plan: 2007–2013*. Dublin: Stationery Office.

Grossman, M. and Kaestner, R. (1997) 'Effects of Education on Health' in J. Behrman and N. Stacey (eds), *The Social Benefits of Education*. Ann Arbor, MI: University of Michigan Press, pp. 69–123.

Habermas, J. (1985) 'Civil disobedience: litmus test for the democratic constitutional state', *Berkeley Journal of Sociology* 30: 96–116.

— (1989) 'Towards a communication-concept of rational collective will formation: a thought experiment', *Ratio Juris* 2(2): 144–54.

HEA (Higher Education Authority) (2008) *National Plan for Equity of Access to Higher Education 2008–2013*. Dublin: HEA.

Heverin, A. (2009) *ICA: The Irish Countrywomen's Association: A History 1910–2000*. Dublin: ICA and Wolfhound Press.

hooks, b. (1994) *Teaching to Transgress*. London: Routledge.

Inkster, I. (1985) *The Steam Intellect Societies: Essays on Culture, Education and Industry circa 1820–1914*. Nottingham: Nottingham University.

Jarvis, P. and Griffin, C. (2003) 'General Introduction' in P. Jarvis and C. Griffin (eds), *Adult and Continuing Education: Major Themes in Education*, Vol. 1. London: Routledge, pp. 1–14.

Kavanagh, M. (2007) 'The Role of Adult and Community Education in Promoting Equality in Education. Flexible and Friendly'. Bray Partnership Conference on

Equality and Education: Across the Spectrum of Lifelong Learning, 4 October. Dublin: AONTAS.

Kenny, I. (1983). *Report of the Commission on Adult Education* (Kenny Report). Dublin: Stationery Office.

Lovett, T. (1997) 'Community education and community development: the Northern Ireland experience', *Studies in the Education of Adults* 29(1): 39–50.

Lovett, T., Clarke, C. and Kilmurray, A. (2003) 'Community Education and Community Action' in P. Jarvis and C. Griffin (eds), *Adult and Continuing Education*: Major Themes in Education VII. London: Routledge, pp. 219–35.

McClenaghan, P. (2000) 'Social capital: exploring the theoretical foundations of community development education', *British Educational Research Journal* 26(5): 565–82.

Mezirow, J. (1996) 'Contemporary paradigms of learning', *Adult Education Quarterly* 46(3): 158–72.

Morgan, M., Hickey, B. and Kellaghan, T (1997) *Report to the Minister for Education on the International Adult Literacy Survey: Results for Ireland.* Educational Research Centre: St Patrick's College.

Morrow, A.R. and Torres, A.C. (2002) *Reading Freire and Habermas.* New York: Teachers College Press.

Murphy, C. (1973). *Adult Education in Ireland: A Report of a Committee Appointed by the Minister for Education* (Murphy Report). Dublin: Stationery Office.

NALA (National Adult Literacy Agency) (2009) *Men and Literacy: A Study of Attitude and Experiences of Learning.* Dublin: NALA

NWCI (National Women's Council of Ireland) (2001) *Women: Knowledge is Power: Women and Education. Report from the NWCI Millennium Project.* Dublin: NWCI.

OECD (Organisation for Economic Co-operation and Development) (1997) *International Adult Literacy Survey.* Paris: OECD.

Sennett, R. (1970) *The Uses of Disorder.* New York: Knopf.

Sennett, R. and Cobb, J. (1977) *The Hidden Injuries of Class.* Cambridge: Cambridge University Press.

Sites, W. (1998) 'Communitarian theory and community development in the United States', *Community Development Journal* 33(1): 57–65.

van der Veen, R. (2003) 'Community development as citizen education', *International Journal of Lifelong Education* 22(6): 580–96.

Whitehead, J. (1989) 'Creating a living educational theory from questions of the kind, "How do I improve my practice?"', *Cambridge Journal of Education* 19(1) 42–52.

CHAPTER 12. 'FROM THE INSIDE OUT': USING PEER EDUCATION IN COMMUNITY DEVELOPMENT PRACTICE

Ajzen, I. and Fishbein, M. (1980) *Understanding Attitudes and Predicting Social Behavior.* Englewood Cliffs, NJ: Prentice-Hall.

Amaro, O. (1995) *HIV/AIDS Prevention Program Evaluation Report*. Prepared for the Massachusetts Primary Prevention Group and the Massachusetts Department of Public Health.

Bandura, A. (1977) *Social Learning Theory*. New York: General Learning Press.

Barry, J. and Daly, L. (1988) *The Travellers' Health Status Study: Census of Travelling People, November 1986*. Dublin: Health Research Board.

Barry, J., Herity, B. and Sloan, J. (1989) *The Travellers' Health Status Study: Vital Statistics of Travelling People, 1987*. Dublin: Health Research Board.

Contento, I. (2011) *Nutrition Education: Linking Research, Theory, and Practice* (2nd edn). London: Jones & Bartlett Learning.

CPA (Combat Poverty Agency) (2004) *Poverty Briefing – Poverty and Health* [online], <http://www.cpa.ie/publications/povertybriefings/Briefing15_Poverty&Health_2004.pdf> accessed 4 April 2008.

CSO (Central Statistics Office) (2007a) *Equality in Ireland 2007*. Dublin: Stationery Office.

— (2007b) *Census 2006 Principal Demographic Results, 2007*. Dublin: Stationery Office.

— (2009) *Measuring Ireland's Progress 2008*. Dublin: Stationery Office.

Declaration of Alma-Ata (1978) [online], <http://www.who.int/hpr/NPH/docs/declaration_almaata.pdf> accessed 20 December 2010.

DoE (Department of Education) (1995) *Report of the Task Force on the Travelling Community*. Dublin: Brunswick Press.

DoHC (Department of Health and Children) (2002) *Traveller Health: A National Strategy 2002–2005*. Dublin: Department of Health and Children.

— (2008). *State of the Nation's Children* [online], <http://www.childrensdatabase.ie/sonc2008/part1/child-mortality.asp> accessed 20 December 2010.

DHSSPS (Department of Health, Social Services and Public Safety) (Northern Ireland) and DoHC (Republic of Ireland) (2010) *Our Geels. All-Ireland Traveller Health Study Technioal Report 1: Health Survey Findings*. Dublin: DoHC.

Fishbein, M. and Ajzen, I. (1975) *Belief, Attitude, Intention, and Behavior: An Introduction to Theory and Research*. Reading, MA: Addison-Wesley.

Foster, G., Taylor, S.J., Eldridge, S.E. *et al.* (2007) 'Self-management education programmes by lay leaders for people with chronic conditions', *Cochrane Database of Systematic Reviews* 4: CD005108.

Freire, P. (1970) *Pedagogy of the Oppressed*. New York: Continuum.

Gilchrist, A. (2009) *The Well-Connected Community: A Networking Approach to Community Development*. Bristol: Policy Press.

Government of Ireland (2000) *Equal Status Act*. Dublin: Stationery Office.

Hardina, D. (2003) 'Linking citizen participation to empowerment practice: a historical overview', *Journal of Community Practice* 11(4): 11–38.

HSE (Health Service Executive) – Mid Leinster (2009) *Oral Health Promotion Programme for Traveller Families in County Offaly*. Clinical Audit Department, HSE – Mid Leinster.

Institut National d'Études Démographique (2010) *Birth and Death Rates (per 1,000 pop) and Infant Mortality Rate (per 1,000 live births)* [online], <http://www.ined.fr/en/pop_figures/developed_countries/birth_and_death_rates_infant_mortality_rate/> accessed 27 October 2011.

Jackson, A. (2009) 'Travellers and Social Care' in K. Lalor and P. Share, *Applied Social Care: An Introduction for Students in Ireland*. Dublin: Gill & Macmillan.

Johns, J. (2007) *Peer Education: Current Literature, Practice and Emerging Trends*. Adelaide: South Australian Community Health Research Unit, Flinders University.

Kavanagh, L. (2010) Informal group dicusssion, Tullamore Primary Healthcare Project, 21 October 2010.

McInerney, P. (2010) Informal group dicusssion, Tullamore Primary Healthcare Project, 21 October 2010.

Midland Health Board (2004) *Primary Healthcare Programme for Travellers, Annual Report 2003–2004*, unpublished report.

Pavee Point (2006) *Traveller Culture* [online], <http://www.paveepoint.ie/pav_culture_a.html> accessed 20 February 2008.

Turner, G. and Shepherd, J. (1999) 'A method in search of a theory: peer education and health promotion', *Health Education Research: Theory and Practice* 14(2): 235–47.

CHAPTER 13. COMMUNITY-BASED YOUTH AND FAMILY INTERVENTIONS: MOVING FROM EVIDENCE-INFORMED TO EVIDENCE-BASED PRACTICE

Barrera, M. (2000) 'Social Support Research in Community Psychology' in J. Rappaport and E. Seidman (eds), *Handbook of Community Psychology*. New York and London: Kluwer Academic.

Canavan, J. (2009) 'Family Support: Policy, Practice and Research into the Future', paper presented at Family Support Now: Reflecting on Contemporary Challenges Conference, National University of Ireland, Galway, 18–19 June.

Cassel, J. (1976) 'The contribution of the social environment host resistance', *American Journal of Epidemiology* 102: 107–23.

Chaffin, M. and Friedrich, B. (2004) 'Evidence-based treatments in child abuse and neglect', *Children and Youth Services Review* 26: 1097–113.

Cobb, S. (1976) 'Social Support as a Moderator of Life Stress', Presidential Address, *Psychosomatic Medicine* 38: 300–14.

Coleman, M.S., Savas, S.A. and Wulczyn, F. (2003) Preface, *Child Welfare* 82: 501–5.

Cutrona, C.E. (1996) *Social Support in Couples: Marriage as a Resource in Times of Stress*. Thousand Oaks, CA and London: Sage.

— (2000) 'Social Support Principles for Strengthening Families: Messages from the USA' in J. Canavan, P. Dolan and J. Pinkerton (eds) *Family Support: Direction from Diversity*. London and Philadelphia: Jessica Kingsley.

Cutrona, C.E. and Russell, D.W. (1987) 'The provisions of social relationships and adaptation to stress', *Advances in Personal Relationships* 1: 37–67.

— (1990) 'Types of social support and specific stress: towards a theory of optimal matching', in B.R. Sarason, I.G. Sarason and G.R. Pierce (eds) *Social Support: An Interactional View*. New York and Chichester: J. Wiley & Sons.

Davis, J. and Smith, M. (2009) 'Refocusing Family Support: A Scottish Case Study', paper presented at Family Support Now: Reflecting on Contemporary Challenges Conference, National University of Ireland, Galway, 18–19 June.

Dolan, P. (2003) 'Adolescents in Adversity and their Networks of Social Support', PhD thesis, Queen's University of Belfast.

Holmes, T. and Rahe, R. (1967) 'The social readjustment rating scale', *Journal of Psychosomatic Research* 11: 213–18.

House, J.S., Umberson, D. and Landis, K.R. (1988) 'Structures and processes of social support', *Annual Review of Sociology* 14: 293–318.

Kazdin, A.E. (2000) 'Developing a research agenda for child and adolescent psychotherapy', *Archives of General Psychiatry* 57: 829–35.

Kazdin, A.E. and Weisz, J.R. (2003) *Evidence-Based Psychotherapies for Children and Adolescents*. New York and London: Guilford.

Office of the Minister for Children (2007) *The Agenda for Children's Services: A Policy Handbook*. Dublin: Stationery Office.

Pawson, R. (2006) *Evidence-Based Policy: A Realist Perspective*. London and Thousand Oaks, CA: Sage.

Petrosino, A., Turpin-Petrosino, C. and Finckenauer, J. (2000) 'Well-meaning programs can have harmful effects! Lessons from experiments of programs such as Scared Straight', *Crime and Delinquency* 46: 354–79.

Pinkerton, J. and Dolan, P. (2007) 'Family support, social capital, resilience and adolescent coping', *Child and Family Social Work* 12: 219–28.

Rosen, A. (2003) 'Evidence-based social work practice: challenges and promise', *Social Work Research* 27: 197–208.

Sanders, J. and Munford, R. (2006) *Towards an Inclusive Approach to Family Support Evaluation*. London and Philadelphia: Jessica Kingsley.

Uchino, B.N. (2004) *Social Support and Physical Health: Understanding the Health Consequences of Relationships*. New Haven, CT: Yale University Press.

Usher, C.L. and Wildfire, J.B. (2003) 'Evidence-based practice in community-based child welfare systems', *Child Welfare* 82: 597–614.

Veerman, J.W. and van Yperen, T.A. (2007) 'Degrees of freedom and degrees of certainty: a developmental model for the establishment of evidence-based youth care', *Evaluation and Program Planning* 30: 212–21.

Weisz, J.R. and Jensen, A.L. (2001) 'Child and adolescent psychotherapy in research and practice contexts: review of the evidence and suggestions for improving the field', *European Child and Adolescent Psychotherapy* 10: 12–18.

Weisz, J.R., Weiss, B. and Donenberg, G.R. (1992) 'The lab versus the clinic: effects of child and adolescent psychotherapy', *American Psychologist* 47(12): 1578–85.

CHAPTER 14. EVALUATION AS A MECHANISM FOR EMPOWERMENT IN COMMUNITY DEVELOPMENT PRACTICE

American Evaluation Association (2007) 'Guiding principles for evaluators', *American Journal of Evaluation* 28: 129–30.

Baur, V., Tineke, A. and Widdershoven, G. (2010) 'Participation of marginalised groups in evaluation: mission impossible?' *Evaluation and Program Planning* 33(3): 238–45.

Carey, P. (2010) Comments by Minister for Community, Equality and Gaeltacht Affairs, Pat Carey TD [online], <http://www.pobail.ie/en/PressReleases/htmltext, 10679,en.html> accessed 10 December 2010.

Cousins, J.B. (2005) 'Will the Real Empowerment Evaluation Please Stand Up?' in D.M. Fetterman and A. Wandersman (eds), *Empowerment Evaluation Principles in Practice*. New York: Guilford Press, pp. 183–208.

Cousins, J.B., Donohue, J.J. and Bloom, G.A. (1996) 'Collaborative evaluation in North America: evaluators' self-reported opinions, practices, and consequences', *American Journal of Evaluation* 17(3): 207–26.

Cox, P.J, Keener, D. Woodard, T. and Wandersman, A. (2010) *Evaluation for Improvement: A Seven-Step Empowerment Evaluation Approach for Violence Prevention Organisations*. Atlanta, GA: Centers for Disease Control and Prevention.

Cronbach, L.J. (1982) *Designing Evaluations of Educational and Social Programs*. San Francisco: Jossey-Bass.

Díaz-Puente, J., Montero, A.and de los Ríos Carmenado, I. (2007) 'Empowering communities through evaluation: some lessons from rural Spain', *Community Development Journal* 44 (1): 53–67.

Fetterman, D.M. and Wandersman, A. (2005) *Empowerment Evaluation Principles in Practice*. New York: Guilford Press.

Floc'hlay, B. and Plottu, E. (1998) 'Democratic evaluation: from empowerment evaluation to public decision-making', *Evaluation* 4(3): 261–77.

Galileo, G. ([1632] 1967) *Dialogue Concerning the Two Chief World Systems – Ptolemaic and Copernican* (1632). Berkeley and Los Angeles: University of California Press.

Greene, J.C. (2002). 'Towards Evaluation as a Public Craft and Evaluator as Stewards of the Public Good or on Listening Well', presentation at the 2002 Australian Evaluation Society International Conference, October/November.

House, E.R. (2005) 'Promising practices: the many forms of democratic evaluation', *Evaluation Exchange* (Harvard Family Research Project's evaluation periodical) 11(3):7.

Motherway, B. (2006) *The Role of Community Development in Tackling Poverty in Ireland: A Literature Review*. Dublin: Combat Poverty Agency.

Patton, M.Q. (2005) 'Toward distinguishing empowerment evaluation and placing it in a larger context: take two', *American Journal of Evaluation* 26: 408–14.

—— (2008) *Utilisation-Focused Evaluation* (4th edn). Sage.

Plottu, B. and Plottu, E. (2009) 'Approaches to participation in evaluation: some conditions for implementation', *Evaluation* 15: 343–59.

Wandersman, A., Snell-Johns, J., Lentz, B., Fetterman, D., Keener, D., Livet, M., Imm, P. and Flaspohler, P. (2005) 'The Principles of Empowerment Evaluation' in D. Fetterman, *Empowerment Evaluation Principles in Practice*. New York: Guilford Press, pp. 27–54.

CHAPTER 15. CONCLUSION: COMMUNITY DEVELOPMENT – MAKING SOCIETY BETTER

Craig, G. (1998) 'Community development in a global context', *Community Development Journal* 33 (1): 2–17.

Daly, S. (2008) 'Mapping civil society in the Republic of Ireland', *Community Development Journal* 43(2), April: 157–76.

Deakin, N. (2001) *In Search of Civil Society*. Basingstoke: Palgrave.

Martin, I. (1999) 'Introductory essay' in J. Crowther, I. Martin and M. Shaw (eds), *Popular Education and Social Movements in Scotland Today*. Leicester: NIACE.

Mayo, M. (1994) *Communities and Caring: The Mixed Economy of Welfare*. Hampshire: Palgrave Macmillan.

Miller, C. and Ahmed, Y. (1997) 'A way forward: community development at the crossroads', *Policy and Politics* 3(25): 269–83.

Mulgan, G. (2010) *Making Good Society: Report of the Commission of Inquiry into the Future of Civil Society in the UK and Ireland*. Dunfermline: Carnegie UK Trust.

New Economics Foundation (2011) *The Great Transition*. London: New Economics Foundation.

Purdue, D. (2007) *Civil Societies and Social Movements: Potentials and Problems*. Abingdon, Oxford: Routledge.

Putnam, R. (1995) 'Bowling alone: America's declining social capital', *Journal of Democracy* 6(1): 65–78.

— (2000) *Bowling Alone*. New York: Simon & Schuster.

Shaw, M. (2004). *Community Work: Policy, Politics and Practice*. Universities of Hull and Edinburgh.

— (2011) 'Stuck in the middle? Community development, community engagement and the dangerous business of learning for democracy', *Community Development Journal* 46(S2), April: ii128–ii146.

Somerville, P. (2011) *Understanding Community: Politics, Policy and Practice*. Bristol: Policy Press.

Walzer, K. (1995) 'The Civil Society Argument' in R. Beiner (ed.), *Theorising Citizenship*. Albany, NY: State University Press.

Index